Praise for
They Don't Represent Us

"The American experiment in representative government is on life support. Lessig provides the medical record and a recommended course of care to save the patient. Every American should read it . . . stat!"

—Roger McNamee, bestselling author of *Zucked*

"Lessig is the thinking man's popular reformer and this book is a powerful, patriotic and above all useful guide to the fixes for American representative democracy. Agree or disagree, every citizen should read this book."

—Tim Wu, bestselling author of *The Curse of Bigness*

"A love letter to the American people and a down-to-earth blueprint of an evolving future in which we work together to fulfill the promise of humanity's most important idea: We the people are endowed with the inalienable right to rule ourselves, free from the tyranny of kings, dictators, plutocrats, or computers."

—Shoshana Zuboff, author of *The Age of Surveillance Capitalism*

"Lessig has long been the leading voice on how corruption undermines American democracy. In this book, he trains his trademark wit and incisiveness on an even bigger problem: Our political institutions, he shows, are deeply unrepresentative. Thankfully, Lessig has an original plan for how to build on the principles of the Founding Fathers to make our institutions serve all Americans."

—Yascha Mounk, author of *The People vs. Democracy*

"A tour de force by one of America's most interesting thinkers about democracy. Lessig finds democratic sclerosis not only in the institutions and arrangements of government, but also among we the people. He offers proposals aimed at getting us out of our silos, educated, organized, and deliberating toward a more perfect union."

—Richard L. Hasen, author of *Election Meltdown*

"American democracy is buckling under the weight of the public's deep cynicism. Professor Lessig's book brings clarity to the many factors feeding this civic deterioration, from our warped campaign finance system to the increasingly balkanized media to the pernicious power of our 'vetocracy.' Charting a new course that can revitalize our Republic will demand a reckoning with these deep-seated challenges. This book is a clarion call to do just that."

—Representative John P. Sarbanes

"In classic Lessig fashion, this book connects one of society's biggest challenges—the impact of technology on our society and democracy—to the evolution of our constitution to show how we've lost our voice in our system of government. But as the reader descends into a spiral of despair, he pulls them up with the hope of potential interventions that could successfully enact positive change."

—Joi Ito, Director, MIT Media Lab

"Lessig eloquently advances his diagnosis of our democratic condition. He then helps us understand how remedies might be possible. A book of lasting importance."

—James Fishkin, author of *Democracy When the People Are Thinking*

THEY DON'T REPRESENT US

ALSO BY LAWRENCE LESSIG

Republic, Lost: 2.0:
The Corruption of Equality and the Steps to End It

Republic, Lost:
How Money Corrupts Congress—and a Plan to Stop It

Remix: Making Art and Commerce Thrive
in the Hybrid Economy

Code: Version 2.0

Free Culture: How Big Media Uses Technology and the Law
to Lock Down Culture and Control Creativity

The Future of Ideas:
The Fate of the Commons in a Connected World

Code: And Other Laws of Cyberspace

THEY

— DON'T REPRESENT —

US

Reclaiming Our Democracy

LAWRENCE LESSIG

DEY ST.
An Imprint of WILLIAM MORROW

HarperCollins books may be purchased for educational, business, or sales promotional use. For information, please email the Special Markets Department at SPsales@harpercollins.com.

FIRST EDITION

Designed by Michelle Crowe

Library of Congress Cataloging-in-Publication Data has been applied for.

ISBN 978-0-06-294571-6

19 20 21 22 23   LSC   10 9 8 7 6 5 4 3 2 1

For all the Katies, Caras, and Helens
who will help claim the democracy that
Samantha Tess (and her brothers) deserve

Contents

Preface

IT'S BEEN TWENTY YEARS SINCE A CLEAR MAJORITY OF AMERICANS acknowledged that climate change is real. Congress has yet to pass any law to address it comprehensively. America has one of the most expensive health care systems in the world, with 25 percent of its budget devoted to administrative costs, and more than 12 percent of Americans still uninsured. Congress is debating whether preexisting conditions should be a ground for denying health insurance, still. The American Society of Civil Engineers grades America's infrastructure with a "D"—meaning conditions are "mostly below standard." The engineers estimate we must spend $1.5 trillion by 2025 to make America safe again. The closest Congress could come to the number "$1.5 trillion" was a $1.6 trillion tax cut, benefiting almost exclusively corporations and the very wealthy. Hopelessness is the one idea that now unites much of the Rust Belt with inner cities across America, as aging populations face a future without retirement savings or a system of social security that can support them. Remove the "-ness" from the first word in that sentence and you have a fair estimate of the chance that Congress will address that problem either anytime soon.[1]

None of these—or a million other—problems are caused by Donald Trump. None of them would be fixed if Donald Trump were not president. These problems are deeper than the occupant of 1600

Pennsylvania Avenue. They signal a failure much more fundamental than the misfiring of an Electoral College crafted at the birth of the nineteenth century.

It is difficult in this moment to recognize that truth. Our attention is drawn to the dumpster fire; we are wired to be distracted by the dramatic. Yet unless we find a way to discipline ourselves, and look beyond the drama, we will find no path to fixing these or any of the other critical problems that this nation faces.

The crisis in America is not its president. Its president is the consequence of a crisis much more fundamental. We tell ourselves that those more fundamental problems must wait, that the urgency of this election trumps everything else.

Yet that is precisely the thinking that got us here. The system that has failed America will not change unless we "challenge it" and make it change.

Those were Barack Obama's words almost a dozen years ago. So too were these:

> If we're not willing to take up that fight, then real change—change that will make a lasting difference in the lives of ordinary Americans—will keep getting blocked by the defenders of the status quo.

A dozen years later, it is blocked still.

Introduction

IN THE LATE 1970S, MAYBE AS LATE AS THE EARLY 1980S, THE IDEA OF "communism" had a funny life within the Soviet Union. On the one hand, communism was a "glorious idea." No one dared doubt its truth, at least to anyone they didn't trust. It was, quite literally, the party line. On the other hand, communism had obviously failed. Everyone recognized it had not worked—at least not in the Soviet Union. Yet skepticism notwithstanding, the parades continued. The praise of Lenin and Marx was never greater. And the system puttered along in pursuit of its glorious ideal—until, suddenly, it collapsed. Almost overnight, the party line flipped. One day, communism was truth. The next day, it was a lie.[1]

We live in a similar time—not at the same scale, not with the same consequence, but with a faint echo of the same dynamic. Obviously, for us, the vulnerable idea is not communism. For us, the vulnerable idea is "democracy" itself.

We live in a time when, on the one hand, democracy is a glorious idea. No one serious (or no one in power) openly questions it. Everyone rallies to its obvious truth. Every problem of government has an obvious remedy—more democracy. Every corruption is simply the corruption of the "will of the people." "The people" are truth. None can deny them. As the famed American political scientist Robert A. Dahl put it almost sixty years ago, "to reject the democratic creed is in effect to refuse to be an American."[2]

On the other hand, and increasingly, most everyone has a sense that this democracy is failing.[3] "The people" are ignorant or stupid. The politicians pander to the worst of both. Serious problems can't be addressed with more democracy. Serious issues can't even be discussed seriously. Confidence in the institutions of democracy has never been lower. And nothing on the horizon of the plausible seems to give any real hope.

This skepticism has more than just grumpiness behind it. Some of the very best in political science argue there is no good reason to trust "the people" to do anything.[4] We not only don't know what we are talking about, but even worse, when we learn something, we seem to know even less. For anyone with courage enough to utter this truth (or if not courage, at least tenure), there is no good reason to recommend democracy, even if, to remix Churchill, there is no obviously better idea.

This is a precarious place to stand. For, as with communism in 1989, I fear that we too are facing a certain collapse. Democracy has battled populism and authoritarianism before. But when it did, there was at least a faith in their alternative—democracy. Today, there is no faith. The best and brightest turn west, not east—to Silicon Valley, not Washington, D.C. The future is technology, and hence technocracy, not a better-functioning democracy. Artificial intelligence (AI) will decide for us. Automatic contracts enforced through something called a "blockchain" will bind us. The very rich will give us the best security they can. It will be good enough, for them at least, given the alternative is so dreadfully hopeless. And for the rest, the operative term is not *hopeless,* but certainly much less hope. The future is not doom. This is America. But without repair, democracy has none of the promise of the democracy in our past.

This is something new. There was a time not so long ago when democracy was obvious; a time when it was the clear solution to the world's ills, to be spread as broadly and as completely as possible. That was the objective of reform across much of the twentieth century. That was its singular achievement. In 1942, there were 9 democratic states across the world. By 1975, there were 34. By the fall of the Berlin Wall in 1989, that number had risen to 63.[5] Democracy had become the default. At the "end of history,"[6] only rogues would deny rule by the people.

Yet if you asked "the people" today anywhere, but especially in America, whether the people rule, most would find the idea somewhat quaint. Everywhere there is the view that society is divided between an elite and "the people." Everywhere there is the view that democracy represents the elite. In the summer 2016, the University of Maryland conducted a massive study of voter "anger" with their government.[7] The study found the highest level of dissatisfaction in the history of polling. It also found an almost unanimous view about the source of that dissatisfaction—both absolutely, and across the parties. Ninety-two percent thought government benefited "big interests" rather than "all people"; 85 percent thought Congress "does not serve the common good"; 89 percent thought "corporations and their lobbyists have too much influence"; and 89 percent believed "elected officials think more about the interests of their campaign donors than the common good of the people." Democracy, we believe, does not work for the demos. Not that it couldn't, in principle, but that in fact it "falls well short in living up to [its] ideals."[8]

This is an astonishing failure that we don't reckon enough. Not at the margins but at the core: the institution governing us—a democracy—lacks the basic integrity of such an institution: that the people rule. That an oligarchy or monarchy would reward an elite is understandable. It's built into the DNA. For a democracy to favor the elite over the people is to add insult to suffering. It is to betray the very promise at the core of the institution. It is to reveal, in a word, that the institution has been corrupted.

That corruption feeds the populism that now rages everywhere. We are angry. We embrace a politics that screams anger. And while the populist demands for intervention are different across the world, what unites them is the sense that this politics is different. That this moment is different. Neither extreme seeks to tinker. Both sides rally to leaders who demand fundamental change—now.

Many of these so-called leaders—or at least the ones who have risen so far—are scary. If they succeed, they will radically alter our future and its promise. Like ignorant urban planners of the 1960s and 1970s, their reforms will be scars on the nations that survive them. Indeed, whether democracy will survive them, in some nations at least, is an open question.

Yet what scares me most is not these populist leaders. What scares me is the elite. Or more precisely, what scares me is an elite sneer at this populist moment. "How can the people be so stupid?" I've heard so many ask that so many times over this past half decade. "Why should we trust our future," one earnest billionaire once asked me, "to people who don't even know our past?"

That question, of course, could be asked the other way around. Nothing that is happening today hasn't happened before. The pace is quicker. The consequences of miscalculation will be greater. The cost of our incapacity to govern is much greater. But the dynamic of this populist moment is the dynamic of populism throughout the ages: When hope fades, anger flourishes. And the puzzle of our history is not why the anger grows, but why those who could address it do nothing.

I am a populist who does not rage. I feel the emotion of this moment as fully as any. But the fearful urgency of now calms me. We don't have the time that fury demands. We don't have the luxury of tantrums. We must find our bearings and march. Whether we believe we can get there or not, we must take up the fight, now, and move.

THIS BOOK IS A MAP that suggests a plan. You can't leave part I without a clear and simple view of the core flaw within our current democracy. That flaw is unrepresentativeness—both of "them," the government, and of "us," the people. How that flaw matters is different from how most see it. Some have grabbed the trunk, and others the tail. By the end of part I, you will see the elephant that stands in the middle of the room of our republic. Its mass will be inescapable.

The remedies in part II then follow, in obvious ways for at least part of that flaw, less obviously for the balance. I can describe and imagine the solutions to the problems with our government. They are obvious, even if their consequence is obscure. The problems with us are more difficult, though they too can be solved. We've never built a democracy for the people that we will unavoidably need to be. We unavoidably must.

The conclusion then seeks inspiration. Drawing upon three stories of unlikely success, it models a bigger victory still. My aim is not to sketch a final plan. I do not write this book to recruit, and this is not truth offered as a ticket to lead. This is a book that crafts a way to see the struggle that we now suffer within, and to see the kind of love that might overcome it.

I am not yet sure we can tap that love. We should recognize that fact as we begin this journey. Our institutions are weakened and corrupted, the parasites that feed on them strong and pervasive. But in the dozen years since I've begun this work, I have been astonished at the progress, first in recognition and then in successes. We are an overloaded plane taking off from a remote runway. We have gotten off the ground. Ahead is a mountain range that we must clear. It is clear we are climbing. It is clear we must climb faster still.

PART I: FLAWS

There is a single flaw that cuts through everything that fails within this democracy: unrepresentativeness. In ways we don't even see anymore, our democracy does not represent us. Part of that unrepresentativeness is tied to the institutions of government. That's the part I call "them." Part of that unrepresentativeness is tied not to them, but to us. Solving the parts tied to us is more critical. We could putter along with the problems with them. We won't survive not solving the problems with us.

For many years, I've written of a different flaw that I've also said cuts through everything: the corruption of money in politics. Even worse, evoking the words of Henry David Thoreau ("for every thousand hacking at the branches of evil there is one striking at the root"), I've called money the root to the problems of this Republic. That was a mistake. While "campaign finance" is a problem, it is just one example of a more fundamental problem: unrepresentativeness. In this part, I map the dimensions of this more fundamental problem, including, but not limited to, the problem of money in politics.

CHAPTER I

The Unrepresentative "Them"

THE FRAMERS OF OUR CONSTITUTION GAVE US "A REPUBLIC." BY THAT term, they meant not a simple democracy, but a "representative democracy."[1] The idea of the people ruling directly was anathema to them—and should be to us. The idea of government unconnected to the will of the people was anathema to them—and should be to us. Instead, the framers mapped a space that stood between these two extremes. They imagined a government guided by representatives selected either directly (the House of Representatives) or indirectly (the Senate and, initially at least, the president). Yet it was *representatives* who were to govern, not the people or the states.

Their constitution was not, however, a philosopher's brief. James Madison had crafted the basic design. He was forced to accept compromises that he desperately wanted to avoid. Most fundamental among those compromises was the United States Senate. It killed Madison that at the core of this constitutional republic was a conflict with principle, necessary to the end of winning over the small states. For a while, he insisted that he would reject that "compromise" in the name of "justice." "The proper foundation of [the government]," he warned, would be "destroyed by substituting an equality in place of a proportional Representation."[2] But when it was clear there would be no constitution without a Senate representing each state equally, Madison swallowed, and a new nation was born. The people would be represented for sure. But as well as the people, so too would the states be represented.

From our perspective, this mixed system is odd. Why complicate what could be represented simply—the people—by adding a layer of representatives—the states—one step removed from the people? But from the framers' perspective, this was not strange at all. They were used to the idea of a government representing different interests, together. The British government was the obvious example: the House of Commons representing the people, the House of Lords representing an aristocracy, and the king representing the monarchy, and hence the nation. All three were equally present in the British system, even if their power was not, over the arc of British history, equal.

America revolved away from the British design, at least with the ideas of monarchy and aristocracy. But it did not reject the idea of a mixed system of representation. Indeed, in the Constitution of 1787, many believed they had perfected the mix. In it, each thing represented—the people and the states—would be represented equally. The House would be "dependent on the People alone," as Madison described it, where by "the People" he meant "not the rich more than the poor,"[3] and with each representative representing the same number of people. The Senate would be "dependent on the States,"[4] at least for its appointment, with each state sending an equal number of senators. Proportionality was thus at the core of this constitution, even if the things to which the institution was to be proportional were to be different. Madison wanted one thing represented equally—the people. The framers resolved to represent two things equally—the people and the states. No doubt, there is a contradiction here: To represent the states equally *means* not representing the people within those states equally. But however we understand this conflict, within each domain, the intent was clear: representative institutions representing equally.[5]

That core principle of equality has been corrupted within our Republic. At least within the domain of "the People," the institutions of our democracy do not represent us equally. That fact presses an obvious question into the fore: Why do we accept unrepresentativeness in a representative democracy? Why do we allow a corruption of the core idea of a republic?

In this chapter, I map that corruption along five dimensions. We do not have (1) an equal freedom to vote; we do not have a vote that weighs the same, in either (2) Congress or for the (3) President. The (4) Senate does not represent the states equally. And the way we fund campaigns means we as (5) voters are not represented equally, anywhere. In every dimension, the core principle of a representative democracy has been compromised. Is it any surprise that having broken its parts, the machine of government no longer works?[6]

I: VOTERS

In 2014, a cofounder of one of Silicon Valley's greatest venture capital firms caused a stir. Not because he announced the next Google. Or Facebook. Instead, this titan of venture capital created a commotion because of an idea that he promoted as a principle of democracy, an idea that practically every American would find just bizarre. According to Tom Perkins, cofounder of Kleiner, Perkins, the right to vote in America should be tied to the payment of taxes. In his view, you shouldn't "get to vote unless you pay a dollar of taxes. [And if] you pay a million dollars in taxes, you [should] get a million votes."[7]

Perkins's idea is not actually completely nuts. Many democracies have had some form of plural voting. In Britain, for example, people affiliated with a university could vote where the university was and where they came from. Same thing with property owners—a vote where their property is and where they live.[8] And Perkins's idea is precisely how democracy works with corporations. Shareholders get as many votes as they own shares (with some shares worth more than others, and some, sometimes, worth no votes at all). Perkins's suggestion simply extended that principle from the corporate boardroom to the ballot box.

Yet as an ideal for democracy, the notion was ridiculed by leaders from across the political spectrum.[9] Whether or not it is good for GM, no one believes it is good for America. In America, everyone gets an equal vote, regardless of the taxes that he or she has paid. This much, at least in principle, is clear.

Indeed, the principle can be stated more generally. All citizens in America, except for felons (in some states) and those not yet eighteen, regardless of income (there can't be a poll tax) and without discriminatory tests (or so requires the Voting Rights Act), have, in effect, the right to vote. The right to vote has become a right of citizenship—not absolute, because never expressed directly as a right within our Constitution, and not defended enough, but bundled within the package that comes with being called an American.

It was not always like this. Voting was not a right of citizenship originally. In the history of its development, it has been limited or conditioned for reasons external to the person—whether he has property, or whether he has paid taxes—and reasons internal to the person—whether he's a he, or white, or a resident.[10] From the beginning, the states defined the scope of the right. Until 1868, they had a pretty free hand. The states could include women or not (New Jersey had done so since 1776, expressly indicating that the right included women in 1790, but then withdrawing it in 1807). They could include black people or not. They could restrict the vote to people holding property or not (as many states did[11]). The Constitution expressly stated that the qualifications to vote for members of Congress (originally senators were selected by state legislatures) was to be the same as the "Electors of the most numerous Branch of the State Legislature." That means it was the states that got to set those qualifications.[12]

At least until the Constitution began to say otherwise: In 1868, the Fourteenth Amendment expressed a soft bias against denying African American males the right to vote (a state's representation in Congress was reduced if it did). In 1870, the Fifteenth Amendment banned that discrimination completely (if fatally imperfectly[13]). In 1920, the

Nineteenth Amendment banned discrimination on the basis of sex. In 1964, the Twenty-Fourth Amendment banned the poll tax in federal elections (the Supreme Court extended that ban to state elections two years later[14]). In 1971, the Twenty-Sixth Amendment banned discrimination against people on the basis of age (at least if you were eighteen or older).

These rules mean identity doesn't determine whether or not you can vote. And in this sense, the right to vote was the first fight of identity politics, as the struggle throughout American history has been to erase franchise exclusions based on identity.

But what about how much your vote counts? Even if everyone must be given a vote, do those votes all have to weigh the same? Can some be, in the words of George Orwell, more equal than others? Could some count for two, or ten, or as Perkins suggested, a million?

For most of American history, the answer to that question was effectively, if indirectly, yes. Even if who you are could affect less and less whether you had the right the vote, how much your vote weighed could depend fundamentally on where you lived, or how the districts were drawn. No one ever adopted Tom Perkins's idea, granting votes based on the amount of taxes one paid. But states systematically allocated representatives so that people living in rural areas had a weightier vote than people living in cities.[15]

The reasons for this difference were many, the most obvious linked to race. African Americans concentrated in cities (slavery didn't end with every slave being given "forty acres and a mule," so property ownership was not common among African Americans). A state desiring to minimize the electoral power of black people could then weight the votes of rural voters, and thus tilt the legislature against the cities.

Many claimed that racism was not the—or the only—reason for unequal votes. In many states, the rural areas were agricultural. It seemed fair to some to give rural voters more power, since the corn and wheat fields would otherwise have weak representation in legislatures. Especially where a state believed that "the values" of rural America should be preserved, the state had a reason to put a thumb on the scale to benefit rural voters over urban.

Yet whatever the reason—benign or not—in the 1960s, the Supreme Court put an end to this inequality. Southern states had allowed differences in the population between districts to balloon; it was not hard to understand that inertia as being driven by animus. Rather than forcing courts to suss out the cases of inequality that were racially motivated from the cases that were not, the Supreme Court adopted a pretty simple rule—one person, one vote. Districts within states had to be drawn to equalize the population between those districts.[16]

We forget today just how controversial that result was. "Few Supreme Court decisions," as the New York Times' Anthony Lewis wrote in 1964, "have stunned this hardened capital city as has yesterday's ruling that state legislative districts must be substantially equal in population."[17] An amendment to reverse the Court's decision was introduced within six months of the decision and came within seven votes of passing the Senate.[18] Many believed that the framers of our Constitution would have rejected the idea of "one person, one vote." And many were quick to recognize that the principle that the Court had imposed on the states was not imposed equally on the federal government. The United States Senate, unlike state senates, was exempted from the rule, as was the Electoral College. This was, the critics insisted, judicial activism on steroids—"making up" a principle found nowhere in the Constitution and applying it differently to different institutions of government.

But the controversy quickly died and the slogan "one person, one vote" came to seem so obvious that few could even imagine a different system. We have come to take the idea for granted (at least as applied to citizens in a democracy): we now assume that voting is a right, and that votes are to be equal.

THAT, AT LEAST, is the theory. But democracy is not a theory. Democracy is a set of practices, embedded within institutions, which themselves have enormous effect on whether its ideals are its reality. The ideal may be that voters are to be equal. The reality in America is plainly and radically different. In no sense is it true that we all have an equal freedom to vote in America. Even within particular states, the freedom to vote is radically unequally distributed.

These differences manifest themselves in the details. How many voting machines does a precinct have? More machines, faster lines. How many poll workers? Or phones to verify challenged votes? Is there parking at the polling place? Is it near public transport? How long are the lines? Are there lines?

Those questions get answered differently, everywhere. How they're answered will determine the burden in voting. Yet burdens alone are not grounds to complain. Voting will always impose a burden. If that burden is equal—not in some academically theoretical way, but in a practical, actual sense, equal—then there is little to complain about in that burden. And where the burden is unequal, we need to ask why. Where the institution of voting crafts the practices of voting to make it harder for some than for others, we must demand that those building those institutions explain the motive. Or purpose. What is the justification?

Here we step into the most obvious and obviously bloody dimension of American political history. Because as many scholars have shown, Carol Anderson most recently and prominently, it is impossible to look at the data about how the right to vote lives across the United States and not see a color skew.[19] (Practically) all black people were denied the right to vote for literally most of American history; half of whites were (women). And when the power of the state to discriminate on the basis of race was removed, the resulting right to vote regardless of race was the most begrudgingly secured right in the history of this nation. To this day, the color of your skin determines how easy it is to vote for way too many Americans. To this day, within the pulse of our democracy, the rhythm and ritual of America's original sin continues to sing.

Not everyone who practices these inequalities experiences them as racism. This is the lesson of Katherine Cramer's great book *The Politics of Resentment* (2016).[20] That gap fuels the fight about whether these differences can even be remedied under the Voting Rights Act, as amended. That law was premised upon racism. It must be defended, or at least the Supreme Court has insisted, by demonstrating racism lives still.[21]

Yet there is another equally rich vein of equality law sitting within our constitutional tradition that need not demand proof of racism to justify a remedy for inequality. That principle comes from the Constitution directly—the first Constitution, before it was amended. It is the principle embedded in Article I, giving Congress the power to ensure that the elections for representatives initially and then for senators (and always, by implication, the president) are equal.

This equality was articulated most forcefully in the case that would ultimately make it possible, constitutionally, to end the white primary—*United States v. Classic* (1941). The details of that case are not important here. What is important is the principle. The Constitution calls voters "electors." The right of "electors" "to choose," *Classic* explains, is "unlike [the rights] guaranteed by the Fourteenth and Fifteenth Amendments." It, unlike those rights, is "secured against the actions of individuals as well as of the states."[22] And whether or not the courts would enforce such equality directly, the Constitution plainly and expressly gives Congress the power to defend that equality, at least in the context of federal elections. The states are given the power to determine the "Qualifications" of electors, as well as the power to regulate the "Time, Places and Manner of holding Elections." But Congress is expressly given the power, under Article I of the Constitution, to "make or alter such Regulations."[23] And Congress would thus plainly have the power to "alter" any regulation that created an inequality in the selection of federal officers.

Thus, under Article I, the question would not be "Has the state manifested racism?" The question instead is simply whether Congress has a legitimate democratic interest in eliminating whatever inequality it has determined is present. And here then is the key: under the Constitution, Congress would plainly have an interest in enacting rules to assure that when the fox is guarding the henhouse, the hens nonetheless have an equal freedom to vote. Or put less metaphorically, when Democrats/Republicans control state government, Congress would have an interest in ensuring that Republicans/Democrats have an equal freedom to vote.

This is a critical point about the nature of American elections. Other nations vest the power to run elections in nonpartisan bureaucrats. It is a bizarre reality that America does not. Instead, in practically every jurisdiction, elections are run by partisan election officials. That doesn't mean that these officials act in a partisan manner. It doesn't mean they are all trying to cheat. It means simply that the rules are crafted and administered by people from one party, to be applied to people from both parties.

Where this is true, Congress has a perfectly legitimate reason to ensure an equal freedom to vote, regardless of party: If the election rules that a state adopts or the election practices that the state administers burden the party that is not in power more than the party that is in power, then Congress should have a compelling interest in reversing the effect of that inequality, to ensure that all citizens have an effectively equal freedom to vote, for federal officers at least.

By "burden," I mean a practical burden. The rule could be the same, but the effect could be radically different. If in a jurisdiction, most Republicans are over sixty-five, then a polling place on the fifth floor of a building without an elevator would be unequal burden. Everyone, Republican and Democrat alike, would be subject to that same burden in principle. But in practice, on average, older people will find it harder to walk five flights of stairs than younger people. Not every older person—my father-in-law could easily beat me, even though he's twenty-some years older than I. But on average, and in most cases.

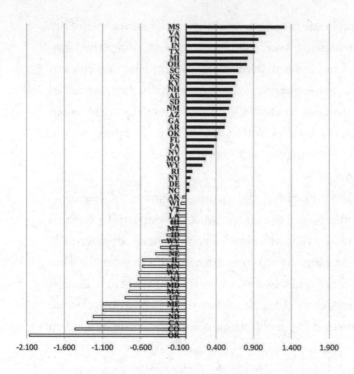

FIGURE 1

Cost of Voting Index values for all 50 American states in 2016

Li et al., Cost of Voting

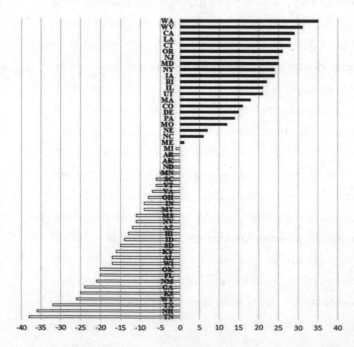

FIGURE 2

Change in state rank on the Cost of Voting Index from 1996 to 2016. Negative values indicate a drop in state rank.

Li et al., Cost of Voting.

So on this measure, does America secure an equal freedom to vote?

The most comprehensive data that we have about how difficult it is to vote measures the burden at the state level. In 2018, three scholars, Quan Li, Michael J. Pomante II, and Scot Schraufnagel, set out to quantify the cost of voting in America. Aggregating the effect of thirty-three different state election laws, they created a "cost of voting index" (COVI) for each state, in each presidential election from 1996 through 2016.[24] That index revealed a pretty striking difference among the different states (see Figure 1).

Yet even more interesting than a simple ranking is their ranking of the changes in the cost of voting over the same period. Were states making it easier or harder to vote? And if there was a difference, what was it?

States at the bottom of Figure 2 have changed their rules to make it harder for people to vote. States at the top have made it easier. Why? At first glance, these changes may seem puzzling. Why would any state make it harder for any one of its citizens to vote? What's the gain?

Yet the answer is obvious: In our democracy, it's not size that matters. It's relative size that matters. The question is not "How many voted?" The question is "Did more Republicans vote than Democrats?" Our system allocates power to the winner, whether or not the winner wins the support of the majority of the population, let alone the majority of the voters. Indeed, as we'll see later in this book, there may be a perverse incentive to reduce the number of voters, at least if that reduction doesn't hurt your side as much as it hurts the other side. The fewer the voters, the cheaper it is to craft a plurality within an election.

So if the burden were felt randomly, or evenly between Republicans and Democrats, the whole effort to increase the costs of voting would be puzzling. But if increasing costs help one side, that side would have an obvious incentive to do just that.

This fact makes the pattern in Figure 2 much easier to understand. The costs of voting are not born equally in America. Instead, they burden the vote of Democrats more than they burden the vote of Republicans. Or put differently, Republicans can bear increases in the costs of voting more easily than can Democrats. On average, Republicans are wealthier; they come from districts where life depends upon having cars; having cars means they have identification, and so on. Thus increasing the costs of voting is a simple technique for suppressing Democratic votes, and thus increasing the chances for Republicans to win.

And thus does the data suggest that Republicans have increased the costs of voting—to make it easier to protect their own legislative majorities—while Democrats have decreased the cost of voting—to make it easier to protect their own legislative majorities.

Don't let this symmetry confuse you, however. Sure, if you're a Democrat, you want to make it easier for everyone to vote. If you're a Republican, you don't. Yet that doesn't mean that acting on either motive is equivalent, either morally or democratically. The question is always "Relative to what baseline?" Is the constitutional norm that all who can should vote? Or not? Does representative democracy demand that more have access to the polls or less? To state the question is to announce its answer: in a representative democracy, all must have an equal chance to vote, regardless of party or ideology.

IN 2013, in *Shelby County v. Holder,* the Supreme Court threw out a whole set of protections against discriminatory voting regimes in targeted districts across the country (though mainly in the South), as identified in the Voting Rights Act of 1965. The Voting Rights Act was enacted to address an obvious need. But in the (most charitably framed) view of the Chief Justice John Roberts in *Shelby County,* there was no showing of any continued need to protect against racism anymore. America had changed, the chief justice insisted. "There is no denying," Roberts wrote for the Court, "that the conditions that originally justified these measures no longer characterize voting in the covered jurisdictions."[25] No doubt, "voting discrimination still exists." But in the Court's view, not enough to justify the continued regulation of Section 4 of the Voting Rights Act. Fifty years after the act was upheld, the Court held, "things have changed dramatically." Justice Thomas agreed.[26]

Many were stunned by the Court's opinion. No doubt America had changed, but to many, the idea that racism had ended was bizarre. In the period between its passage and 2013, as Ari Berman writes, "more than three thousand discriminatory voting changes had been blocked by the courts and Justice Department," using the rules of the VRA.[27]

Yet whether or not John Roberts was right about America, certainly election law changed dramatically after *Shelby County*. All across the nation (though mainly in the South), states began to adopt techniques that have had the clear effect of burdening some citizens more than others. That burden may well be motivated by race. It was certainly beneficial to one political party. Zoltan Hajnal, Nazita Lajevardi, and Lindsay Nielson studied the effect of voter identification laws in the thirty-four states that have some form of ID law. The net effect of these laws is, they found, plainly partisan.

> The findings presented here strongly suggest that these laws do, in fact, have real consequences for the makeup of the voting population. . . . Strict voter ID laws appear to diminish the participation of Democrats and those on the left, while doing little to deter the vote of Republicans and those on the right. They produce a clear partisan distortion.[28]

The same consequence flows from new techniques to purge voting rolls. Crosscheck, for example, is a program designed to identify fraudulent voters and purge them from the voting lists. Launched with three states in 2005, the project quickly grew. In 2017, it analyzed 98 million voter records, returning 7.2 million "potential duplicate regis-trant" records to member states. But the name-match techniques bur-den different races differently. As Carol Anderson reports, minorities are "overrepresented in 85 of 100 of the most common last names."

As a result, when Crosscheck zeros in on name matches, whites are underrepresented by 8 percent on the purge lists, while African Ameri-cans are overrepresented by 45 percent, Asian Americans by 31 per-cent, and Hispanics by 24 percent. According to *The Root*, "[r]oughly 14 percent of all black voters were purged from databases under the guise of preventing 'double voting' and 'fraud.'"[29] Though grounded in race, the differences have an obvious partisan bias.

In theory, these efforts are meant to eliminate so-called voter fraud. Yet there is no evidence of substantial voter fraud in America—at all[30]—and no good evidence that having a voter ID requirement increases voter confidence.[31] In practice, whatever these changes were meant to do, they have in fact simply eliminated the ability of thousands to vote. As the Brennan Center for Justice summarized the changes since *Shelby County,* there have been a "flood of new barriers to voting that would have otherwise been blocked," with the consequence that "thou-sands upon thousands of would-be voters were thwarted at the ballot box over the course of multiple elections."[32]

This suppression has had an obvious effect. In 2000, President Bush prevailed in Florida with 537 votes. Yet as the United States Civil Rights Commission concluded, "it was widespread voter disenfranchisement, not the dead-heat contest, that was the extraordinary feature in the Florida election."[33] Just one example gives measure to the consequence: The company that had purged voters before the 2000 election ran their purge again, after the election, with a more exacting matching rule. That means a rule that is more demanding before it identifies two names as the same individual, and thus subject to exclusion. That "exercise turned up twelve thousand voters who shouldn't have been la-beled felons—22 times Bush's 537 vote margin."[34] Likewise in Ohio in

2004: "Overwhelmingly Democratic precincts in Columbus received seventeen fewer voting machines in 2004 than 2000, while heavily Republican precincts got eight more machines."[35] Postelection surveys in Ohio found that "3 percent of Ohio voters left their polling places without voting because of the long lines"—lines that took almost three times as long to clear as lines with predominantly white voters.[36] That number was almost 50 percent greater than the margin of victory by Bush.[37] The stories here are endless, and cataloged meticulously by many, including the Brennan Center and authors such as Carol Anderson—in 2016, a five-hour wait in Maricopa County, Arizona; in 2012, a line with four thousand people stretching for a quarter mile in Cincinnati; in 2017, lines in Miami-Dade County that bent "beyond the photographer's lens and meld[ed] into the horizon."[38] Ari Berman, reporter at *Mother Jones* and author of *Give Us the Ballot,* counted 868 fewer voting places in 2016, in half the counties that had been subject to the Voting Rights Act before *Shelby County.*[39] No fair review of the facts since 2013 could turn up anything other than a massive effort to make inequality within this representative democracy even more real. Whether or not intended because of race, the effect on party is clear.

This partisan bias is just wrong. A representative democracy at a minimum must ensure that the burdens of citizenship are born equally. Any difficulty in voting must be shared in common. And any difficulty for difficulty's sake (because of the predictable political consequences) should be illegal whether or not you can prove it is driven by hate. Whatever the scope of Congress's continued power under the Fourteenth Amendment to address racial discrimination, it should have a clear power to banish partisan discrimination in the opportunity to participate in federal elections.

My effort to speak beyond race will be resisted by some. There is an important lesson that America has still not learned about the extraordinary harm that continues because of our long history of racism and worse. The fight for voting rights is a resource in that lesson. The idea that jurisdictions are tilting the rules again to make it harder for blacks to vote is astonishing to many whites. That surprise motivates support.

I don't mean to interfere with that economy of activism. But I do mean to tap into an idea of equality that should be even more fundamental. We should not have to prove that election officials are racists in order to attack a system that makes it harder for some to vote than others. The inequality is wrong regardless. We can fight that inequality, at least at the federal level, without proving it is driven by racism. Racism is a particularly odious wrong. It is one that we, as Americans, have an ongoing duty to fight. But it is not the only wrong of inequality. And long before we rid America of racism, we can make American elections equally free.

No doubt, not every American believes that all citizens should have an equal right to vote. The first director of the conservative think tank the Heritage Foundation, Paul Weyrich, told a gathering of evangelical Christians supporting Ronald Reagan: "I don't want everybody to vote. Elections are not won by a majority of people,; they never have been from the beginning of our country and they are not now. As a matter of fact, our leverage in the elections quite candidly goes up as the voting populace goes down."[40]

That same view was apparently behind Senate majority leader Mitch McConnell's vitriolic attack on Democratic reforms proposed in 2019 that would enable more people to vote more easily.[41] It was, he said, a "power grab"—a charge that only makes sense if you don't believe that everyone should have an equal freedom to vote. And it is the thesis behind Jason Brennan's *Against Democracy* (2016), which proposes a form of "epistocracy," to weigh votes differently based on the knowledge of the voter.

Some have this view because of racism, though not all. And whether it's racism or not, there is a substantial number of Americans who believe that some of us shouldn't be voting. Or that it should be differently difficult for people to vote, so that only those who really want to participate, do. According to a study conducted by the Pew Research Center, a significant number of Americans (32 percent overall, 63 percent of Republicans) believe citizens should have to take steps, such as registering, to "prove they want to vote."[42] Those who believe in the importance of education and "epistocracy" worry whether a system that doesn't filter any voter on any knowledge can produce great leaders. How can a citizen who hasn't a clue about history or trade policy or economics select among candidates who will have learned from history, especially as to trade policy and the techniques of sane and constructive economics?

I get the intuition of some that the vote would be better if it were earned rather than given. Or if we could filter those who know nothing from those who know lots. Indeed, as a teacher and a student of American history, I ought to like such a system. The views of people like me would have much more weight than the views of people I often disagree with.

Yet understanding is not agreement. A representative democracy should ensure at the very least that every citizen counts equally. It can do that only if every citizen has an equal freedom to vote. Today, we have obviously and grotesquely failed in that commitment. In this way, today we are not equal, and our democracy is unrepresentative.

2: REPRESENTATIVES

In 2018, almost a million residents of Massachusetts voted for the Republican running for Senate (out of 2.6 million votes cast), and almost half that number voted for Republicans running for Congress. On January 3, 2019, there were zero Republicans from Massachusetts sworn in to office on Capitol Hill.

In 2018, almost a quarter of a million residents of West Virginia voted for Democrats running for the House (out of about 572,000 votes cast). On January 3, 2019, not a single Democrat from West Virginia was sworn into office.

These numbers are the consequence of a system called "gerrymandering." Named after Massachusetts governor (and the fifth vice president of the United States) Elbridge Gerry, gerrymandering describes a technique for drawing electoral districts. More pejoratively, it is a way for politicians to pick the voters rather than the voters picking politicians. Gerry had been elected governor in 1810. In his second term, the legislature redrew the legislative districts to benefit Gerry's party. The public likely hated the idea then as much as it does now. Gerry was defeated in his next election, but the victory of having this awful practice named after him survived.

Every congressional district in America is drawn with an eye to a certain result. Or at least, a result beyond the baseline objective of minimizing the difference in population between the districts. In the most extreme cases, that objective is simply to maximize the number of seats held by the party drawing the district. It can do that in a way that can be shown in a graphic:[43]

The Choices of Gerrymanderers

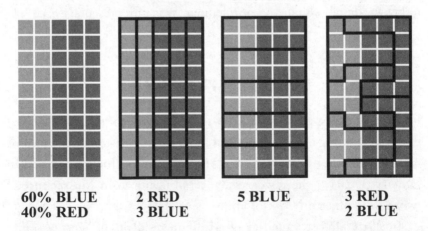

| 60% BLUE
40% RED | 2 RED
3 BLUE | 5 BLUE | 3 RED
2 BLUE |

FIGURE 3

Lawrence Lessig, CC-BY-SA, derived from Steve Nass, CC-BY-SA.

As the image makes clear, how lines are drawn matters fundamentally to who gets the seats within a district. One set of lines yields one party in control; another set of lines yields the opposite.

Pennsylvania's redistricting in 2010 was a pretty good example of how bent the system can be: In 2008, Obama had won Pennsylvania by 1.6 million votes (54 percent vs. 44 percent). Pennsylvania Democrats in turn won 12 congressional seats; Republicans got 7. In 2010, the Republicans gained control of the legislature and redistricted, to favor themselves. Then in 2012, even though Obama again won the state by more than 300,000 votes, and the Democrats got 2.7 million votes in the House against 2.6 million for the Republicans, the Republicans captured 13 of the 18 seats. Democrats got more votes; Republicans got more than twice the number of seats.[44]

The same story could be told the other way around. In 2018, there were 2.3 million votes cast in Maryland's congressional races. Sixty-five percent of those votes were for Democrats. Thirty-two percent were for Republicans. But because of gerrymandering, 87.5 percent of the congressional seats in Maryland are Democratic; 12.5 percent are Republican. As Neal Simon, an independent who ran for United States Senate in Maryland, describes it:

> If our state's eight House seats were divided proportionally—that is to say, if they represented the entire spectrum of Maryland voters—our congressional delegation would consist of: one far-left Democrat, four moderate Democrats, one independent, two moderate Republicans, and one far-right Republican. Instead, after the districts were redrawn under Democratic Gov. Martin O'Malley, who admitted doing so to most effectively elect party members, the state is represented by six far-left Democrats, one moderate Democrat, and one far-right Republican. In other words, instead of the five seats they should hold, Democrats control seven. Worse yet, instead of six moderates and two extremists, we have one moderate and seven extremists.[45]

These gaps are viewed by most as deeply unfair. They are, and they could get worse. As David Daley describes in his book *Ratf*cked*, the ability to render this gap has been made a million times more powerful by the emergence of technology and big data. The consequence of these technologies together is a constant struggle by the parties in control to twist the lines to inflate their own power, and thus to protect themselves from the threat of an actually competitive democracy. When voters from one party are all packed into a single district, those lines deny them their representation. These citizens are rendered irrelevant—by a map. The system denies them an equality that a representative democracy demands.

The consequences of this kind of distortion are not small. As Samuel Wang, a Princeton professor of neuroscience and molecular biology and the director of the Princeton Gerrymandering Project, explained to me, while the wrong from voter suppression is visceral and real, the "representational harm in gerrymandering can be quite large, and I think it's underappreciated how large those harms can be." For example,

> [In the *Bethune-Hill* case[46]] . . . if the African-Americans were less packed into those 12 [Virginia] districts, they would have had as many as 15 districts. . . . So . . . that's more like a 20% loss of representation [because of the gerrymandering].
>
> Another example [is] the State of Pennsylvania. [A]fter the court case, the delegation there is 9–9 Democrats to Republicans, and before it was five out 18. . . . Going from five out of 18 to nine out of 18 is a shift of four seats. That's 44% loss out of nine seats.

The single most important effect of this gerrymandering is to increase the number of "safe seats." Close to 85 percent of Congress is so crafted, meaning in 85 percent of the districts, it's almost impossible for the other party to win. If you're a Republican in a safe-seat Republican district, you know, barring some scandal, that your representative is going to be a Republican. Or if you're a Democrat in a safe-seat Democratic district, you know, barring some scandal, that your representative is going to be a Democrat. According to the *Cook Political Report,* in 2017 there were only 72 "swing districts" in the House of Representatives—while two decades ago, there were 164.[47] That means that in all but 70 or so seats, the party of the winner of the election is set before the first vote is even cast.

Call this "safe-seat democracy," and notice one obvious effect. For even if a congresswoman within a safe seat doesn't need to fear a challenger from a different party, she still needs to fear a challenger in her own party. That is, a challenge in the primary. A Democrat in a safe-seat Democratic district is not going to be beaten by a Republican. But she might be defeated by another Democrat, challenging her in the primary. The contest is thus the primary, and the objective of every incumbent is to avoid any challenge in the primary.[48]

Yet primaries are oddly unrepresentative elections. Very few voters actually vote in most primaries. In 2014, for example, Republicans had a 9.5 percent turnout of voter registration. Democrats had 8.1 percent.[49] 2018 was slightly better, if reversed: 9.9 percent of voters cast ballots for Democrats, while 8.8 percent cast ballots for Republicans.[50] And those who do vote are very particular—they are the wonks, or the politically engaged. They are also the most extreme ideologically.[51] And so if the incumbent is to avoid a successful challenge from a member of her own party, she must ensure that there is no hook for the even more extreme members of her own party to leverage to defeat the incumbent.

Thus the Republican in a safe-seat Republican district must ensure that there's no hook for an even more extreme Republican to take him or her on. And a Democrat in a safe-seat Democratic district must ensure there's no hook for an even more extreme Democrat to take him or her on. The attention is thus to the flanks—not to the base of the party and certainly not the middle voter in the district. The power is in the extremes, not in the middle.

This dynamic is "certainly conventional wisdom," as a recent Brookings report put it, among politicians and many scholars.[52] And as Robert Boatright has found, over the past decade at least, "the pre-dominance of ideological challenges is unmistakable."[53] "[M]embers of Congress must now pay more attention to partisanship than before,"[54] as Boatright concludes—even if the data don't actually establish that primary challenges are more frequent or consequential now than be-fore.[55] And as the 2018 election reveals, the practice of the Tea Party right to challenge moderate Republicans is now being copied by pro-gressives or "democratic socialists" on the left: organizations such as Justice Democrats have made "primarying" a key technique for shift-ing the balance of power in Congress to the left. The effect of this copycat strategy is obvious, even if its actual effect on votes in Congress is not yet manifest.

The easiest way to avoid a primary challenge, of course, is to be extreme yourself. And so, the systematic effect of a safe-seat Congress

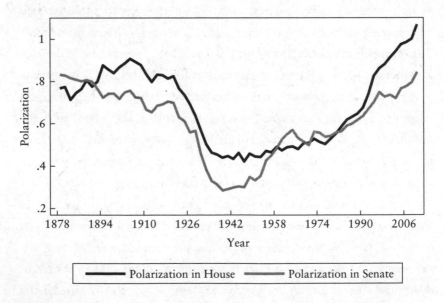

FIGURE 4

Average distance between positions across parties. The y-axis shows the difference in mean positions between the two parties in both the House of Representatives and Senate from 1879 to 2011 using the DW-NOMINATE measures.

Barber & McCarty, Causes and Consequences of Polarization.

with the emergence of the wing-driven primaries may be to push Congress to the extremes. On this account, our representatives will become both more liberal and more conservative than we as Americans are. That fact, in part, may be a consequence of this gerrymandering, especially when linked to the dynamic of primaries.

I say "may" to acknowledge that the point is contested among political scientists. Some believe there is such an effect.[56] Others do not.[57] According to the analysis of political scientists Michael Barber and Nolan McCarty, "polarization relates more to the difference in how Republicans and Democrats represent moderate districts than the increase in the number of extreme partisan districts."[58]

The dynamic here is importantly compounded. It is clear, first, that polarization in Congress is greater now than at any point in the past 125-plus years. As Barber and McCarty map, the gap was high just after the Civil War. Then there was a long period—call it the "era of getting along"—when congressmen learned to work together. And then, since roughly the mid-1980s, there has been a significant rise in the difference between the two parties.

But that story hides an important change in both the character of the parties, and the context of the media within which parties operate. We'll consider the media in chapter 2. Consider here the character of parties.

The political party in America during the "era of getting along" was a very different animal from the political party today. As Sam Rosenfeld describes in his book *The Polarizers*, political parties in America were not ideological. Polarization (or, alternatively, ideological sorting)[59] has increased as they have become ideological. During the 1950s and early 1960s, for example, the Democratic Party was still a deeply divided party ideologically. The New Deal liberals were resisted strongly by southern Democrats. Southern Democrats were genuine conservatives (mainly about race, but not just), while many northern Republicans were genuinely liberal (especially about race, but not just).

That reality imposed a certain discipline upon the politicians.

Nothing happened unless it was cross-partisan. Lyndon Johnson, perhaps the most successful, and certainly the most important Senate majority leader in American history, made bipartisanship a rule. As his press secretary George Reedy would comment, "there were practically no circumstances under which Johnson would countenance a 'Democratic' bill" when he was majority leader.[60] And as Rosenfeld describes,

[The] mores [of Johnson and Sam Rayburn] tended to emphasize attitudes antithetical to vigorous discipline and programmatic commitment. The social world and professional values of midcentury congressmen and senators were focused around collegiality, compromise, deference, and bipartisanship. "Integrity crosses party lines," a Republican told one scholar studying the issue. "You rely on some of your Democratic colleagues equally." The intensely self-conscious internal culture of the Senate in particular venerated civility, reciprocity, and a peculiar combination of individualism and conformity. It instilled a primary commitment to the Senate as a body.[61]

This kind of politics was not captured by big ideas. As Johnson once said, "what the man on the street wants is not a big debate on fundamental issues; he wants a little medical care, a rug on the floor, a picture on the wall."[62] That implied, as Rosenfeld puts it, that "Americans shared core premises and sought from politics only incremental improvements."[63]

The rise of ideological political parties threatened the politics of incrementalism. Johnson helped trigger this development by becoming the century's most important civil rights president. When he got Congress to pass the Civil Rights Act of 1964 and Voting Rights Act of 1965—*finally*—Johnson knew that he had destroyed the Democratic Party in the South. That shove then pushed both parties down an ideological sorting mountain, as the Democrats became more consistently committed to equal rights and the Republicans became more adept at appealing to the hidden racism of American whites.

Race of course was not the only—and certainly not the edifying—dimension along which the parties sorted themselves. Inspired by Barry Goldwater, and realized by Ronald Reagan, the parties also developed clearly different positions on the role of government, and the inherent virtues of the market. Those differences crystallized when Reagan was elected president. And in response, not only were Republicans becoming more consistently ideological, but so too were Democrats.

My purpose in recounting this evolution is not to take sides. I lament the loss of Congress's ability to function, yet I don't feel pulled by a politics of ideological incoherence. It may well be that the culture of politics that we have evolved just does not fit with the constitutional structure that we have inherited. That is a serious threat to our long-term capacity to govern.

The flaws that I am focusing on here, however, are those we can tie to the actions of government *within* the structures of separated powers. The question I am asking is not whether we, as a people, are getting it right. The question instead is how might the rules of the government be steering us wrong? Or more specifically, how are the rules making the problem worse? And how could different rules help?

This is where gerrymandering becomes difficult. Barber and McCarty report that polarization is stronger in swing districts, at least as measured by roll call votes. We can flag, and then bracket, one important concern about that methodology: what gets voted upon is a small and skewed measure of the influences within Congress.[64] What helps signal and cement a congressman's loyalty to either extreme is often not captured in that single dimension of influence. That's the nub of the criticism from political science that suggests that campaign money doesn't affect Congress. (Yes, there are those who think that, too.) It too measures roll call votes and finds in those little evidence of an effect by money. But studies that reach beyond that dimension certainly do find an effect, a point that, bizarrely, political science still just ignores.[65]

Yet assuming Barber and McCarty are right—assuming that swing districts are triggering the polarizing behavior among members of

Congress—that difference could well be driven by the strong need to turn out general election voters. Competitive districts can go either way; the need for candidates in competitive districts—especially when turnout is low generally—is to turn out their base. Safe seats have less urgency to turn out the vote in the general election. Regardless of who votes in a safe-seat district, the majority-party candidate is going to win. This suggests that the drive to polarizing behavior may be a function of the need to get people to vote, not the nature of the seats as safe-seat districts. Or more powerfully (and pointedly), it suggests that if we actually achieved the result that the anti-gerrymanderers want, namely more competitively drawn districts, we might well increase the result that none of us want, namely an even more polarized political culture.

Or relatedly, the extremism could be a function of fundraising: in the age of Internet fundraising, candidates for Congress appeal widely for campaign funds. Small-dollar giving is relatively polarizing, given the politics of those who give.[66] Extremism here may thus be the most effective technique for raising campaign funds.

These are important and fair concerns that qualify anxiety about gerrymandering. They suggest, as mentioned above, that if we don't fix anything else and just fix gerrymandering, we could well see polarization increase. That seems right, though the implication is not clear. We should fix gerrymandering—so that every voter has as close to an equal shot as we can craft—and fix the other flaws that feed the politics of polarization as well. And more important, for the purposes of this part of the analysis, Barber and McCarty's data can't distinguish between the addition to polarization caused by the need to turn voters out or raise money, and the addition caused by the need to keep the extremes in a party happy. Indeed, as the Brookings Institution's Thomas Mann concludes, that is the toxic cocktail for our democracy: the mix of redistricting, primaries, and campaign finance together.[67]

If Mann is right, then the political character of the House of Representatives is in part a product of the government's decision to draw districts in one way rather than another. The consequence of this is to render certain citizens within a district as lesser citizens within that district. The Republican in a safe-seat Democratic district counts less than a Democrat. And a moderate Democrat in a safe-seat Democratic district counts less than an extreme progressive. I say "counts less" in just the sense that a differently drawn district would increase the weight of their votes. This way of drawing districts thus produces citizens who are not represented equally.

The consequence of this inequality is different from the inequality caused by voter suppression. For the beneficiaries of this inequality are different. In the last section, it was the party controlling the state that benefited from the unequal access to voting. In this case it is the extremes within both parties that benefit from the dynamic of safe-seat gerrymandering. Thus the suppression of the vote in Georgia benefits Republicans over Democrats. But safe-seat gerrymandering benefits both progressive Democrats (like New York's Alexandria Ocasio-Cortez) and conservative Republicans (like Texas's Mike Conaway).

It's this difference that begins to explain the staying power of gerrymandering within our political system. Both sides, in their heart of hearts, kind of like it. Campaigns are expensive. Competitive campaigns are really expensive. It's hard enough for the parties to support the 70-odd competitive races that there are every two years. God forbid there were 270, let alone 435!

But whether the politicians like it or not, the consequences seem increasingly clear. This is a system crafted by insiders to benefit insiders. It is a system that has the consequence of rendering most voters less important than some, certainly members of the minority party in every safe-seat district (more than 12.5 million voters[68]), and maybe even adding to that the members of the majority party not drawn to vote. Close to 60 percent of Democratic primary voters in the 2018 primary called themselves "liberal" or "strongly liberal," while about a third called themselves moderate. That difference was greater for Republicans— close to 75 percent were "conservative" or "very conservative" compared to just over 20 percent who said they were "moderate."[69] Yet nationally, there are just as many "moderates" as "conservatives," according to Gallup, around 35 percent, and about 26 percent who call themselves "liberal."[70]

The problem of representativeness is not that some people have more influence than others. The problem is when the rules crafted by the state *make it so* that some people have more influence than others.

For example, if you're a Stalinist in America today, your views don't matter much. There is not a Stalinist Communist Party in America. Even if there were, there would be a tiny number of people who would join. That tiny number will translate systematically into exactly zero political influence. Because of your views, you don't matter.

But that fact is a function of you, not the state. It is the unpopularity of your views that makes it so your views don't matter much, not the rules drawn by the state for counting your vote or reckoning its influence. Put differently, there is no method for reckoning the influence of your vote equally with the votes of others that could give you any more influence than the ideal system we will consider below. Your lack of influence is wholly on your views.

Gerrymandering is different. When the state crafts safe-seat districts, it is creating the conditions that depress the significance of the minority vote. If the state could draw the districts differently, to increase the significance or influence of that vote, then, all things being equal, citizens would be more equal. As it is, they are not.

3: SENATORS

California has two United States senators. Wyoming does, too. Each senator in California represents almost 18.5 million citizens. Each senator in Wyoming represents fewer than 275,000 citizens. For every 15 people represented by a senator from Wyoming, a senator from California would represent 1,000. A citizen in Wyoming is thus 66 times more powerful in the United States Senate than a citizen from California.

(By contrast, in 1800, the power of a citizen from the smallest state (Delaware) was just 13 times the power of a citizen from the largest state (Virginia).) Yet despite representing *the people* in each state unequally, formally, the Senate represents each *state* absolutely equally.

The Senate is an odd duck—for us, now, as we conceive of a representative democracy. We think today of senators as representing people. For the framers, senators represented states. Each state had two senators. The Constitution expressly forbid any amendment that would deny each state equal representation (at least without its consent). That equality is the basic premise of any republican form of government: that an entity represented be represented equally.

Over time, however, the nation learned that the framers' design for the Senate was fraught. Vesting the appointment of senators in state legislatures was an open invitation to corruption. A legislature as a collective could not be held responsible for a bad or corrupt senator, but individual legislators could benefit enormously from selling Senate seats to the highest bidders. By the end of the nineteenth century, the institution had become a complete embarrassment.

Montana was just an extreme case. Montana became a state in 1889. A decade later, a local industrialist, W. A. Clark, decided he wanted to be its senator. The Montana legislature accommodated his wish in 1899—"in the wake," as the Montana Supreme Court has written, "of a large number of suddenly affluent members [of] the Montana Legislature." Clark admitted to spending $272,000 (about $8 million in current dollars) to secure his seat. Estimates by others put the number at more than $400,000 ($12 million). When the United States Senate learned of the bribes, it refused to seat Clark. Clark returned to Montana and secured a second appointment. When the Senate threatened to unseat him again, he resigned. In 1901, he finally secured a seat in the Senate, by funding the election of a friendly legislature. This time the United States Senate acquiesced. In response to the charge of corruption, Clark is said to have said, "I never bought a man who wasn't for sale." Of Clark, Mark Twain would write:

He is as rotten a human being as can be found anywhere under the flag; he is a shame to the American nation, and no one has helped to send him to the Senate who did not know that his proper place was the penitentiary, with a ball and chain on his legs. To my mind, he is the most disgusting creature that the Republic has produced since [Boss] Tweed's time.[71]

Clark may have been "the most disgusting." But as David Graham Phillips wrote in *Cosmopolitan* in 1906, in his series "The Treason of the Senate," there were many like Clark.[72] Indeed, as the *New York Times* would write in a highly critical editorial describing the time, a millionaire could buy a Senate seat "just as he would buy an opera box, or a yacht, or any other luxury in which he can afford to indulge himself."[73]

The framers might have avoided this flaw by vesting the appointment of senators in the governor. At least he or she could be held responsible for a badly behaving senator, and thus suffer in his or her reelection if the appointment was flawed. But at the moment the problem manifested itself most clearly, the obvious solution to the problem in most people's minds was not to give power to an executive, but to give power to the people. By the end of the nineteenth century, the progressive movement had exploded across America. Its simple (and simplistic) message was that the people could solve any problem of democracy, if we could bring them in more closely. Some states began holding state elections for senators, at least indirectly. Those elections were not binding, but they were very persuasive. And they helped build a movement that in 1912 finally got Congress to propose an amendment to the Constitution to give "the People" the right to select the senators.

When the Seventeenth Amendment passed, however, it rendered the theory of the Senate ambiguous. Did the Senate represent the states still? Or did the Senate now represent the people in the states, if unequally, at least between states? On the former theory, the equality of senators from each state made perfect sense still. On the latter theory, it did not. If the Senate had become yet another representative body, representing "the people," then the Senate was badly apportioned, given the wildly different populations of the people between the states.

What's important in this story is not just the theory of the Constitution, but also the conscience of the nation. We were born a nation of states. The loyalty of the people was to their states, first. It was an astonishing moment in 1850 when Daniel Webster spoke on the floor of the Senate and declared, "Mr. President, I wish to speak today, not as a Massachusetts man, nor as a Northern man, but as an American. . . ."[74]—astonishing because to most Americans, such a claim was as bizarre then as Senator Ted Cruz declaring today that he stood on the floor of the Senate "not as an American, nor as a Texan, but as a citizen of the world." Our loyalties then were local, because our lives then were local.

If anything has changed in America, it is this ideal of locality. Most Americans today think of themselves as Americans first, and citizens of a state second, if at all. And that evolving consciousness renders an unequal Senate more and more troubling. Given the rules of the Senate, the vote of 41 senators can veto absolutely anything. That's not true with a presidential veto, which can be overridden by a vote of two-thirds of each house. A senatorial veto is absolute. Neither the president nor the House has any power to reverse it.

Yet 41 senators could represent as little as 10 percent of America. Thus, in principle at least, the will of 90 percent of America can be blocked by the will of 10 percent. In a world where we took for granted the idea of the states being represented as states, that 41 votes means just over 40 percent can veto any change—not a perfect democracy, but not an embarrassment, either. But a representative democracy in which 10 percent can block the will of 90 percent is not, in any sense, representative anymore.

Even on the original understanding of the Senate, the rules of the Senate do not make sense. Even if we believe that the Senate represents the states equally, the rules of the Senate betray that equality. Majoritarianism is the default within democratic institutions; unless expressly modified in the Constitution, it should prevail. But the weird rules of the present Senate betray this majoritarianism. They effectively give to a minority (of states) the power to block the will of a majority (of states). Thus even accepting the compromise that Madison lamented, the Senate has evolved to deny the core equality that the framers meant to secure. It too, as an institution, is unrepresentative, both of the states *and* of the people within those states.

4: PRESIDENTS

The idea of the president was a work in progress for our framers. They knew they didn't want a king (though Hamilton wanted an elected monarch[75]). They knew they didn't want a puppet of the states (though some in many states did). And at least many knew they didn't want a president elected by the people directly: nothing like that had ever happened before in the history of humanity, and for a nation as diffuse and expansive as the United States, at least given the technology of the time, there was a genuine fear that the people would have no clue whom to choose as president.[76]

So the framers crafted a pretty clever compromise. There would be no king. And there would be no puppet of the states. Instead, the states were given the power to select "electors" who were themselves then given the power to select the president. How the states selected those electors was completely up to the states. But by using the word *elector,* the framers were signaling pretty clearly that those people being selected were being selected to exercise judgment. They were not potted plants. There were not rubber stamps. There were not simple delegates or agents of the people in a state. And just to make that point perfectly clear, the electors were directed to vote by "ballot," which in the framing context meant by "secret ballot."[77] Why would you give the elector the chance to hide his vote if you meant him to act as a simple clerk?

This point is important, and it bears emphasis. The Constitution speaks of two kinds of "electors" only—what we could call legislative electors and presidential electors. The legislative electors were the people who selected members of Congress. The presidential electors were the people who selected the president.

Legislative electors, under the Constitution, were to be those with the "Qualifications requisite for Electors of the most numerous Branch of the State Legislature." So, for example, if a state (before the Twenty-sixth Amendment) said anyone twenty-five or older could vote for a state representative, then anyone twenty-five or older could vote for a United States congressman in that state. Very quickly the states converged on a fairly standard formula.[78] But still, it was the states rules that determined who had the power to vote for federal representatives.

It is clear that a legislative elector (i.e., a voter) has the right to choose how he or she will vote. As is clear from its etymology, an "elector" is a "chooser." Dictionaries at the time of the founding defined an elector as a "chuser"—he who has the "choice of any public office."[79] "Elector" thus implies choice. If they could be forced to vote one way or another, they would not be exercising any choice.

The same should be true for presidential electors as well. The state gets to "appoint" presidential electors. In exercising that choice, the state gets to discriminate in lots of obvious ways. But however the state chooses, the elector retains the right to vote however the elector wants. Across the history of presidential electors, there have been almost two hundred electors who have voted contrary to how they were pledged. In every case, their unpledged vote was counted as a legitimate vote.

If "electors" are electors, and hence, if they have the right to vote as they choose, then it is not difficult to imagine their choice altering an election. In 2016, seven electors cast their vote contrary to how they were pledged. In 2000, George W. Bush won in the Electoral College with just one vote. If just two had had the same idea that seven did in 2016, history would have been radically different. This fact rightly concerns many Americans. That concern does not negate its being a fact.

Yet that's not the feature of the Electoral College that I want to focus on here. Instead consider how the electors get pledged to one candidate or another. Today, all but two states (Maine and Nebraska) allocate all of their electors to the winner of the popular vote in their state. Thus, in 1992, though Bill Clinton received less than 40 percent of the votes in Maine, Montana, Nevada, and New Hampshire, because of the third-party candidate, Ross Perot, Clinton still received all of the Electoral College votes from those states. In 2016, a third of the electoral votes that Donald Trump received were from states where he won a plurality only.

This is the consequence of the "winner take all" (WTA) system. Critically, that system is nowhere described in the Constitution itself. The Constitution leaves it to the states to allocate their electors as they choose. Initially, most states either allocated electors by district, or the legislature allocated electors as it wanted. WTA began to be the rule at about the time of Andrew Jackson. Once one state did it, others followed pretty quickly, and for a pretty obvious reason: if your state, allocating electors by district, is dividing its electors between two candidates, but your neighboring state is giving all of its electors to just one candidate, then your neighbor could matter more to the candidates than do you. This created a race to the bottom, as each state shifted to WTA to ensure that it mattered as much as the next.

It is difficult for us to see today exactly what the framers imagined the states would do in 1789. That's in part because the framers had no real clue. But it's also because the very idea of the presidency changed pretty radically pretty quickly. We've actually had two very different conceptions of the Electoral College, because we've had two very different conceptions of the president. At the beginning, the ideal of the president was George Washington—a man above politics, a man who united the nation, a man who was the clear consensus candidate for every faction in the nation. Given that ideal, the Constitution gave electors within each state two votes to cast; the winner would be president, and the runner-up would be vice president.

But once the likely candidates were no longer individuals who stood above politics, politics created an obvious incentive for the system of selecting the president to be hacked. The election of 1800 is a pretty good real-world example of just how.

In 1800, Thomas Jefferson challenged the incumbent, John Adams. The two had been friends for more than twenty-five years; they would be friends again (both dying within hours of each other on the fiftieth anniversary of the Declaration of Independence, July 4, 1826). But at this moment in their mutual history, they were not friends. Adams had beaten Jefferson in 1796. Under the rules as they then existed, that made Jefferson vice president. It didn't take long for people to realize how idiotic it was to imagine the loser serving in the winner's administration. So by 1800, the pols had devised a pretty clever hack to avoid this obvious mistake: Candidates for president would run with running mates; the electors would cast one vote for the candidate and their second vote for the running mate. One elector from the running mate's list would then cast his ballot for someone else. That would give the running mate at least one less vote than the candidate, and hence make the running mate the vice president.

That's exactly how the system worked in 1800—at least on the Federalist side. Adams received 65 electoral votes. His running mate, Charles Pinckney, received 64. An elector from Rhode Island cast his second vote for John Jay, assuring Pinckney would not tie with Adams.

But the election nonetheless was tied—not between Jefferson and Adams, but between Jefferson and his running mate, the conniving, future assassin of Hamilton, and eventual traitor to the nation, Aaron Burr. Though Jefferson had won the popular vote, and, with the legislatures that allocated their electors directly, won 73 electoral votes as a consequence, Burr's team "forgot" to arrange to have one of its electors vote for someone else. Thus Burr received the same number of votes as Jefferson, forcing the election into the House of Representatives for it to be resolved. After thirty ballots, eventually the House decided to award the election to the candidate who everyone knew was the one candidate actually running for president—Jefferson.[80]

That story, however, hides the real disaster that was just narrowly avoided. Because imagine that the elector from Rhode Island who voted for Jay (so as to ensure that Pinckney would not tie with Adams) had instead voted for Burr. No doubt, going into the vote, most who know anything knew Adams had lost. But if Adams had lost, why not cause some real trouble? Making Burr president would just embarrass the Republicans. Or at a minimum, why not force the election into the House, because again, everyone would have expected that New York would have done as Rhode Island had done. But of course, because New York hadn't done so, a vote for Burr by the delegate from Rhode Island would have made Burr president. And thus the man no one was expecting would become president would become president, all because of the anomalous vote of a Rhode Island elector.

Everyone understood in 1801 that the nation had dodged a bullet. Very quickly, Congress began considering an amendment to the Constitution to correct the framers' error. The Twelfth Amendment separated the vote for president from the vote for vice president, so that the majority's preference could not be hijacked by a conniving minority (or vice president). Now the simple question was whether and who received the majority of electoral votes. That candidate would be president. If no one received a majority, then the top candidates would be considered by the House. And the candidate who received the most votes in the House would be president, every state getting one vote.

There's a subtlety to this system that we are likely to miss. As law professor Ned Foley has described brilliantly, the core value that the framers of the Twelfth Amendment were trying to protect was majoritarianism. The idea of a plurality deciding who would be president was anathema to them. They thus required that the president achieve a majority of electors, and if he didn't achieve a majority, then a majority of the states—which would mean a majority of the congressmen and senators within each state. Theirs was thus a double-majority system: their presumption was that the candidate who would win would have won in every state that gave him a majority.

And so it has worked for most presidents over the last 220 years. As Foley has calculated, in only three elections—1844, 1884, and 2000— has the Electoral College clearly awarded a victory to the candidate who was not the Jeffersonian compound-majoritarian winner. In another 13 elections—1848, 1888, 1892, 1912, 1916, 1948, 1960, 1968, 1976, 1980, 1992, 1996, 2016—it is unclear whether the winner was a Jeffersonian compound-majoritarian winner. And in the remaining thirty-two elections, the president was a clear compound-majority winner.[81]

But this winner-take-all system also encouraged an instability. It enabled the winner of a mere plurality within a state to get all of the Electoral College votes from that states. And when that fact is added to yet another fact the framers of the Twelfth Amendment did not contemplate—namely, that there would be more than two candidates running for president—it created the conditions for the election of presidents who did not in any meaningful sense represent the majority of America. That was certainly the case in 2000. It may well have been the case in 2016.

A president who doesn't represent the majority of America is obviously a president who doesn't represent America. Foley's book *Presidential Elections and Majority Rule* makes a powerful argument for reforms that would fix the flaws that cause this particular nonmajoritarian result.

Yet *these* flaws don't happen in every election. Indeed, historically, in most elections, the candidate selected has been the majority candidate. A second flaw caused by WTA, however, is different. It affects *every* election. And this flaw, unlike the first, has no foundation in our constitution's text.

This flaw, ignored by many but identified clearly by law professor Samuel Issacharoff, is the way that WTA selects an obviously *unrepresentative* president,[82] and not just when the president happens not to win the popular vote, but in *every single* election that is governed by this system.

Just think about what happens when the states choose to allocate their electors under WTA—what is the consequence for the nation as a whole?

You don't need to be a Karl Rove or Paul Begala to understand what will happen politically. If states allocate their electors according to WTA, then the only states that it makes sense for either candidate to campaign in are states whose electors might flip from one side to another. To campaign in any other state—or to care about winning the votes of voters in any other state—would be a catastrophic waste of effort.

Think for example about California. It would make no sense for a Republican candidate to campaign in California, since, ordinarily, regardless of how well that candidate does, she or he is not going to get enough votes to win the state. Under WTA, if he or she doesn't win, he or she gets nothing. And the same is true for the Democrat. The Democratic candidate knows he or she is going to win California. So why (except to raise money) spend any time campaigning in that state? The electors from California are already in the Democrat's column. Any money spent there is money that could have been spent where it could have changed the vote.

This means that the rational campaign manager for both the Republican and Democratic parties will never spend any time campaigning in any solidly red or solidly blue state. The only states that those campaign managers will campaign in will be the so-called swing states or battleground states. Those are the only states that could go one way or the other. That is therefore where the fight will be waged.

Yet these states don't represent America. The voters in the swing states are older, and whiter.[83] Their industry is more traditional. There are 7.5 times the number of people working in solar energy in America as mine coal. Yet we never hear anything about solar energy in a presidential campaign because those people live in states like Texas and California. Coal miners live in battleground states. They become the central focus of the candidates running for president.

And not just during a campaign. As Andrew Reeves and Douglas L. Kriner have demonstrated in their powerful book, *The Particularistic President*, presidents bend their policies to benefit the battleground states. As they observe, "electoral and partisan incentives combine to encourage presidents to pursue policies across a range of issues that systematically target benefits to politically valuable constituencies."[84] Those constituencies are determined by the way states allocate their Electoral College votes. As a president is heading into his reelection campaign, he becomes focused on the battleground states. Thus, in 2008, four states, Kriner and Reeves estimate—Florida, Ohio, Michigan, and Pennsylvania—received "more than a billion dollars in additional grant spending simply by virtue of being swing states."[85] "All voters are not," as they summarize their findings, "of equal electoral importance. . . . [Instead] the existence of the Electoral College, coupled with the adoption of winner-take-all apportionment of electoral votes in forty-eight states, results in some Americans having greater electoral clout than others."[86]

Because of WTA, "presidential candidates are all but compelled to value and vie for the votes of some Americans more than others."[87] So, for example, when the Trump administration lifted the federal ban on offshore drilling, almost immediately, Florida got an exemption. New Jersey could barely get a hearing. What was difference between the two states? Florida is a swing state; New Jersey, not.[88]

The battleground states have more power per voter than the rest of the country does. Or put differently, the system of electing a president with the Electoral College and with states using the WTA method means that some voters are worth more than others—simply because of the decision that governments have made for how their votes will be counted. It's thus no surprise then that Pew found voters in battleground states prefer keeping the Electoral College, while voters in nonbattleground states prefer selecting the president through popular vote.[89]

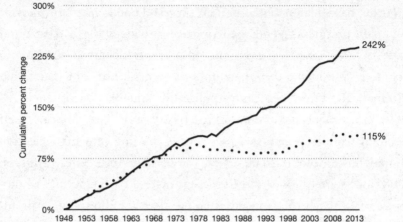

FIGURE 5

Wage Gap

Lawrence Lessig, CC-BY, derived from Economic Policy Institute analysis of data from Bureau of Labor Statistics (BLS) Labor Productivity and Costs program, BLS Current Employment Statistics public data series, BLS Employer Costs for Employee Compensation, and Bureau of Economic Analysis National Income and Product Accounts.

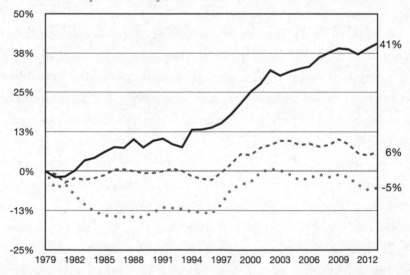

FIGURE 6

Different Growth by Class

Lawrence Lessig, CC-BY, derived from Economic Policy Institute analysis of Current Population Survey Outgoing Rotation Group microdata.

The framers may well have intended the Electoral College to benefit small states. No doubt the per capita electoral power in small states is higher than in large states. But swing states are not small states. The swing states are the states that just happen to be so divided politically that the election in that state could go one way or another. Pennsylvania, Florida, Ohio, Michigan, Wisconsin, Colorado—these are large states, not small states. Granted, New Hampshire and Iowa are small states (in population at least). But the average size of a swing state is 7.5 million, which would make it the thirty-ninth-largest state in the union.[90] As Kriner and Reeves put it,

> ironically, the Electoral College, an institution created by the Founders in large part to promote geographic equality, has become a major source of geographic inequality as presidents have systematically pursued a range of policies designed to disproportionately benefit voters in swing states, particularly in election years.[91]

So the power that this system grants to swing states was not intended by the framers. It doesn't help select a president who cares about the nation as a whole. It doesn't even help select a president who represents the majority. And it has the added weakness of increasing the probability that the president who is ultimately elected does not actually win even the plurality of the popular vote. Indeed, given shifting demographics, the probability that the president will be selected by the Electoral College after losing the popular vote will only increase. According to some estimates, in a close election, that probability is almost 20 percent.[92]

Thus the rules adopted by the institutions of our democracy—here, the states—for allocating the electors who select the two national offices within our Constitution—the president and vice president—produce a president who is unrepresentative of the nation he or she is to lead.

5: VOTES

Middle-class middle America has suffered greatly over the past two decades. Not that poorer people around the country did any better. But certainly, people who are wealthier did do better. Much better.

This is something new. Until the middle of the 1970s, America was a middle-class nation. Growth benefited everyone, the middle class especially. The middle class lived with real promise, as parents could imagine their children doing better than they, and as families felt and were, over time, wealthier.

All that has now changed. Since the middle of the 1970s, middle-class and lower-middle-class workers have done worse than upper-middle-class workers and the rich. A now-famous graph tracks how wages and productivity grow together through the middle 1970s. Then productivity climbs radically, while wages stagnate and fall.

In 2007, the U.S. middle class household had $17,867 less income than it did in 1979, measured in constant dollars. Middle-class wages are stagnant since 1979; lower-class wages have fallen. Yet upper-class wages have climbed substantially.

Today, it is likely that children of middle-class families will not do better than their parents. Many will do much worse. And the future for the former middle class across the Rust Belt of the United States has, quite profoundly, rusted.

Hopelessness drives addiction. Thus with this decline has come the rise of a most dramatic epidemic—opioid addiction. Since 1991, opioid prescriptions internationally have tripled, from 76 million to 207 million. The United States is the largest consumer globally, accounting for 100 percent of Vicodin consumption, and 8 percent of Percocet. From 1999 through 2017, almost 218,000 people have died in the United States from opioid overdoses, with almost 50,000 dying in 2017 alone—about a third higher than the number of people who died in automobile accidents in the same year.[93]

People talk endlessly about the effect of money in politics. There's no clearer example—both about the corrupting effect and its dramatic consequences—than the opioid crisis. Our government bent its standards and allowed a completely predictable epidemic to arise because of the enormous amount of money that was made available to the key actors in this tragedy.[94]

Standing behind the opioid crisis is a single firm, Purdue Pharma. Standing behind that firm is an extraordinarily wealthy family, the Sacklers.[95] Most of the money the Sacklers have collected is from the profits on OxyContin. Millions are addicted to these drugs, which have earned the family $35 billion.

At every stage in the development and marketing of OxyContin, there was corruption.[96] The Sacklers perfected an extraordinary drug development, marketing, and regulatory machine. They perfected the ability to leverage influence into sales. First, doctors paid by Purdue Pharma argued that medicine was not open enough to the good of opioids. Pain doctor and professor Russell Portenoy praised this "gift from nature" that he said should be "destigmatized." "Opiophobia," he declared, had to end. Portenoy was paid by Purdue.[97]

Other doctors were also paid to promote the drugs and to write papers that affirmed their safety. "The marketing," writes Patrick Radden Keefe for *The New Yorker*, "relied on an empirical circularity: the company convinced doctors of the drug's safety with literature that had been produced by doctors who were paid, or funded, by the company."

And not just doctors: regulators who found reason to give this drug special treatment also found themselves the beneficiary of special treatment by Purdue Pharma later. When the Food and Drug Administration (FDA) approved OxyContin, it took the unusual step of declaring that it was safer than other pain medications. The examiner who made that extraordinary declaration, Dr. Curtis Wright, Keefe writes, "left the agency shortly afterward. Within two years, he had taken a job at Purdue."

Since 1999, more than 200,000 people have died from OxyContin overdoses. That's four times the number of American soldiers killed in

Vietnam. When addicts find the drug too expensive, they often move on to other cheaper opioids. "According to the American Society of Addiction Medicine," Keefe reports, "four out of five people who try heroin today started with prescription painkillers." The company had declared that "fewer than 1%" of OxyContin patients developed addiction. The actual number was thirteen times greater.

Yet most striking for our purposes here was the effort by the company to leverage its influence in the political space to assure an essentially unchallenged opportunity to addict America. According to Keefe, between 2006 and 2015, Purdue and other painkiller producers and nonprofits spent "nearly nine hundred million dollars on lobbying and political contributions—eight times what the gun lobby spent during that period."

That money did not go to Republicans alone. Indeed, Democrats on average received more. Since 1996, Purdue and the Sacklers have contributed to more than three hundred candidates and political organizations.[98] Joe Lieberman was the number one recipient. Number two was Chris Dodd, who left the Senate in 2011 to become the chief lobbyist for the Motion Picture Association of America. Nine out of ten members of the House, and all but three members of the Senate, have taken money from pharmaceutical companies. One of those legislators, Congressman Tom Marino, nominated to be President Trump's drug czar, had to withdraw when it was discovered that he had pressed legislation that made it harder for the Drug Enforcement Administration to move against those illegally distributing opioids.[99]

Notice one thing about this example of money corrupting politics: there was never a campaign ad that ran in any campaign ever that tried to persuade voters to vote for a candidate because he or she was liberal about opioids. There was not a single case when a candidate gave a speech to the public that tried to persuade the public to support him or her because of his or her liberal opioid policy. All of the influence about this issue was in the background. And all of it came from the effect of money, yet money's effect here was not on the people. Money's effect was on the people's representatives.

This is a critical distinction, not noted enough by those who rail against the effect of money on politics.

It's one thing to worry about how campaign spending might affect the voters. It's a completely different thing to worry about how campaign contributions or spending might affect candidates. There's a very good reason for us to worry about giving the government the power to worry about how political speech affects us. There's a very different reason for us to worry about how campaign money affects representatives.

That difference goes to the heart of our First Amendment. It's not the government's role to police the speech market—especially the political speech market. If the government got to decide which speech was good speech and which speech was bad, it would become very tempting for the government to suppress the speech that was critical of it. Such has been the history of governments since the beginning of time. Such is precisely the reason our constitution meant to keep that power off the legislative table.

But when the government polices the effect of campaign money on representatives, its objective is at least conceivably very different. From the beginning of the republic, we've understood that there's a compelling reason to avoid the corruption of representatives. That's because from the beginning of time, we've understood that private vice can steer public officials away from the public good. It has long been an important function of ethics rules and regulations to keep representatives focused on the straight and narrow.[100] Indeed, there is even some evidence that voters themselves cannot root corrupt officials out, making rules to avoid corruption even more important.[101]

The simplest example of corruption regulation is laws against bribery. From the beginning of time, the government has been free to ban or regulate bribery. It hasn't always done so (not until 1853 in the House of Representatives[102]), but no one ever doubted that it could. The Constitution itself lists bribery among the reasons why the "President, Vice President and all civil Officers of the United States" might be impeached and removed from office. Certainly it can't violate the First Amendment for Congress to impeach a federal judge who accepted money in exchange for a particular judicial decision—even if the offer ("I'll give you one million dollars if you acquit me.") and the decision ("The defendant is acquitted.") are both plainly "speech."

What, beyond bribery, Congress can regulate, is a more difficult question. However, before we try to answer that question, we should understand a bit more how money actually matters in Washington. What is the economy of influence? Where does it have its effect?

Because the truth is, our Congress is not bribed. Our Congress is influenced through a much more subtle—and much more effective—technique than that. We must understand that technique if we are to ensure representativeness.

BOSS TWEED IS ONE of America's most colorful political figures. He was also one of the most corrupt. From 1858 until 1877 (when he was sent to prison), Tweed ran New York's political machine, "Tammany Hall," which means he effectively ran the city of New York, controlling its government and profiting enormously from graft and blatant corruption.[103]

Whatever else Tweed knew, he knew about power. He understood, that is, how power in a democracy gets made and hence leveraged. And in a famous quip he gave us a perfect picture of that dynamic—a picture that will explain much about the nature of American politics today. As Tweed said:

I don't care who does the electing, as long as I get to do the nominating.[104]

The insight is brilliant and, once seen, obvious. If a person gets to choose who gets to run in a political system, then that person has enormous power within that system. The people may get to vote among the small list of people nominated. But if there is one person—or one type of interest—that is nominating that small list, *that* person, or interest, has a dominant influence over those nominees, and more important, over the person ultimately elected. The person elected recognizes that she must keep the nominator happy. That recognition gives the nominator unequal power.

So in honor of Boss Tweed, let's give those nominators a name: "tweeds." Formally, a "tweed" is any individual or interest that qualifies a candidate to be a candidate. So understood, you are a "tweed" if to be elected, the candidate must first satisfy you. The "tweeds" within a political system are thus the people in that system who get to (at least effectively) nominate the candidates who get to run in that system. They are the veto point. They are the interest that the candidates must satisfy before the candidates get the chance to persuade the voters.

Every political system has its tweeds. And a democracy is not corrupt simply because there are some with more power than others (at least depending on how that power gets built). But the question in every case must be whether the characteristic that makes you a "tweed" can be justified against the background principles of your particular democracy. Sometimes it can. Often it cannot.

For example, in our system, the primary is a tweedist process. It wasn't always. First, it didn't always exist. Primaries only entered upon the American political stage at the end of the nineteenth century.[105] But once the progressives had made it irresistible for the parties to embrace the primary, practically every state followed suit. By the end of the twentieth century, even nominations for the presidency were determined by primaries. Primaries are therefore tweediest, but they are justified if political parties are justified.

That's not to say there have not been arguments on the margin. There is a constant fight against "closed primaries" by citizens who believe that it violates equality to deny any citizen the right to participate in critical primaries. There is a regular and serious fight within the parties about the power of party leaders within mixed systems of nomination: In 2016, early in the primary season, Bernie Sanders supporters were upset that "superdelegates" would have the power to vote independently of party primaries. Later in the season, his supporters were upset that "superdelegates" did not exercise their independent power to vote for Sanders, contrary to the votes in the party primaries. And finally, there is the unavoidable and undeniable effect of primaries that I have already described when discussing gerrymandering—that given the low participation by citizens less interested in politics, primaries bend unmistakably to the extremes within either party. These are all grounds for serious skepticism about the advisability of using primaries to nominate candidates. They don't, however, constitute grounds to reject the primaries as inconsistent with our democratic principles.

Consider, however, three examples that do constitute grounds to reject a particular kind of tweedism. As I will argue, all of these examples share a common form. In all of them, the qualification that makes you a tweed arguably cannot be justified in the terms of the democratic principles within which it exercises its power. In these examples, in other words, tweedism cannot be justified.

White Tweeds

In 1870, America determined that the right to vote could not be denied on the basis of race. The Fifteenth Amendment was the last of the Civil War amendments. For a brief and noble period, it helped secure to African American males an equal right to vote.

Within a decade, that right was almost dead. White terrorists throughout America's South rallied white racists to use force to keep African Americans away from the polls. At first, the federal government defended the newly enfranchised ex-slaves. Over time, its resolve weakened. By the end of the nineteenth century, southern states had hatched a gaggle of techniques to keep black men away from the polls. When the Supreme Court was asked to invalidate one particularly grotesque example of this exclusion—Alabama had completely nullified the Fifteenth Amendment by refusing to register African Americans—Justice Oliver Wendell Holmes practically laughed at the absurdity of the idea that the Court would intervene.

One of the racist techniques used was the "white primary." Adopted by a number of states indirectly in 1923, the white primary was embraced quite explicitly and directly by the state of Texas. By law, beginning with the election of 1924, only whites could vote in the Democratic primary. Black men were free to vote in the Republican primary (if they could register). They were free to vote in the general election (again, if they could register). But they were barred from the choice among the Democratic candidates to become *the* Democratic candidate, in a state that was overwhelmingly Democratic. In 1924, not a single Republican won any federal office, and in the House, in all but one district, the Democrats won by at least a factor of 5. The Democrat won the Senate by a factor of 6. Only the Republican running for governor, George C. Butte, dean of the University of Texas Law School, did relatively well, winning more votes as a Republican than any since the Civil War. Yet Miriam "Ma" Ferguson beat Butte 59 percent to 41 percent.[106]

The white primary may seem puzzling, given the Fifteenth Amendment. How could it be that denying someone the right to vote on the basis of race in a primary isn't "denying or abridging" the "right of citizens of the United States to vote" "on account of race, color, or previous condition of servitude"?

The answer is pretty straightforward, even if hard for us to accept. The "right . . . to vote" that the Fifteenth Amendment was speaking of was the "right . . . to vote" in an election. Obviously, not every "vote" is a vote within an "election." No one in 1870, for example, believed that the elections of a private club were "elections" for purposes of the Fifteenth Amendment. The Union League was free to exclude African Americans—or not—without fear of violating the Fifteenth Amendment. So the critical question was whether "a primary" was "an election" for purposes of the Fifteenth Amendment.

As bizarre as this idea is to us today, the argument that it wasn't "an election" for purposes of the Fifteenth Amendment has a pretty compelling logical structure. "An election" selects the elected officials of a government—either legislators, or executives, or in some states, and stupidly, judges. "A primary" does not select anyone to government. The winner of a primary is not a government official. The winner of a primary is a candidate to become a government official. Thus, when Texas banned African Americans from voting in the Democratic primary, it wasn't, it claimed, excluding them from "voting in an election." It was simply excluding them from the choice among Democrats about who would be the Democrats' candidate in "an election."

Amazingly, this crazy logic survived in American law for more than a generation. It was explicitly endorsed by the Supreme Court in *Newberry v. United States* (1921). And while its demise is interesting, the details of its decline are beyond our scope here.

Instead, what's important is to recognize the tweedist effect of Texas's all-white primary. For most of the twentieth century, the only party that mattered in Texas was the Democratic Party. That meant that the only primary that mattered was the Democratic primary. If only whites could vote in the Democratic primary, then in this sense, whites were the tweeds of the Texas democracy. They did the nominating, regardless of who did the electing. And every elected official in Texas knew that if he (and it was primarily "he") wanted to keep his job, then he had to keep whites in Texas happy.

Texas had thus produced a democracy that was responsive to whites—that is, first within the primary, and then because of the significance of the Democratic Party, in the general election as well. And

whether its structure violates the Fifteenth Amendment or not (and today it clearly would), the question that we must focus on here is whether
the inequality it created can be justified. Can a democracy justify a
system that weights the power of a vote on the basis of race differently?

Of all the easy questions in constitutional law, this ought to be the
easiest. The race of a citizen should not matter to the power of that citizen's vote. Of all the qualifications, race, in our history, should be the
most obviously not allowed. So the white primary is a clearly tweedist
structure that could not be justified.

Okay, but what about the filter of simply being a Democrat in Texas
(in 1940 at least). Imagine there was no filter of race. Imagine anyone—
white or black—could vote in the Democratic primary. But imagine
(because this was true) that the only party that mattered in Texas was
the Democratic Party. So the Democrats didn't need to worry about
who did the electing, as long as they did the nominating. That, too, is
a kind of tweedism. And if the tweedism of a white primary is invalid,
why is the tweedism of a Democratic primary not also invalid?

Both are instances of tweedism for sure. The difference is in the nature of the discrimination. There's a good reason for a political system to
filter on the basis of a political party—so long as individuals within the
system all still have an equal vote. But there's no good reason to filter on
the basis of race. With respect to race, we ought to be equal. My vote
should count as much as yours, regardless of the colors of our skins. But
with respect to ideas, all bets are off. Your crazy ideas have no claim in
justice to having the same weight in every part of our political system as
mine (thank heavens!). The only equality question is whether it has an
equal weight within the election.

The white primary is thus a clear example of tweedism gone bad:
we can clearly understand the effect of this tweedism, and we can understand why it should be invalidated.

Consider now a second example, more contemporary if politically
more remote.

Red Tweeds

In October 2014, the province of Hong Kong was brought to a halt. Hundreds of thousands of citizens joined the "umbrella protests," challenging a proposed law for selecting Hong Kong's chief executive.

Hong Kong had been a British colony—leased from China in 1898 for a term of ninety-nine years. Throughout the twentieth century, China made it clear that when the lease was up, it wanted Hong Kong back. As 1997 approached, the citizens of Hong Kong grew more and more anxious as they contemplated being absorbed by a nation that, let's say, was less convinced of democratic virtues.

To allay these concerns, China promised that the citizens would be free to elect their own chief executive. The law that brought Hong Kong to a standstill in 2014 was the law that described the process for selecting that chief executive.

That process had a familiar (at least for readers of this book) form. The citizens of Hong Kong were guaranteed the right to vote for the chief executive. But to become a candidate for chief executive, you had to get the approval of a "nominating committee." That nominating committee was to be composed of some 1,200 citizens. That means for a population of 7 million, .02 percent had the power to select the candidates that the rest of Hong Kong got to vote among.

That fact triggered the protests. For the 1,200 were not randomly selected citizens. Instead, while chosen through an immensely complex process, the protesters believed the 1,200 would represent "the business and political elite." This was not "a democracy," as Martin Lee, chairman of the Hong Kong Democratic Party, objected. It was "democracy with Chinese characteristics."[107]

Yet of course, those "Chinese characteristics" were not just Chinese. They were tweedist. The structure China wanted to impose on Hong Kong was precisely the structure Boss Tweed imposed on democracy in New York. Sure, the people could vote. Have at it. But they could only vote among the candidates that China selected. This, as Western observers were quick to note, was thus not a democracy. As Chris Patten, the last British governor of Hong Kong before the handover, wrote in a *Washington Post* op-ed,

> No one told the people of Hong Kong when they were assured of universal suffrage that it would not mean being able to choose for whom they could vote. No one said Iran was the democratic model that China's Communist bureaucracy had in mind, with the Chinese government authorized to exercise an effective veto over candidates.

The Hong Kong model is not troubling because of the relatively small number who are doing the nominating. It is troubling because of the bias in the small number who are doing the nominating. If Hong Kong convened a convention with 1,200 citizens, randomly selected and representative of Hong Kong, there'd be nothing (from this perspective, at least) wrong with that system. The nominations would be done by a "few," but those "few" would be representative.

But could the proposed Chinese system be justified nonetheless? No doubt, it isn't representative of the people of Hong Kong. But why would that make it corrupt?

The answer, of course, depends on your conception of Hong Kong's democracy. If you read the deal that was struck as a promise for self-determination, then obviously, China choosing the candidates that Hong Kong gets to choose among violates this principle of self-determination.

But if you read the deal as a kind of kludge—a way of preserving some aspects of "democracy," while ensuring China some control—then the argument for the protesters becomes more difficult. Yes, the bias burdens the people of Hong Kong. But the bias was a compromise with the nation that now rules Hong Kong. It's like each state getting two senators within a constitution that otherwise respects political equality.

My point here is not to resolve that question (though my own biases are with the people of Hong Kong). My point instead is simply to identify what needs to be justified if indeed one wants to justify the obviously tweedist structure of Hong Kong's democracy. There are tweeds in that system. Does their power cohere with the constitution of that system or does it not?

Green(back) Tweeds

We take it for granted in America that campaigns for federal office will be privately financed. For many years, there was public funding for presidential candidates. Obama put the kibosh on that, when he became the first candidate for president since Nixon to turn down public funding. But most people didn't seem to notice, and most politicians didn't seem to care. Since 2008, every major candidate for federal public office has relied on private funds to fund his or her campaigns.

At the presidential level, this might not matter much. Candidates like Bernie Sanders have found it possible to raise ungodly amounts of money in small contributions. Yet no one thinks Sanders is beholden to anyone—except maybe to the millions who contributed to him, which, in a democracy, isn't a terrible thing. And while Donald Trump certainly exaggerated his reliance on his own money obscenely, it is also true that the SuperPACs—political action committees that can accept unlimited donations—didn't get him to where he got.

But we should neither exaggerate the insignificance of losing presidential public funding nor, and more important for our purposes here, imagine that the economy of influence for funding presidential campaigns is anything like the economy of influence for funding campaigns for Congress.

First, presidents may well be able to fund their own campaigns privately—but only by turning the office into a permanent fundraising operation. When Ronald Reagan ran for reelection in 1984, he attended eight fundraisers. When Barack Obama ran for reelection twenty-eight years later, he attended 228 fundraisers![108] How does the leader of the free world do his job while attending 228 fundraisers?

But, second, and more important, we cannot confuse the business model of fundraising for (at least populist) presidential candidates with the business model of fundraising for the vast majority of members of Congress. Bernie Sanders may have been able to crowd fund a presidential race. And a handful of candidates for Congress—Michele Bachman or Alexandria Ocasio-Cortez—may be able to raise the funds they need in small contributions only. But the ordinary candidate for Congress cannot rely on small contributions alone. That is why the ordinary member of Congress spends anywhere between 30 percent and 70 percent of his or her time raising money for his or her campaign from big funders primarily.[109]And what do we know about these funders? As law professor Nicholas Stephanopoulos put it, summarizing the research, "If there is one thing that political scientists have learned about the small slice of Americans who give money to candidates, it is that they are nothing like their peers who do not give money."[110]

Just think about that fact for a second: Imagine the life. Imagine you had to spend even just half your time sucking up to powerful people to get the money you need to run your campaign or the campaigns of others from your party.

Is that a discipline likely to produce leaders? Is that the way to produce representatives keen to represent us?

This was a point that Donald Trump made repeatedly—at least early in his campaign. It was a good point. When he was still keen to attack Jeb Bush, Trump repeatedly emphasized this human dimension to this fundraising nightmare. How could Jeb Bush think about the public interest, when he knew the decision he was going to make might affect someone who had just given his SuperPAC $1 million? The politicians, Trump insisted, were beholden to their funders. "Everybody that puts up that money wants something for it. It's not good for the United States. It's not good for the country."[111] He knew that. He had been a funder. The politicians could not, Trump insisted, act for the public good without constantly worrying about whether that act would be, for a funder, a private bad. They were thus compromised by this private dependence. That compromise makes it, Trump insisted, "a corrupt system."[112] "SuperPACs are a disaster," Trump declared.[113] "Very corrupt." They "are controlling your Senators, they're controlling every candidate, they'll only do what's right for those people that gave them money."[114]

What is right about this perspective is that it focuses us on how the funding affects the representative, not how the funding affects the voter. Too often, reformers tell us that campaign money is bad because it distorts "the speech market" and therefore distorts us. Even the Supreme Court has sometimes fallen into this trap. In *Austin v. Michigan Chamber of Commerce* (1990), for example, the Court allowed the state to regulate corporate speech because of "the corrosive and distorting effects of immense aggregations of wealth that are accumulated with the help of the corporate form and that have little or no correlation to the public's support for the corporation's political ideas."[115] Here the problem was not simply wealth; it was wealth accumulated through the indirect help of the state, with no "actual public support for the political ideas espoused." Yet the idea that one's freedom of speech depends upon public support for the idea spoken is the negation of free speech, not its defense.

But in a constitutional republic that protects free speech, it can't be the government that decides which speech to allow or disallow based upon its view about whether that speech "distorts" us. Obviously. In this respect, "We, the citizens" have to take care of ourselves. And while I'd be the first to agree that the effect of SuperPAC spending is not more, but less, understanding in the public, I don't believe it's the government's job to pick sides in a political debate. Some tasks are just too dangerous for people or institutions with a monopoly on legitimate violence.

That's why Trump's perspective is so helpful here. The point isn't that this dependence on big funders corrupts *us*. The point instead is that it corrupts *our representatives*. Or as Stephanopoulos puts it, the "distortion of *voters* is different from the distortion of *representa-*

tives."[116] A constant discipline of sucking up to money makes representatives sensitive to the views of those with money—and convinced that the public is more conservative than it is.[117] And that sensitivity gives those with money much greater influence within our government than their numbers would allow. As Stephanopoulos puts it, "politicians' [policy] positions reflect the preferences of their donors to an uncanny extent."[118] And in "combination, donors' abundant resources, policy extremism, and ideological giving contribute to severe misalignment in their favor."[119]

This is the democracy that Tom Perkins was begging for: the funders get as many votes as they give, and the big funders are getting a lot of votes in the money primary. They control the money primary, even if the extremists control the actual primary. They don't represent us, any more than the extremists represent us.

This is true for Democrats as much as for Republicans. The clash between the "establishment" Democrats and the progressive or Bernie Sanders Democrats is almost exclusively, in its essence, a fight about money. Establishment Democrats recognize they need to keep certain interests happy, if they are to fund their candidates' campaigns. Those interests aren't political; they are financial. Democrats are against Wall Street, but they can't be too much against Wall Street. They are in favor of lower-price drugs, but they can't actually press for more competition in drug pricing.

In none of these examples do we have to believe that anyone has been "bought off." That's not how politics—or life—works. To offer someone a bribe is to insult that person. Insults, it turns out, are not the most effective mode of persuasion. Instead, this bending in Washington comes through the subtle nudge of perpetual fundraising, tied to the cuddling and collaboration with lobbyists. Persuasion is through favor, not bribe. It comes through obliging someone, not from purchasing them.[120]

This point should be obvious, yet lawyers and judges just can't stop looking for corruption in all the wrong places. Think about your own life, and where you use money to get what you want, versus favors or relationships. The bargain is the tool we use when that's all we have, at a store or at a gas station. But when we develop a rich and robust relationship with someone, it's not bargains that get us what we want. It's friendship. I do this for you, knowing that someday, you'll do something for me. As the great modern theorist of the gift economy Lewis Hyde describes it,

> It is the cardinal difference between gift and commodity exchange that a gift establishes a feeling-bond between two people, while the sale of a commodity leaves no necessary connection. I go into a hardware store, pay the man for a hacksaw blade and walk out. I may never see him again. The disconnectedness is, in fact, a virtue of the commodity mode. We don't want to be bothered. If the clerk always wants to chat about the family, I'll shop elsewhere. I just want a hacksaw blade.[121]

And that is ultimately and precisely the dynamic that works in Washington, too. No one need bribe anyone, for everyone to become responsive to the needs of Congress. And as responsiveness begets responsiveness, Congress bends to the needs of those with the money.[122]

So let's recap a bit, to link all this back to the point about representativeness.

If the funding of campaigns is private, then funding is its own contest. We could say the funding is its own primary. It takes time. It has an effect. It has a qualifying effect—the only people who can run are those who do well in this funding primary. It makes members dependent on those who fund their campaigns, just as candidates for chief executive in Hong Kong are dependent on China, or candidates for office in Texas (circa 1923) were dependent on whites.

This dependence is thus a kind of tweedism. Like every tweedism, it gives the tweeds a special power within the democracy.

In our democracy, this tweedism means the rich have that power. Their views are worth more than those of the rest of us, because we've allowed a system for funding campaigns to develop in which the candidates are dependent on them. They are the nominators, in Boss Tweed's sense, while we are the electors.[123]

Of all the inequalities that mangle *them*, this is the most corrupt, because in a real sense, it is the most invisible. We all have a sense that the politicians' focus is elsewhere. But focus is a hard thing to track. Who knows why they do what they do, really? All we can say for sure is they don't seem to be attentive to what most Americans want. Yet when you account for the money, you can account for the (lack of) attention.

The tweeds of our democracy are not just white. We are not Texas, 1923. Nor are they red. We are not Hong Kong, 2014. The tweeds in this democracy are green—as in the color of money. The people who don't care about who does the electing, so long as they get to do the nominating, are the holders of great wealth in America. They benefit from a system in which they have more political power, because that system helps them preserve their endless economic power, too.

CONSEQUENCES

Such extreme inequality not only threatens our economic well-being; it undermines our democracy. Since the Supreme Court's disastrous *Citizens United* decision in 2010, billionaires have poured huge amounts of money into the political process. In return, they are getting policies that serve their interests at the expense of working families, the environment, and our national security.

—SENATOR BERNIE SANDERS, 2018[124]

There's a common view that the problem with our democracy is that it benefits rich people. That this system is designed to support "the billionaires." That the core corruption of the idea of our democracy now is that it benefits the elite alone.

This view is too simple—and indeed, too hopeful. If the system can't be representative, then would that it were a system that benefited the elite. Then at least it would be a system that had a rational end, even if it wasn't an end that was supported by a democratic majority.

Yet our actual system is actually less hopeful or rational than even this. Our actual system doesn't benefit the elite (on balance); it benefits no one. Our actual system is not an oligarchy leveraging its power to steer government to the wealthy's ends. Our system is vultures feeding on the carcass of a dead water buffalo.

For work through precisely who is benefited by each of these inequalities:

No doubt the inequality in votes—because of private funding of public elections—benefits the rich. Funders must be rich to afford the level of funding that now matters. The consequence of that funding is to bend policy in a direction that benefits them (especially the crony capitalists[125]). One could well argue that even the funders of campaigns are not representative of the rich. Funders are typically those who have something special to gain from government. Certain industries—telecom, IP—are keen to engage. Others are not. So while the rich, as Benjamin Page, Jason Seawright, and Matthew Lacombe demonstrate, are already more conservative, regardless of their politics, it is the especially interested who spend the most to drive the politics of rent-seeking, the practice of manipulating public policy to increase individual profit.[126]

But the inequality from gerrymandering does not benefit the rich. Safe-seat gerrymandering skews to the extremes and the extremes are not necessarily the rich. On the left, the most progressive push policies not favored by the rich (higher taxes). On the right, the Tea Party types push policies that benefit the rich though not necessarily the cronies. No doubt there is overlap between a politics sensitive to the extremes and a politics sensitive to wealth (especially when, as happened, the wealthy work to capture one of those extremes—the Tea Party[127]); but there is no necessary connection between the two, and no guarantee to the rich at least that the populism of the extremes will inure to its benefit.

Likewise, with the Senate: No doubt expensive campaigns benefit the rich. But small-state senators are not necessarily captured by the rich. The people in small states are not wealthier than the people in large states.[128]

Likewise with the Electoral College: winner-take-all benefits battleground states, not the rich. The battleground states are the most purple states. The interest of those states has no obvious connection to the interests of the wealthy. The support for tariffs to benefit steelworkers does not benefit the rich (or anyone for that matter). The support for farm subsidies benefits only a slice of rich—agribusiness. No doubt the mix of policies necessary to win the support of battleground states is eclectic and shifting. But it is not a mix designed to make "the billionaires" happy. It is a mix designed to attract the most purple votes.

And finally, with endless efforts to suppress the vote: While there is some evidence to suggest that both parties play games like this, it is clear the Republican Party has embraced voter suppression as a fundamental strategy. The primary beneficiary of such suppression is political, not economic. If it means Republicans win, then maybe that means the rich do better. But if the technique of suppressing the vote of your opponent were open and notorious, the beneficiaries would turn on local political control, and not the economic interests of the most wealthy.

What these five differently distorting inequalities do together is not easy to predict. Along some vectors—tax cuts—they may be additive. But along a wide range of issues, they conflict. Tea Party Republicans hate crony capitalism. The rich don't. Swing-state Democrats turn a blind eye to steel tariffs. Democrats generally don't. Rather than a bias that runs in an obvious direction, the sum of these different inequalities bends consistently in no particular direction. This is not the physics of a plutocracy. It is the dynamic of a vetocracy—a "veto-ocracy," as Francis

Fukuyama puts it.[129] As Fukuyama describes, the American Constitution already embeds many veto points for any substantial legislation. A law can be stopped in either house. A law can be slowed by the president. A law can be struck down by the courts. A president can refuse to enforce a law. All of these constitute the ways in which the constitutional system makes change difficult. This much (small-*c*) conservatism is built into the plan.

Yet when you add the dimensions of inequality described in this chapter together, you multiply the points of veto. The rich get special power because of the way we fund campaigns. The extremists get special power because of gerrymandering (just ask Paul Ryan or John Boehner, each of whom found it impossible to govern because of the extremism of the Freedom Caucus). The small states get special power because of the Senate. The battleground states get special power because of the Electoral College. The dominant parties in the states get special power because of the corruption we've allowed to come to voting. Each of these "special powers" gives someone a way to stop something. Each is another veto point in an already veto-rich republic.

The consequence together is thus not a democracy that always bends to the rich. It is a democracy that cannot bend, or function. Regardless of the issue, there are interests who want nothing (rather than something) to happen. Because of multiplied veto points, those interests can practically always succeed. As author and historian David Van Reybrouck observes, "Whilst the US government's plans to overhaul its infrastructure have been stuck in Congress for almost a decade, China has built the Three Gorges Dam and thousands of miles of new railways and roads."[130] A similar comparison could be made with many countries and many projects many times over.

So the question in the end becomes, How much do we suffer because we have a government that cannot govern?

There may have been a time when it wouldn't have mattered much. America in the antebellum period was a nation governed by its states. If the federal government failed, or had been rendered inoperative, no doubt on the margin things would have been worse. But the world would have puttered along just fine. Nothing critical required critical thinking or smart governance, at least at the national level.

But even if there was such a time once, that is not our time now.

Only the most committed partisan could continue to believe that climate change is not real or serious. Yet our vetocracy will not allow us to address climate change sensibly, and it will not, until that corruption is repaired.[131]

America continues to spend almost $700 billion a year on "defense," including more than $80 billion for the growing military-intelligence-industrial state.[132] We are the largest arms exporter in the world—by far. Those exports are extraordinarily destabilizing. Yet they will never end, so long as so many in Congress depend upon the millions in support, direct and indirect, provided by these industries.[133]

The American economy has become fat and huge; markets are highly concentrated, and, when accounting for institutional investors, highly coordinated. That fatness is a consequence of antitrust law in hibernation. Yet the law hibernates because its application is so effectively vetoed.[134]

The Internet in America is slow and expensive—compared to other nations, and not just Korea or Japan. That is the consequence of a regulatory system bent to benefit incumbents. The Federal Communications Commission (FCC) is easy to capture. Under the Trump administration, it was obviously captured by FCC commissioners keen to do the telecoms' bidding. Their demand was to continue to weaken competition among broadband providers. The consequence of weakened competition is always higher prices and lower quality. Congress will never respond to this obviously absurd policy choice because the power of the telecoms, even among the Democrats, ensures that a reversal of FCC policy will not happen.

And twenty years after the Columbine massacre, we *still* to this day have no comprehensive regulation to keep dangerous weapons from deranged men—again, and obviously, because of this vetocracy.

The list is endless—and too depressing to continue. You get the point: Other nations can govern themselves. Their policies might be flawed; their insights might be incomplete. But at least they can move. They can make strategic judgments, and get their people turned in a different direction. They can manage, given an increasingly foreign future. They can adjust.

We cannot. Like a battleship that cannot steer itself, we float listlessly, or we barrel along without regard. Either way, it's the same consequence. We as a nation—we as a democracy—will fail if we cannot fix "them." The government's inability to govern is the first step to that death.

The high costs of that incapacity are increasingly recognized, even, and maybe especially, in centers not traditionally focused on politics. By far the most influential recent entry in this debate was a devastating report from the Harvard Business School, authored by Katherine Gehl and Michael Porter. "Why Competition in the Politics Industry Is Failing America" analyzed the functioning of our government the way any business school professor would analyze the functioning of any business or industry. Not surprisingly, Gehl and Porter conclude that our government is failing our nation. And not just in some modest, or marginal sense. To the contrary, in their view, the political system is *the most prominent* "weak and deteriorating factor" in the American economic environment. Our Congress faces increasing gridlock; there is declining cross-partisan support for landmark legislation; and not surprisingly, given those two factors, confidence in our Congress has never been lower. "Our political system has become the major barrier to solving nearly every important challenge our nation needs to address," Gehl and Porter write.[135]

Great nations always fail. That is the history of humanity. The constant struggle of any people is to fight against this inevitability. Our only question then is whether we will fight or whether our time is up. If we cannot govern ourselves, then we have given up.

Have we given up?

CHAPTER 2

The Unrepresentative Us

AS AMERICA APPROACHED ITS 1936 ELECTIONS, MOST AMERICANS, OR AT least most reading Americans, had a pretty clear sense of what was going to happen. The president, Franklin Delano Roosevelt, had been elected in 1932. Already three years into the Great Depression at the start of his first term, his administration had not made America great again. Ordinary Americans were not significantly better off. Roosevelt was attacked by many, especially on the right, both for his "fascist" and "communistic" policies.[1] The elite was not happy. Many wanted him gone.

And most thought he would be gone. In 1936, the then-dominant method for measuring the public's view about a national question— such as, who would be elected president—was quite certain about the answer. In each election since 1916, the *Literary Digest* had run a presidential straw poll. As professor and author Jill Lepore describes, while the *Digest* "regularly miscalculated the popular vote . . . for a long time it got the Electoral College winner right."[2] In 1932, the magazine mailed more than 20 million ballots. It had come within 1 point of the final result. As it pressed on to the 1936 election, the *Literary Digest* increased its spread and depth. By October, 2.3 million ballots had already been returned.[3] Those ballots spoke loudly and clearly: Roosevelt would be defeated; Alf Landon would become the thirty-third president of the United States.

If you don't know the name "Alf Landon," then you know the *Literary Digest* was wrong. Not only did Landon not win, but Roosevelt won in the biggest landslide in a contested presidential election in American history. All but two states went with Roosevelt, and even in those two states the vote was close. The *Digest* had blown it, predicting Landon, 55 percent, and FDR, 41 percent, versus the actual: Landon, 36 percent, FDR, 61 percent. Within six months, the *Literary Digest* was shuttered.

In the months leading up to the election, there had been at least one person who had insisted that the *Literary Digest*'s prediction would be wrong. A PhD in applied psychology, and a professor of journalism at Northwestern University, George Gallup had predicted not only that the *Digest* was going to be proven wrong; he also predicted the percentage for Landon that the *Digest* would predict.[4] The problem, as Gallup diagnosed it, was that the population that the *Digest* had surveyed was skewed. The *Literary Digest* got its list from registration records for telephone subscribers and automobile owners. Obviously, the people who owned cars and leased phones in the 1930s were not a random or representative sample of America. They (the relatively rich) may not have liked FDR. But they were not the only people who were going to vote. Gallup saw that, and with that vision, Gallup struck gold.

With a small—but representative—sample, America could be understood. That fact was enormously significant. If an accurate picture of America required millions of ballots, there were very few questions that could ever rise to a level of significance enough to produce millions of responses. But if a thousand people could be said to speak for America, a business model for listening to America was within the reach of many—in both politics and marketing. Gallup had proven his point; his point launched an industry.[5]

The idea of such a technology had been a fantasy of democratic theorists for many generations. Almost exactly fifty years before, the British academic Viscount James Bryce had written in his masterful *The American Commonwealth* that the final stage in the evolution of democracy "would be reached, if the will of the majority of the citizens were to become ascertainable at all times, and without the need of its passing through a body of representatives, possibly even without the need of voting machinery at all."[6]

George Gallup had now delivered that final stage. No longer would democracies need to rely upon interpretation or guesswork. We could "know" the "will of the people" directly, through the magic of public opinion polls. That fact, Gallup insisted, had democratic significance. Four years after dethroning the *Literary Digest*, he published *The Pulse of Democracy*, and pressed a campaign proselytizing this new technology of democracy.[7] He had found a way "to monitor the pulse of America," and now America could hear from the people directly. As David Moore, author and former senior editor of the Gallup Poll describes, "When in the mid-1930s George Gallup, Elmo Roper, and Archibald Crossley unveiled their scientific method of conducting public opinion polls, they expected that the people's voices would now be heard not just at election time, but continuously."[8]

Gallup crisscrossed the country, selling the technology that he had helped birth. As he wrote,

It is the fashion today in some circles to bemoan the lack of intelligence of the American electorate. Pessimistic critics of the social scene assert lugubriously that whatever may have been the condition in the past, the American voter today is incapable of self-government. We have all heard that "the majority is always wrong," and that "the average American has the intellectual ability of a child of 12." . . . But as far as I am concerned, I am willing to trust the people to make the correct decision when they have a chance to express themselves on one issue at a time.[9]

The combination of "populist democracy, scientific authority, and marketing know-how," writes academic Daniel Robinson, "coalesced to form an ideological defense of polling equating it with the public good."[10]

Of course, neither Bryce nor Gallup had invented the idea of the "will of the people." Something like that idea had been with democratic theory from the very beginning, though it was Rousseau who gave us the term "public opinion" in 1744 to identify the "customs and manners of all members of society (as opposed to some elite)."[11] Alexis de Tocqueville had described its role in the American mind forty years before Bryce. Politicians and writers had long insisted that they knew and hence spoke for the people. They knew, they told us, through their experience and exposure to ordinary souls, just what the people wanted. Indeed, though Bryce fantasized about Gallup's poll, he was nonetheless quite convinced, even in 1888, that there was a way to understand the public's will even without a scientific poll.[12] And of course there had been straw polls since the beginning of the republic.[13]

Yet these efforts at divining a will before Gallup's science were interpretations, not findings—a "mysterious vapor," as political scientist V. O. Key would put it, "that emanated from the undifferentiated citizenry."[14] They were experts reporting on the public's view, as a Catholic priest reading a Latin Bible might have reported on the divine's view. We had to trust the priest, just as we had to trust the politician, because "we" ordinary sorts had no other access to the truth that they interpreted. They were the experts. We had to yield to them. As de Tocqueville would put it, "in worshipping the deity, you learn to conciliate the priest."[15]

But then Martin Luther and George Gallup gave us access. Direct access. Access that (at least pretended to be) without interpretation. With a Bible translated into the "vulgar" languages, ordinary people could read God's word directly. And with a simple method to know what a representative sample of a public thought, ordinary people could read the "will of the people" directly. Democracy had been liberated from the politicians and the pundits, just as religion had been liberated from the priests and the pretenders. And while Gallup's revolution didn't trigger the wars that Luther's did, it was resisted, too, for it too "threatened to topple one local priesthood and replace it with another."[16]

It is hard for us today to realize just how profound George Gallup's invention was. We live at a time when polls are ubiquitous—and when they have, as political scientist Philip Converse notes, "had a major impact not only on our understanding of . . . opinion, but also on the conceptions which all of us hold . . . as to what 'public opinion' is best taken to mean."[17] After a slow start, the news is now filled with gaggles of competing polls.[18] Anyone with a thousand dollars can get any question asked nationally. The website FiveThirtyEight.com aggregates "all the polls it can find," weighted according to method and accuracy, to measure, for example, the popularity of Donald Trump. It is as hard for us to imagine a time when policy could be guided without a constant signal directly from the people, just as it will be hard for our kids to imagine navigating on a highway without GPS. We take the public opinion poll for granted. It is part of the furniture of modern public life, as familiar as interstate highways or satellites. And it's almost unimaginable today that many had questioned even whether polls should be allowed—and some countries to this day forbid them.[19] Polls, one congressman insisted, are "in contradiction to representative government."[20] To save representative democracy, some thought they should be banned outright.

Yet we don't think enough about *who* these polls are polling. What do *they* know? Or, more important, how do they know what they know?

That changed dramatically across the arc of the twentieth century. And that change was the product of another technology: broadcasting.

BROADCASTING

In its most capacious sense, the concept of "broadcasting" had its birth long before radio or television. The broad-street or penny press made it economically possible to convey the same information to, if not millions, then at least a huge slice of the reading public, at the same time. But that conveying was limited by the medium. It was people who read who were broadcast to by newspapers. Reading is a choice. It is something we opt in to.

The broadcasting I focus on here is the technology of transmitting electromagnetically the same content at the same time to a wide range of people. Radio did this first, after a slow and Internet-like start. In 1927, 3 percent of radio content was news—and that included weather reports and police alarms.[21] World War II changed that mix dramatically, and quickly made radio central to social and political life. In 1939, 60 percent of Americans got their news from the radio. By 1944, that number had grown to 74 percent.[22]

Yet there is a coincidence here that we should not overlook: broadcasting in the sense that I mean is born just at the moment that polling is growing up. Americans come to hear a common story and understand a common set of facts just as they get asked a common set of questions.

This coincidence is critical, because whatever differences there may have been in the understanding of public issues and exposure to public debates, they get flattened as broadcasting increases. Walter Lippmann was a prominent skeptic about the public's capacity during the turn of the last century and into the two world wars. The public he came to see was one easily manipulated; he was therefore skeptical about "democracy's dependence on it."[23] It could well be that the public was as ignorant as Lippmann charged; yet that wouldn't negate a claim about what the public would eventually become—because of broadcasting.

Radio is important to this dynamic. Television is fundamental. Invented in 1927 and struggling for many years in a regulatory battle with the radio-protective FCC, it wasn't until after World War II that television began to have a significant audience. But once it truly launched, it took off like a rocket. In 1949, 2 percent of households had a television set. Fifteen years later, that number had climbed by 90 points.[24]

Television changed everything, not just because there were just a few stations that a huge population was exposed to, but also, and more important, because it was the most addictive technology in the house. People would turn the television on and leave it on. Its attractiveness trumped anything else. And thus what television ran became what America watched. Audiences that were literally unimaginable fifty years before became the ordinary pattern of prime-time TV.

This reality radically affected politics, argues Princeton political scientist Markus Prior.[25] TV changed the mix of people who were engaged in politics. Before television, information about politics was primarily conveyed through writing. When television became dominant, and television covered politics, information about politics became more equally distributed. This was not so much because people wanted to learn about politics, but rather because people wanted to watch TV, and the news was all that there was during certain times of the day. The general public thus became more generally informed because the technology of choice at the time was inefficient. Many who watched the news would have been happier watching something else. But between the news and the crickets out on the front porch, most picked the news.

The consequence was a wider range of informed voters. And the consequence of more informed voters was higher participation at the polling booth. Ignorance breeds passivity. Knowledge breeds engagement. During the 1960s and 1970s, Prior demonstrates, there was a marked increase in the participation of middle- and lower-class voters. The technology of TV had had the unintended consequence of making them more politically active. Broadcast television thus "narrowed the turnout gap" between upper- and lower-income voters; it also increased "the proportion of less partisan voters."[26]

As television broadcasting began to dominate American life, American understanding about everything—including matters of public import—changed. We saw things we hadn't seen before. We were forced to see things we could ignore before. We were brought into a national conversation, curated by a small number of media executives, that radically affected how we understood the world. Central to every major issue that transformed over the second half of the twentieth century is a technology that taught the story to practically every American, everywhere.

This point is obvious as applied to culture. The attention share of broadcast media throughout the 1970s is unimaginable today. *Amos 'n' Andy* attracted 40 million listeners on radio "each and every evening—with some episodes reaching 50 million" in the 1930s. The total population in the 1930s was about 122 million.[27] This pattern only grew with television. Throughout the 1970s, the broadcasting networks would compete for the prize of an audience that could be 60 to 70 million people at one time. The peak attention in American history was on September 9, 1956, when Elvis Presley appeared on *The Ed Sullivan Show:* 82.6 percent of viewers watched that single episode on television. This was a technology that grabbed the attention of the whole nation. And if, as law professor Tim Wu remarks, this was the "decade of conformity," can one really exclude the most salient possible reason: "the historically anomalous scale of attention capture effected by television, together with the homogeneity of the stuff created to do the capturing"?[28]

This peak attention affected more than culture. Consider just one example that will suggest the more general pattern.

On March 7, 1965, beginning at 9 P.M. Eastern, America was watching *Judgment at Nuremberg.* Based on an episode of *Playhouse 90,* the film told the story of a kind of greatness that was America after World War II.[29] Based on principles of natural justice, America had prosecuted German Nazis after the war. The film was an account of the trial of those criminals. Almost 50 million Americans were watching that show—just about 25 percent of the population.[30]

About thirty minutes into the program, the broadcast was interrupted. News reports had just begun to tell the story of incredible violence in Selma, Alabama. For three years before that Sunday, the

Student Nonviolent Coordinating Committee (SNCC) had conducted voter registration campaigns in Selma and throughout the region. Their work was resisted forcefully by local election officials. Martin Luther King Jr., as well as the Southern Christian Leadership Conference (SCLC), agreed to help SNCC to get the officials to register black voters. In 1965, just 19.3 percent of African Americans were registered to vote in Alabama.[31]

So in January and February, King and the SCLC led a series of protests in Selma. On February 17, one of the protesters, Jimmy Lee Jackson, was shot and killed by a state trooper. In response, King announced a march from Selma to Montgomery, Alabama, on March 7, 1965, to protest the killing and demand an equal right to vote. Six hundred marchers assembled that morning, led by future congressman John Lewis. As they approached the Edmund Pettus Bridge, they saw on the other side state troopers mounted on horses. They were told to go back. They believed they were entitled to march. So they marched. The Alabama state troopers launched an attack. Using tear gas and billy clubs, the troopers tried to push the marchers back. Many, including Lewis, were beaten severely. More than fifty people were hospitalized.

Astonishingly, all this happened even though there were television cameras covering the march. And so, on the evening of "Bloody Sunday," *Judgment at Nuremberg* was interrupted, and 50 million Americans got to watch not just the story of German racism but of American racism as well. Right smack in the middle of their living rooms, white Americans were viciously attacking black Americans, simply because black Americans were exercising their constitutional right to peaceably protest for a constitutionally guaranteed right to vote free of racial discrimination.

One doesn't have to be a social psychologist to understand that this event would have affected the psychology of Americans profoundly. At one moment, we were at our best. At the next moment, we were at our worst. The hypocrisy alone, whether recognized or not, would have moved people. The idea that this is who we were would be too much for many Americans to accept.

What is striking here is not that television covered this event and many others, but that practically everyone saw it. The public was saturated with information—and, critically, saturated from and by very few sources. Few could escape the news. And the news told these stories while adhering to journalistic principles that aspired to what they considered to be neutrality. Not neutral in some absolute sense, whatever that would mean, but neutral in the sense that the networks steered to avoid seeming partisan while reporting critically important stories of political struggle.

As the public's understanding evolved on this issue, and many others, the public was quizzed on its views. The polls evinced the public's progress. That progress made sense. Or at least to a certain elite, against the background of what the world then understood, it made sense. The public was coming to understand these issues; its sensible response was driven by this understanding; that understanding in turn, as Converse put it, manifested a "growing acceptance in practicing political circles of the kind of populist measurement" of polls.[32] As Robinson describes it, the poll, "construed rhetorically as the voice of 'The People,' came to command both political and moral authority in a country whose progressive tradition embodied strong democratic and scientific currents."[33]

Yet the critical point to see is that the public's understanding was driven by one technology, broadcasting, and then measured by another technology, polling. Broadcasting brought the news to our living rooms; polling queried us at our phones. The public grew; its growth was recorded and reported. And as that growth seemed sensible—at least to a public grounded in these same views—that sensible public became normatively significant.

Reasonableness begat respect. The public seemed eminently reasonable.

This is the public described by Benjamin Page and Robert Shapiro in their classic work, *The Rational Public: Fifty Years of Trends in Americans' Policy Preferences*. Surveying the period from the 1930s to the beginning of the 1990s, Page and Shapiro argue forcefully that American attitudes over this period were "rational"—meaning they were real (not random, nonattitudes), stable, coherent, and made sense. When these attitudes change, Page and Shapiro insist, they change in understandable and predictable ways—"sensible adjustments to the new conditions."[34] These conclusions are important, because, as Page and Shapiro remark, "Americans take for granted that citizens' preferences should be the chief determinant of policy-making." In countries like the United States, "citizens' policy preferences have a substantial impact on what governments do." "Our point," they write, "is that the public as a collective body is capable of holding sensible opinions and processing the information made available to it."[35]

Yet the critical point here is left unsaid—*how* is "the information made available to it"? Because the signal contribution of Prior is that the information ecology for much of the period that Page and Shapiro review was quite special. As Prior writes, describing the consequence of the rise of broadcast television, "it is difficult to imagine that differences as stark as these have no effect on politics."[36] Likewise, we could say that it is difficult to imagine that the ability of the public to "hold sensible opinions and process information made available to it" is *unrelated* to the character of the information environment. If broadcasting matters to politics, then broadcasting must matter to understanding more generally.

This is an age in which most of America saw the same thing, and that "same thing" exposure had an obvious effect. The point is not that we lived through a time of perfect information or perfect education. I don't mean to argue that the sources were not biased. The point instead is that we lived through a time of concentrated information and concentrated education. The technology of television tricked most Americans into a daily lesson about public issues. That lesson informed them. It set a baseline of understanding. And as they were informed, their views evolved. That evolution was measured in the polls. It would be "gratuitous to refuse to believe," as Converse put it, that the evolution in actual public policy was unrelated to these polls.[37]

We don't have a similar record from a hundred years before the 1960s. Before broadcasting, of course, there was certain information that traveled broadly and completely. The *Congressional Record* (born as the first official publication of Congress recording its debates in 1873) was given away for free to newspapers. Many published the debates on the front page of their papers.[38] The Associated Press, founded in 1846, provided a critical service to help spread the news of the world across America.[39] And no doubt, American culture at the end of the nineteenth century reached out "for printed information which could take them beyond the bounds of their local community."[40]

But however impressive these efforts at national informational integration were, we can be confident that only a slice of America read and understood the most important stories of the nation. In the main, America was fragmented, culturally and epistemologically, and we could not see what America knew. There were no polls capturing everything America thought. What "America thought" was instead interpreted through the charitable eyes of America's politicians.

No doubt it was not always done charitably. When one reads how, during the Civil War and afterward, southerners spoke of Yankees and Yankees spoke of the South, it is hard to believe, Lincoln notwithstanding, that the nation held together. And when one reads how whites for most of this period characterized the understandings of African Americans, it is easy to understand how racism continued throughout the twentieth century and to the present day. The point is not that people are always generous. It is that when "we the people" are interpreted by politicians who mean to rally us to their cause, that interpretation of necessity takes on a rosy tint. You don't win supporters on the campaign trail by telling the audience, "You know you're all idiots; you know you don't know diddly squat; so stop pretending you have an informed view, and just let us get on with our work." Charity is how we speak of those we're speaking to. And when interpretation is all that there is, charity gets a very long leash.

POST-BROADCAST DEMOCRACY

And then technology changed. Again.

Beginning in the 1980s, as cable began to spread, television in America fragmented. The choices increased faster than the market increased, so that market share fell. It did so slowly at first—the patterns of life are hard to change—but then extraordinarily quickly: in 1980, more than 90 percent of television viewers were tuned in to one of the three major networks during prime time. By 2005, that number had fallen to 32 percent.[41]

At first this competition seemed good. Broadcast news was limited, in time and depth. There were evening shows and then morning shows. When Iran took fifty-two Americans hostage in 1979, journalist Ted Koppel gave us the late evening news. But it took an extraordinary entrepreneur to tap the real potential for television news on cable. That potential, it turned out, required satellites. In 1980, just as cable was being born, Ted Turner launched the first twenty-four-hour news channel, CNN. The immediate effect was to make it seem as if the new technology—cable—would give us new and better access to news than the old technology of broadcast.

And in an important sense, it did. For anyone interested, there was more to consume. The "more" that was available was more international and more continuous. Stories could be covered as they unfolded. Unfolding stories were in their nature more compelling.

Yet still, there was a norm that governed this news. That norm was inherited. It came from the professional ethics of those who wanted to believe themselves journalists. It would take an extraordinary norm entrepreneur to explode that inherited norm. The absurd coverage of O. J. Simpson's car chase in 1994 may have surfaced the idea; Bill Clinton may have created the conditions; but it was Roger Ailes who made the leap. In 1996, Fox News was born, and with it, the news returned to the news of the nineteenth century.

For in the nineteenth century, news was partisan. The organs of news production were partisan. There was no embarrassment in the nineteenth century with the idea of a newspaper spinning the news to their side. Spinning was the business model, the necessary market dynamic to make loyalty to newspapers possible.[42]

This nineteenth-century partisan ethic returned to television news as the twentieth century passed to the twenty-first. This result is perhaps an obvious consequence of competition. When CNN was born, it was alone. It was network news, but better. But when Fox became a competitor, the question became "what strategy would help us compete in the cable news business." A distinctive brand became the key. A way to channel political anger became gold. The idea of wresting the truth from a "biased" and "corrupted" "mainstream media" became the morality play that would energize the Fox News generation. Fox News then inspired MSNBC. Each step was responsive to consumer demand. Each step was just giving us what "we" wanted.

The point is critical. No doubt the market was fragmenting. But we don't know whether that fragmentation alone would have been enough to change the conclusions drawn by Page and Shapiro about a "rational public," because the change was not just fragmentation. Layered onto the fragmenting market was a new business model for media—a model that profited from polarization. The news reached fewer, but it steered the story both to the left and right. The news had an interest not just in telling us the news. They had a commercial interest in spreading the news in a way that made the left hate the right, and the right hate the left. There was a strategy to recruiting us, and that strategy had no necessary connection to the truth or to what was important. Why or how that changed incentive matured we will consider below. That it changed is the critical point now.[43]

And then the technology changed again.

Starting in the 1990s, running across the telephone and cable wires, a new network of communication was launched—the Internet. As that network took off, the very idea of "channels" became fundamentally different. No longer was a channel something that *channeled* people. A channel was just another book on an endless shelf of content, competing with every other book to be read.

Endless writing has reflected on the history of the Internet. Much of it has been optimistic and hopeful. Much of it has been dark and pessimistic.[44] As we look back now, we can see that optimists were focused on what the Internet would *add* to culture; we ignored what it would *take away*. And not the Internet alone, but the Internet as a continuation of the fragmentation begun with cable TV.

Yes, we would have access to blogs, and Twitter, and Facebook and YouTube. Yes, podcasts would open a world of new content unimagined twenty years before. Yes, Wikipedia would become an incredible source literally unimaginable in its scope even when launched. And no, the end of copyright extremism did not mean the end of cultural creativity. Without doubt, the Internet would add something critically new to culture and politics. And like children falling for a magic trick, all of our attention was on the flashy cool right in front of our faces.

Yet these additions were on top of what was being removed. For giving people a million choices meant that the choice we had all been "forced" to make before was no longer going to be forced upon us now. Before, we had all been "forced" to watch the news—because the news was all that was on, and television was so irresistible. Now we were free. We could watch the Home Shopping Network, or the History Channel, or YouTube, or Vimeo or Netflix. We were free to do as we wished, and the reality is, first, not everyone wished to watch the news, and second, because of who they were, those who wished to watch the news watched an increasingly biased or slanted version of news.

That freedom continued on the Internet as well. We could read the *New York Times* or the *Wall Street Journal*. Or we could just get our news from our friends' Facebook feeds. Everything was available. In the slogan of the day, the Internet "interprets censorship as damage and routes around it."[45] Using a protocol called "RSS," people could mash together their own newspaper. And as artificial intelligence (AI) got great, the newspapers themselves would evolve to give us what we wanted in real time. The news no less than anything else on the Internet became part of the "Filter Bubble," to use CEO of Upworthy Eli Pariser's powerful and apt description of the epistemology of the emerging Net.[46] We were as we wanted to be, and the technologies of the Net worked hard to give us exactly what we wanted to see.

No doubt the Internet had banished the censor (at least for relatively developed democracies: the authoritarians were quick to learn how to use the technology to better control their people). But it had also banished the editor. In the era of broadcast, the editor had assured us that at least within the narrow range of the "appropriate," the news covered all sides. And in the era of broadcast, the editor had assured us that the crazy just did not appear. No self-respecting news editor at CBS or NBC would have covered a Donald Trump campaign for president in 1976. No one would have taken him seriously enough to even repeat his name. But in the world of today, there is literally no one to resist or who could resist. When Breitbart, and then, reluctantly, Fox made Trump irresistible in 2015, everyone had to follow. There was no editor. There was no capacity for any network to be an editor. We, in aggregate, were the editor. We got what we wanted. As Zeynep Tufekci describes it in her powerful account of the evolution of activism, "[n]ow that mass media no longer hold a monopoly on attention, neither censorship nor the competition for attention operates in the same way." "Attention" is the "key resource," "no longer to be conflated with mass media, and no longer under the sole control of traditional elites."[47]

In the culture space, this freedom is an unambiguous good. In the democracy space, it is not. In the culture space, we are free to watch as we want, and what we want is a wider and more interesting range of stuff than the stuff of television circa 1976. Freedom here has inspired an extraordinary diversity—not despite the technologies of the Internet, but because of them. No one familiar with television forty years ago would think it could compare well with practically any television today. We might yearn for the days of Walter Cronkite. We don't yearn for prime time TV of the 1970s. Culture has become wildly more creative and expressive and diverse—and that's a wonderful thing that we should celebrate loudly and repeatedly. And its diversity flows from the same technological features—a radical fall in the costs of creativity, and a radical increase in the access to audience. Competition here is unqualifiedly good; it has made us, culturally, a richer and more interesting society.

But when we switch from the culture channel to the democracy channel, the consequences of this diversity are very different. They are, in a word, awful. If fragmented news media means a more polarized democratic public, that weakens the capacity of democracies to progress. If the public is more relevant—because visible and polled—but the public is more divided, then the divided public becomes a brake on change. A divided public becomes a tool that the status quo can invoke to block changes that threaten the status quo. It becomes a reason to do nothing, because doing anything is, for some group, "antidemocratic."

This result is driven by an obvious dynamic. We watch what we want—individually. But what we want individually has no obvious link to what we might need, collectively. In the age of broadcast democracy, broadcast news had guided us to an understanding that was shared. Whether true, or rich, or sufficient, or balanced, it was shared. And on the basis of that shared understanding, which could still, as Page and Shapiro showed, respect the "expert" and the commentators, broadcast democracy had been possible.

That shared reality is now just gone. Consuming what we want individually has rendered us isolated collectively. Think lounge chairs in echo chambers. We are ideologically alone, together. We are divided and ignorant (at least about the other side) and driven to even more division and ignorance.

Ignorant. I mean that term in a very precise sense. I am one of the very rare white males over fifty in America who could tell you almost nothing about football. I used to watch it with my dad, but only because I loved my dad. I didn't love football. When I was in college, I could probably have told you the rules. I had a basic sense of the game. I certainly didn't have the courage to avoid the political correctness of the time—that white guys went to football games. But as I write these words, I could not name three of the top ten teams in whatever league dominates America. I couldn't even name that league. I could not tell you who won the Super Bowl last year. I would have no clue about whom to bet on this year. I am, in this sense, profoundly ignorant.

But to say that I am ignorant is not to say I am stupid. I may be stupid, but stupidity is not implied by ignorance. I assume (though I've not really tried) that I could learn about football. I assume I could learn about the teams. I assume I could follow the results each week and get a better sense about who's likely to win. I could study the statistics. I could listen to the other white males over fifty (even at Harvard Law School) and learn something.

This is the sense in which I say that "the people are, inherently, ignorant." We know not nothing, but not enough collectively. That does not mean we are stupid. No doubt there are some of us who know tons. But on average, we—or more precisely, a representative sample of us—do not know even the slightest bit about critical issues of national import. Most Americans have lives that are far from the substance of American public policy. They live those lives in happy ignorance of that policy. As David Moore, a former senior executive with the Gallup poll, described it in 2008, "The hard truth is that on most policy issues, large proportions of the public know or care little about the specifics, and thus have developed no meaningful opinion about them."[48]

This is the point that political scientist Anthony Downs formalized seventy years ago, and that sparked generations of engagement and resistance among his colleagues.[49] A rational citizen, "under Downs's formulation, . . . would remain uninformed and disengaged"—

"because of 'the infinitesimal role which each citizen's vote plays in deciding the election,' the returns to acquiring political information 'are so low that many rational voters [will] refrain from purchasing any political information per se.'" Voters in this theory are ignorant, not stupid. Indeed, they are ignorant because they are smart—at least about how to maximize their own individual preferences. We have lives and passions and interests. Some have more than one job. Some have children. Some have more than one child. Some want to read novels. Some want to binge-watch Netflix. Some work out for hours a day. Some work out at least an hour every day.

Downs didn't mean that the public would be completely ignorant. It's just that any cure for its ignorance would be accidental, not planned. People were exposed to political knowledge as a by-product of doing what they otherwise would want to do. As someone flips through to the sports section of the newspaper, he might notice Congress's declaration of war. ("Oh, man, we're at war with North Korea. Yea, that's bad. But damn, did the Cubs lose again?") Or when he goes to the movies, he will see the newsreels that run before the movie. (Remember, Downs was writing in the 1950s.) Those inadvertent exposures would teach something. But not enough, Downs believed, to produce a public well informed about matters of public import.[50]

Broadcast democracy increased this inadvertent exposure. This is Markus Prior's point. Americans didn't choose to watch television news. They chose to watch television, even when the news was on. Even more than the age of newsreels, broadcast television produced an enormous by-product effect that brought the news to America whether America wanted it or not.

But then cable TV and then the Internet changed this by-product effect again. Cable allowed us to self-sort, into those very few who like cable news, and those very many who like sports or the Home Shopping Network. And the Internet enabled us to self-sort yet again. And while it's quite possible that the Internet has returned us to a world where we are all exposed to the news whether we want it or not—

through the "news feeds" of our "friends" on Facebook—that inadvertent exposure is architected to be anything but unbiased.

No doubt the public's ignorance has always been a problem. But here is the key: Before polling, it was invisible. When polling was born, it was feared. But as broadcasting prepared us to be polled, we became better. We had a foundation. That foundation in understanding could drive us.

Yet that foundation has now been removed. We don't live in the same information ecosystem. We don't understand the same facts. "If you watch Fox News," Barack Obama declared, "you're in one reality, and if you read the *New York Times,* you're in a different reality."[51] And so the truth as it is reflected from us is a truth that is increasingly divided and partial. We know less. What we know more, we know more dividedly. The machinery that we have for teaching us what we need to know to make decisions for our democracy is clearly failing to convey what needs to be taught. Not in a small way, but in a huge way. It won't be fixed simply by reforming Fox or Breitbart. The basic structure of incentives for political journalism has no obvious connection to conveying the information that we need. As Tufekci puts it, describing social media, these platforms "are in the business of monetizing attention, and not necessarily in ways that are conducive to health or success of social movements or the public sphere."[52]

"Junk food" is the analogy here. We are children of the processed food revolution. Two generations ago, people ate food prepared at home. That food, in general, was healthy and nutritious. That's not to say everyone could afford either the time or the food. But it is to note a simple and fundamental fact—that home-cooked food retains most of its nutritional value, and is, on balance, healthy.

It's just not as good, as in as tasty, or compelling, or as easy or as addictive as processed food (and not to mention, it seemed to entail a sex-based servitude for those within the kitchen). So for the past forty years, the pattern of food consumption by Americans has changed dramatically. More people eat out. More people eat processed food while eating in. In 1889, there was no fast food, and less than 10 percent of America ate out. Today, 30 percent are eating out, and another 20 percent are eating fast food.[53]

The market incentive for this transformation is quite clear: The producers want to addict (not in a formal or medical sense but in the sense of habit) consumers to their product. "Food science" is thus the study of how food can be made more addictive. The very best learn how to tweak the ingredients to produce a maximum desire for repeat consumption. The elixir of salt/fat/sugar becomes the method for pulling an audience in and keeping it committed. Think french fries or potato chips or popcorn rather than broccoli or bell peppers or almonds.

All of this would be just great for us if processed food were also good for us. If we could eat as much of what tasted great as we wanted and still supply the nutritional requirements of our bodies, without consuming too much, that would be food heaven.

But of course, that is not our fate. The food that is most compelling or addictive to a food-processed nation is not the food that is most healthy. What's good for (the profitability of) Kraft is not good for (the health of) America.

For some, the remedy to this is to imagine food companies becoming virtuous. That hopeless story is told well in Michael Moss's *Salt Sugar Fat: How the Food Giants Hooked Us*. It's hopeless because food markets are competitive, and the ability of one company to do good is constrained by the incentive for others to do bad (and then eat the good company's lunch, so to speak). So as Moss tells it, company after company has been enlightened—by the desire to do good—only to be reenlightened by the stock market's insistence that it let others be good and that it focus on doing well.

For others, the remedy is powerful and pervasive government regulation. Think Michael Bloomberg and the regulation of soda in New York: these sorts want to see the government controlling the size of

Coke bottles, or limiting the amount of sugar in children's cereal, or banning the advertisement of candy or sugar-infested "health foods" on Saturday morning TV. They want to see the heavy hand of the state steering us back to a healthy diet.

No doubt the objectives of these regulators are good. Yet I am skeptical that regulation alone would be enough (though I realize that much in the unhealthy mix we have now comes from a mix of unhealthy and corrupted regulation).[54]

In my view, the real remedy must begin and end with individuals choosing to eat differently. The law could make that choice easier (by, for example, not subsidizing schools to buy and serve the worst food possible). But the essence of any solution must be a different choice by individuals.

Yet whether I'm right or not about the solution, the part to keep focused on is the consequences for the nation of this processed food culture. The consequences of these bad choices by individuals are felt by the individual primarily. But in the age of socialized medicine, it is also felt by society. Your unhealthy eating harms me to the extent that my health insurance costs are higher because of the chronic diseases of people like you. If you smoke, I pay a price. If you live on Twinkies, our health system is going to pay a price. The magnitude of this externality—the effect your behavior has on others—may be hard to measure. Yet there is certainly an externality. Our challenge is how to account for that externality and correct for it.

The information ecology follows a similar dynamic. Here, too, there is a market incentive. Here, too, the market incentive is unconnected to a public good. With food it was unconnected to healthy eating. With the ecology of understanding, the market incentive is unconnected to understanding. Indeed, it may be worse than with food. For here the market incentive is not just unrelated to the public good. Here the market incentive may well be tied to a public bad. Frito Lay doesn't do better the more unhealthily we are. But Fox News and MSNBC may well do better the more partisan and ignorant we are.

THE INCENTIVES OF ATTENTION

Any democracy requires that the people know what is and what is not, so the people can decide, based on their values, what to do or not to do. If you want to save for your retirement, you need to know what the interest rate is. The choice to save rather than to spend is a value choice. Regardless of the value chosen, you need facts to determine how best to go on.

That understanding requires institutions. There's no pill that delivers truth. There's not a single class that we could require in high school. Instead, understanding within a society requires institutions that convey understanding. That conveying is more art than science. It is certainly not simple. If America needs to understand the facts about nuclear power, that is not a trivial task. To the contrary, how one conveys the information that's required for understanding is a very complicated question.

This is the challenge at the core of what I do for a living. I am a teacher. My job is to understand what's true, and to work out how best to convey that truth. I'm not so stupid as to miss that what I think of as true will be affected by my values or politics. I'm not so smart as to know exactly how to convey what I believe is true to everyone at any time. But I do know that the objective is to convey the truth, at least where there is truth to convey. That objective constrains what I do. The institutions within which I work constrain what I do to that end as well.

How such institutions should be structured is an impossibly hard question. It is a great virtue of America that we have many different models that compete. There are public institutions and private, religious and secular, formal and informal, libraries and Wikipedia. Anyone who said they knew how best to convey the truth would be lying. We don't yet know even a fraction of what we would need to know to answer that question with any integrity.

But we do know how not to do it. We do know what would not work. Consider just one example: Imagine a school of medicine that was established to train doctors. And imagine that the dean of the medical school decided that the compensation of professors should be determined by drug companies. The drug companies would review the syllabus of the professor and watch her teach. They would review the examination results of the students and even administer their own test to fill in gaps that the exams did not cover. And then, based on their evaluation, the drug company would decide how much the professor was to be paid. The dean signs up for this program because the drug companies have agreed to provide the professors' salaries. It's good for the (budget of the) medical school, and good for the drug companies. But literally *no one else* would think that this scheme was good for medicine. This might well be naive, but we all have a sense that the job of a medical school is to educate doctors independently of drug companies. No doubt drugs are important and often essential to treatment. But equally without doubt, there are treatments that don't require drugs that are sometimes even better.

The point is not that the facts a drug-company-sensitive professor would convey would always be false. Or even that they would mostly be false. To the contrary, most of the facts uttered by such professors would be true. The point instead is that we can see that tying the institution of medical education to an influence that has no necessary connection to the truth of medicine is an effective way to corrupt the institution of medical education. Not in every case. Not with every fact. But with enough to show us why we need a different way to convey the truth. Maybe a single drug-company-sponsored course would be okay. (Not in my view, but I may be extreme.) But you don't need to be an extremist to see why a whole medical education tied to the interest of drug companies is not an appropriate education for doctors.

So then think about the institutions we have evolved for conveying information about matters of public policy. I don't mean to students in a university. I mean to the public generally. The democratic presumption that the twentieth century left us with is that our views are all, at any one time, equally relevant. That means that our views, at any one time, are to count, equally. What is the institution we have built for conveying the information necessary to construct those views? And what are the incentives of that institution?

There's no simple way to describe that institution. It has no simple structure. Yet there are dominant players, and hence dominant patterns of play, within that institution, at least now. Consider just two institutions, cable television and the Internet, and consider the incentives that affect each.

These two institutions have evolved to have a common and critical dependence—upon advertising. And the question we need to ask—as a nation that depends upon an understanding public for its democracy to survive—is whether the incentives of that dependence are consistent with the incentives of understanding and truth.

Put more sharply, can an ecology of information driven by advertising provide the balance of information necessary for democracy? Or is it—as I increasingly believe—like the medical school with drug-company-compensated professors?

The answer to this question has been clear to many for a very long time. In 1922, Herbert Hoover declared that advertising would never be allowed to corrupt radio: "It is inconceivable that we should allow so great a possibility for service, for news, for entertainment, for education, and for vital commercial purposes to be drowned in advertising chatter."[55] Hoover was wrong.

In 1963, the famed historian of broadcast media Erik Barnouw asked, in testimony to Congress, "whether we can afford to have our culture and our artistic life become a byproduct of advertising? My answer," he continued, "is that we can't."[56] We did.

The question was clear to the founders of Google, Larry Page and Sergey Brin, at least at the beginning, when they wrote, "advertising funded search engines will be inherently biased towards the advertisers and away from the needs of the consumer."[57] They were right.

It was clear as well to one of the most important media figures in the Internet age, John Battelle, cofounder of *Wired* magazine: the advertising model for distributing news, he wrote, "was in clear violation of every ethical boundary known to media."[58] It was.

Yet this clarity and insight, with real anxiety, has not stopped the evolution of advertising at the core of our attention economy. This is a problem. I didn't begin this work focused on the damage done to our democratic culture by the industry of advertising. Yet I have become convinced that this industry is at the center of all that ails us. We have not begun to reckon the consequences to the ecology of information, and hence to democracy, rendered by advertising. This chapter is but the hint of a start.[59]

CABLE NEWS

For reasons we can leave to one side, I spent a bunch of time in cable newsrooms in August 2015. That was just at the moment that Donald Trump was first breaking through. Cable stations would cover every word that man uttered. He'd give a speech—typically long and rambling and barely coherent—and the cable networks would cover it, from start to finish. It was all Donald, all the time.

In practically every interaction I had with producers or the like during that month, they would complain about that reality. That complaint was a trigger for me. "How can *you* complain? You're the one covering the man?" "We have no choice," was the generic response. "If we don't cover him, our viewers will just switch channels. And if the viewers defect, the advertisers will defect as well."

There are many of us who have complained extensively about the concentration of media in America. I'm one of those many.[60] We complainers had a certain threat in mind: the fear was that there would be one person who could steer a nation according to his (and it was always his) own extreme views. The villain, for our side at least, was a Roger Ailes—a monstrous and monstrously powerful force that would steer media and therefore politics.

What we did not consider was that *we* would be the villain. Not "we," as in me or my colleagues. But "we" as in all of us. What we were not imagining was that as the technology of media became more and more sensitive to us individually, it would become more and more responsive to what we individually would want. And that that responsiveness itself would be a problem. The point is not that the idea was never there. In one of the first "law of cyberspace" conferences that I attended at Yale in 1994, Professors Eugene Volokh and Cass Sunstein were already debating the consequences of "the daily me."[61] Yet none of us then had any rich or deep sense about how this crafting would evolve, or what the consequences in the end would be.

For the reality is this: the world of cable television is insanely competitive. The markets are small (by comparison, historically) and the drive for ratings is fierce. The primary technique for earning strong ratings is to give the customer what the customer wants. But for news, that means the customer for news. That customer is not the average citizen. He isn't responsive to the average desires or needs. Instead he is the hyperpartisan, eager to be fed the partisan news. And in a competitive information market, the market will feed those desires, repeatedly and reliably over time.

The incentives in this market, like every market, drive the news to what the audience wants. That means if the audience is biased, the news follows the bias. It plays to its base, whatever its base might be. Success is measured by ratings, for ratings drive advertising revenue. The question the advertising executive asks is not "What's true?" The question the advertising executive asks is "What drives eyeballs?" From this perspective, what's good for CBS News is not what's good for the nation; what's good for CBS News is what drives the nation to watch CBS. That was the plain meaning of perhaps a joke by CBS's former CEO Les Moonves. As he said in the summer of 2016, "Sorry. It's a terrible thing to say. But, bring it on, Donald. Keep going . . . It may not be good for America, but it's damn good for CBS."[62]

The actual pattern of polarization on cable news supports this hypothesis. In a massive study of the influence of cable news networks, economists Gregory J. Martin and Ali Yurukoglu considered the relationship between what they call "slanted news" and voting behavior. Their question was "How much could slanted news contribute to increases in ideological polarization?" Their finding was that "cable news channels can explain an increase in political polarization of similar size to that observed in the US population over this period." Put differently, under the model they test, it is the polarization of the networks that drives the polarization of the public. And using an exceptionally clever independent variable, they are able to show that it is not just self-sorting that explains this difference.[63]

More significantly for our purposes, Martin and Yurukoglu find that the pattern of polarization for cable news outlets follows the path predicted. The difference in the partisan slant among these networks increases, with Fox beginning the move, and MSNBC joining in later on. "Cable news does increase ideological polarization among the viewing public," they conclude. And that effect is increasing over time. One graph demonstrates the slant of the networks (see Figure 7.)

These slanted networks, they find, succeed in switching the votes of nonideologically aligned viewers. Fox is much more effective in winning over liberals than MSNBC is in winning over conservatives. My own analysis, drawing on Gallup surveys, finds similar partisans differently affected, depending upon the media they watch. So, for example, "very conservative" viewers of MSNBC had higher approval ratings for Barack Obama than "very conservative" viewers of Fox (21.1 percent versus 3.1 percent); likewise, "very conservative" viewers of Fox had a higher approval rating of Donald Trump than "very conservative" viewers of MSNBC (90.8 percent versus 73.7 percent).[64] But regardless of relative success, the general effect of news network polarization is clear: polarized networks make for a more polarized nation—in at least the minimal sense of being more consistently sorted along ideological lines than before.[65]

Indeed, it might even be worse than this: if the partisan valence of

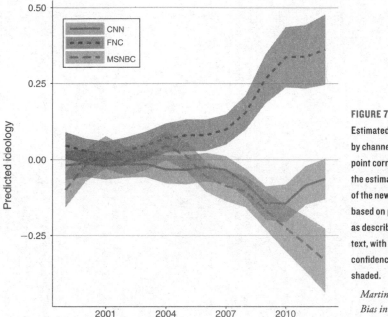

FIGURE 7
Estimated ideology
by channel year. Each
point corresponds to
the estimated ideology
of the news channels
based on phrase usage
as described in the
text, with 95 percent
confidence bounds
shaded.

*Martin & Yurukoglu,
Bias in Cable News.*

a story makes the story more profitable, then there's an obvious interest in both rendering a story partisan, or worse, rendering an audience
even more partisan about the subject of a particular story. That's not
enough to claim that any outlet will actually act on that interest. But
it is to recognize a continuing incentive to steer not just a television
network but "reality" itself away from the "truth."

Consider a particular example of this more general dynamic. Not all
domains of science render politically. A map of science topics produced
by Yale law professor Dan Kahan shows some that have a partisan valence, and others that do not (see Figure 8). Your views about climate
change or GMOs will be a function of your politics. Your views about
cell phone radiation will not.

Yet while this map might seem hopeful—as only a minority of the
issues identified seem vulnerable to partisan bias—it could also map a
certain strategy. Those issues that do not now skew politically could

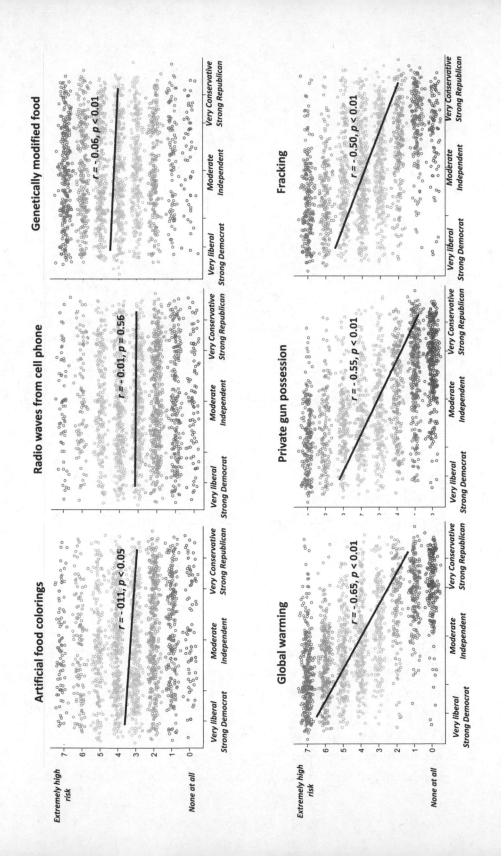

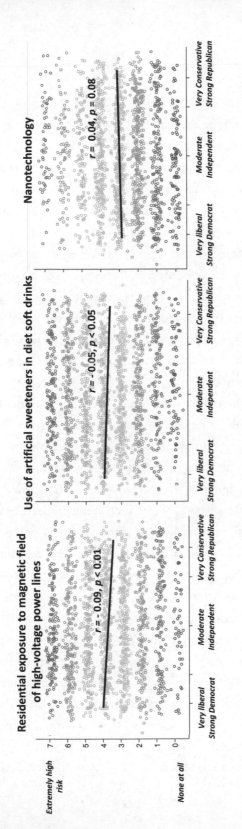

FIGURE 8

"Polarized" vs. "unpolarized" risk perceptions. Scatterplots relate risk perceptions to political outlooks for members of nationally representative sample (N = 1800).

Dan Kahan, What is the "Science of Communication"?

be rendered political. If Fox News could make concerns about cell phone radiation an issue of "the far left," then it could leverage a partisan spin around cell phone radiation stories (not to mention encourage cell phone companies to advertise with Fox News more heavily). Again, that's not to claim that this rerendering is possible or cheap. But it is to remark that there's an ongoing bias to bias that is unrelated to truth. If antiscience distortion pays, or pays more than the truth, then we can expect there will be more antiscience distortion.

The point is—and is always—about the incentives. In an ecology of advertising, the incentive of news is not necessarily truth. It is truth if it pays. Likewise, the incentive is not a judgment about significance. It is significance if it pays. Thus the domain we rely upon the most to inform us about the issues that we, as a democracy, must reckon is a domain that is dependent not on truth, but on attention. Attention has no necessary connection to truth.

Incentives will guide cable news, as it makes sense to guide them. That's not to say that they will be guided in the same way, necessarily, regardless of the network. But it is to say that we should stand skeptical about the capacity of cable news to stay focused in a way that advances understanding, or at least the understanding a democratic public would require. Truth or significance *may* be a by-product; it may as well not.

The 2016 election is a perfect example of this more general point.

At Harvard, Yochai Benkler and his colleagues have done extraordinary work to understand the pattern of news consumption during the 2016 presidential election. After the 2016 election, they mapped the flow of stories and information across both cable television and the Internet. The strong conclusion that they draw is that, contrary to conventional wisdom, the problem with news in America is not symmetrical. The right, they argue, has gone off the rails, while the left continues to produce news that conforms to basic standards of journalism. The right lives in an echo chamber; the rest of media, both left and centrist, "operates as an interconnected network anchored by organizations, both for profit and nonprofit, that adhere to professional journalistic norms."[66] As they conclude, "partisan falsehoods thrive on the right not as errors but as design features of the network, and why these design features have made the right-wing ecosystem a richer breeding ground and receptive ecosystem for propagandist efforts, foreign and domestic."[67]

The evidence for this difference is compelling, even if uncomfortable. It is never easy for an academic to conclude there is a partisan bias in the problem that he or she is addressing. The insistence on symmetry makes it easier to remain relevant to all sides. But like Thomas Mann and Norm Ornstein reviewing Congress, the strong conclusion of Benkler and his colleagues is that one side has gone off the rails, and that side is taking our democracy down.[68]

Yet there is a second story less emphasized in Benkler's data that says a lot more about the hopelessness of now. It may well be that the right was less constrained by truth. But the left no less than the right was obsessed with empty information calories. Even publications such as the *New York Times* found it impossible to resist coverage of news that had no relevance to informing Americans about the issues.

The so-called Clinton email scandal is the clearest example. Let's start with the facts: There was no "scandal." Period. No doubt Clinton should not have used a private email server to conduct State Department business. That was bad judgment (yet for anyone who has used State Department technology, completely understandable). But this was the sort of bad judgment practically every secretary of state in the age of email had committed. No secretary of state has ever been prosecuted for that bad judgment.

Once the emails were discovered, Clinton wanted to be transparent about what content had flowed across her private servers. No one else *ever before* had tried to be transparent in this way. We know that Secretary Colin Powell, for example, had used an AOL account for his email.[69] We don't know anything about the content that he shared on AOL. Powell never released his emails. Clinton did.

But of course, she didn't release all of her emails. When the decision was made to release the emails, Clinton instructed her staff to separate the work-related emails from the private emails. Following those instructions, her lawyers identified thousands of emails that they deemed not relevant. Those emails were excluded. Stupidly, they were also deleted. But the point that anyone familiar with legal process recognizes is that this sort of determination is made by lawyers all the time, and that in the ordinary case, it is wholly unremarkable. No doubt they should have recognized that this was not an ordinary case. Indeed, what's most astonishing about Secretary Clinton is her repeated assumption that her behavior would be interpreted in good faith.

When the Clinton team determined to release the emails, however, they were informed by the State Department that the emails needed to be reviewed before they could be released. No one who knew anything about the facts believed that Clinton had shared any documents marked "secret." But secrecy law doesn't turn upon the markings. It turns upon the substance. And even something deemed not secret at the time it is released could, later, be deemed secret and therefore not able to be released. What the State Department lawyers thus insisted upon was that they had to review the emails before they were released, to determine whether any emails, though not marked "secret," should nonetheless be considered "secret."

In the course of that review, not surprisingly, there were a number of emails that were determined to have been secret, or more precisely, emails that *should have been marked* as secret and therefore not shared on Clinton's server. Those emails were not released to the public. But what was released was the fact that there were emails that Clinton shouldn't have sent across her private email server. That quickly transformed into the suggestion that she was sharing classified information illegally. That morphed into, "Lock her up."

But here is the critical point: The emails determined to be secret were determined to be secret *after* they were shared. They were not marked secret. No one sharing them was therefore sharing them knowing they were secret. Yet I am certain that this critical bit of the story—critical, that is, to any fair understanding of any Clinton "wrongdoing"—is not understood even to this day by more than a fraction of America. And this is despite the fact that the so-called Clinton scandals were *the most reported stories* about Clinton in the 2016 general election cycle.[70] Not just by the "off the rails" right. Benkler's data shows that it was also the left that couldn't resist these information Cheetos either. Story after story created the impression in America that Clinton was a criminal who should have been "locked up," even though I am certain that anyone armed with the actual facts would never have come to that conclusion.

This point is critical and bears repeating. There is plenty in the class of things that we are ignorant about that is just not covered by the news. We don't know squat about Central Africa. That's because there is no news about Central Africa reported in the American press. Americans have little understanding about the history of India and Pakistan. That's because no network has covered that conflict in the past two decades.

But here is the number one story reported on during the 2016 election cycle, and the most basic fact about its nature was simply not conveyed to most Americans. This is like reporting on the Super Bowl without reporting who won. (Or I imagine, given that I am ignorant about football.) Or a story about the rise of George W. Bush that omits the fact that his father was president (and one of the most important figures in American political life) before him. That this, the most covered story, omits conveying the most critical facts about the story tells us not that Americans are stupid, but that the economy of influence driving the production of news has little connection to an interest in conveying understanding, or even—and at least—the information we would need to make the judgments we need to make as citizens in a democracy.[71]

The point reaches far beyond the so-called email scandal. As the Shorenstein Center has documented quite powerfully, the media coverage of 2016 election did anything but help the public understand the issues.[72] That observation alone may not be anything new: the vast majority of news coverage focused on the horse race (42 percent). That was more than four times the percentage covering policy positions (10 percent). Yet this pattern has been with American journalism since the general deployment of the public opinion poll.

More striking was the tone of the coverage: almost universally negative. This, too, has been a trend, though this last election was an extreme. As Harvard professor Thomas Patterson describes in the Shorenstein report:

> Negative coverage was the order of the day in the general election. Not a week passed where the nominees' coverage reached into positive territory. It peaked at 81 percent negative in mid-October, but there was not a single week where it dropped below 64 percent negative.[73]

Even those numbers, however, are exaggerated, since they count horse race coverage (for the leading candidate) as positive coverage. If you narrowed the scope to stories about fitness for office, 87 percent were negative, and 13 percent positive—*for both Clinton and Trump.*[74]

That negativity was true regardless of the news outlet. Trump's most negative news outlet was CBS (89 percent versus 11 percent); his most positive (though still negative) was Fox (73 percent to 27 percent). Clinton's was similar: her most positive coverage (though still negative) was the *Los Angeles Times* (53 percent versus 47 percent); her most negative was Fox (81 percent to 19 percent).

Yet most striking of all is the general frame the media brought to each candidate. Clinton was the scandal candidate. As Patterson reports: "Clinton's alleged scandals accounted for 16 percent of her coverage—four times the amount of press attention paid to Trump's treatment of women and sixteen times the amount of news coverage given to Clinton's most heavily covered policy position."[75]

By the end of the campaign, almost 40 percent of the coverage of Clinton was coverage of her alleged "scandals." Here again, among outlets, there was relatively little difference. The *Los Angeles Times* was the least scandal-obsessed, focusing just 7 percent of their coverage of Clinton on scandals; Fox News was the most scandal-obsessed at 27 percent; but even CNN was a close second to Fox (18 percent), and the average of the broadcast networks together was 16 percent.

So what accounts for this systematic failure to cover an election in a way that might help us understand whom we should select for president? The answer, Patterson insists, is quite familiar to anyone reading these pages—incentives.

> The incentives in journalism today, everything from getting a story to go viral to acquiring a reputation as a hard-hitting reporter, encourage journalists to engage in criticism and attack. As Kathleen Hall Jamieson put it, journalists have become conditioned to "find the wart [and] make it stand for the whole."[76]

And just as warts are caused by viruses, the best/worst of these journalistic warts spread like viruses. Think of the extraordinary moment when, on December 4, 2016, "a young man carrying an assault rifle walked into Comet Pizza in Northwest Washington, D.C., to investigate reports that Hillary Clinton and her campaign chief were running a pedophilia ring from the basement of the pizza parlor."[77] Half of Trump voters "gave some credence" to the rumors behind that insanity.

That same dynamic explains why Trump dominated the news from the very beginning of his campaign. His "words and actions were ideally suited to journalists' story needs." Patterson writes, "The news is not about what's ordinary or expected. It's about what's new and different, better yet when laced with conflict and outrage. Trump delivered that type of material by the cart load."[78]

Trump was a reality TV star, rendering the reality of a presidential campaign much more compelling—for TV. Thus it made sense—for the media—to cover an empty podium in Palm Beach, Florida, as the networks waited for Donald Trump to give a victory speech on Super Tuesday, rather than cover an actual speech by Bernie Sanders in Phoenix, Arizona, after his disappointing showing.[79]

And thus are we entertained, entertained to the death of democracy. We understand lots. We just don't understand what we would need to understand for our judgments about critical issues of policy to be sensible.

The point is not just about ignorance. It is about the poison of a cocktail of ignorance with more than a dash of partisan spin. We, as a people, have long been ignorant—maybe less so in the age of broadcast democracy, but even then. Yet as ignorance is ordered according to partisan spin, the ignorance becomes toxic. Our confidence in our tribe covers our uncertainty about the facts. And the identification of a side with our tribe makes it more likely that we believe the story and resist the other side.[80]

And this is true not just for the remote facts or obscure issues. Think again about the rise of Donald Trump. What was most striking to Republican policy wonks about Trump was how far he and his policies were from core Republican values. He spoke about the corrupting influence of money in politics. The last time a GOP candidate for president did that (Buddy Roemer, 2012), he was pushed off the national debate stage. Trump had no time for free trade. No respect for interventionist foreign policy. He promised universal health care—better than Obamacare. He attacked Wall Street. He loved Russia.

This gap signaled to the wonks that Trump could not be the Republican nominee. But of course, most Republican voters—like most voters generally—know nothing about "Republican policies." Beyond vague clichés (which, like "fiscally responsible," have no connection to reality), most Americans identify with identities, not policies; with tribes, not truth.[81] Political parties are attitudes, not collections of party platforms. They are social meanings, as Yale law professor Dan Kahan frames it, that define identity and membership.[82] And when Trump rewrote the policies that were considered to be Republican, only the wonks even noticed, and certainly, only the wonks cared. Bill Kristol, Max Boot, David Brooks—these were the deeply principled policy Republicans who were astonished to discover that the loyalty of their fellow travelers had very little to do with the ideas in the Republican platform.

This is not a point about Trump supporters. It is a point about America. We don't know—in a nonpolarized, sustained way—jack shit about policy, and we ought to be more open and honest—and proud—about what we don't know. We don't know it not because we're stupid. Not because we couldn't. We don't know it because for the vast majority of us, it makes no sense to know it.

Without doubt, there was more information available to Americans about the candidates running for president in 2016 than was ever available in any election in American history. From Twitter to Wikipedia, anyone with access to the Internet had access to endless content. The Net is the largest library ever—and we should think of it as a library. One gets to select whatever one wants. And that selection is unimaginably broad.

Yet the question is always and only not what is available, but what is consumed. Most upper-middle-class Americans have access to incredibly healthy food. That fact says nothing about what they eat. So too with information about the political choices that Americans must make. The issue is not what we could have consumed. The issue is what we did consume. And more important, why.

Defenders of the media, whether "mainstream" or Fox (as if a regularly dominant platform is not "mainstream"), will insist that this is just too cynical. Producers don't produce lies. The reporters don't make up the facts.

Certainly, that is true. Nothing I'm describing here is necessarily willful or intended. Everything is the consequence of a system of incentives. The bending to what the meter of return tells you is profitable is never direct or obvious. Yet over time, institutions get very good at steering to the bottom line, however they may justify it. Fox

News aims to be "fair and balanced" by including liberals "who are either poorly equipped for televised combat with conservatives or are willing . . . to validate right-wing narratives."[83] The pressure may be invisible; that doesn't mean there isn't pressure.

There may be one critical caveat to this story about incentives—though the caveat is not reassuring. In Martin and Yurukoglu's work discussed before, they were able to compare the optimal level of polarization to maximize ad revenues versus the level to maximize electoral influence. Or put differently, between making more money and having a greater political effect, which did the networks select? According to their data, the networks wanted political effect more than money. Or again, they were willing to lose viewers in order to increase the political commitment of the viewers who remained. Martin and Yurukoglu are not certain of this effect. Differences in advertising rates could ultimately show that the networks are maximizing revenue and not political effect. But the data does suggest that on the margin, it may be more than just money that explains what we're seeing, even if it is clearly money that pushed the networks down the path they've gone.[84]

One clear example will suggest the general pattern. Without doubt, one of the most important commentators on Fox News today is Tucker Carlson. Carlson is relatively young. The network has a strong interest in protecting his brand. He is also clearly identified, ideologically. He has come to replace Bill O'Reilly; he depends upon maintaining the same loyal following that O'Reilly was forced to give up.

That following has a certain view of the world. It's not that Carlson never challenges that view. Instead, like a slot machine revolving to three jackpots, sometimes Carlson surprises everyone with episodic right-wing skepticism. (On January 2, 2019, for example, he launched into a fifteen-minute monologue attacking the free market.[85]) But in the main, Carlson (like the great Rachel Maddow) enables his audience to live within their relatively comfortable worldview. He brings gifts to his audience that rewards them for their worldview.

Sometimes he'll do whatever it takes. In a segment about criticism of the Electoral College, for example, by the right's favorite target du jour, Alexandria Ocasio-Cortez, Carlson tried to defend the college. Presidents, he insisted, had been elected without a majority of the vote before. Lincoln, for example, "did not win a majority," Carlson informed us. And then Carlson said this: "I mean I'm not that old, but I covered both of Bill Clinton's campaigns and he never won the popular vote."

So what, the implication was, was the difference with Donald Trump? Clinton didn't "w[i]n the popular vote," and neither did Trump.

Carlson is no dummy; he knows the difference between "winning a majority" (which Lincoln and Clinton did not do) and "winning the popular vote" (which Lincoln and Clinton certainly did, while Trump and George W. Bush did not).[86] A plurality is not necessarily a majority. Indeed, never has a Democrat been elected without winning the popular vote; the only presidents ever selected without winning at least a plurality were all Republicans (or Federalists).

Tucker knows that truth. He let the truth slide. Sliding the truth helped fit the story into the box that Tucker Carlson occupies— comfort food for conservative viewers.

The point is this: Sellers give volume discounts. Even, maybe especially, in competitive markets, a seller will give a much lower price to those who will buy in bulk, since those buys cement a market for the seller that ensures it can survive.

I'm suggesting a similar discount in the world of competitive news media. Fierce competition forces every network to battle for attention. One clearly effective strategy in that fight is a partisan discount. If we don't all have to sit in the same news audience, then we can divide ideologically. That division is enabled by offering the audience the furniture that fits. A network is a home; it should be comfortable for the people who you want to live there. That doesn't mean that there's never any mix. It does mean that the mix is treated as adventure or as the exotic. "Look, it's a liberal!" "To understand that view, we've invited conservative commentator blah blah blah."

This is true even if Benkler and his colleagues are correct. This dynamic can exist even if there is not perfect symmetry in the distortion of news on the right and on the left. The left may well adhere to journalistic standards more than the right, as Benkler and his colleagues argue, but count the number of identity politics stories on the left: does their proportion have any connection to the relative importance of that issue compared with income inequality or climate change? I am not saying that the issue of transgender bathrooms is not important. God forbid you misunderstand me here, and I get banished from polite society (at least my side of society). What I am saying instead is that the poverty of black children in inner-city schools is also important. As is the hopelessness of blue-collar workers in Ohio. Or the families drinking poisoned water in Flint, Michigan. These are important stories, too. They are just not quite the clickbait that identity politics is.

It is useful to think why. On both sides, we are driven to the simple and the clear. Both sides cater to certainty. On the right, it is identity politics—so clear is it to the base on the right that the left has gone off the rails in its focus on those issues. On the left, it is identity politics—so clear is it to the base on the left that America must *finally* come to terms with these great injustices of society, and that anyone who disagrees must have a white-hooded robe stuffed in his closet. Neither side wants to wade into the muddle of the middle—into issues that have no clear valence or answer, because they are genuinely difficult public policy issues. Those issues just do not pay—either the politicians or the media.

Yet *these* are the issues that a democracy must address, even if neither side nor the media has any incentive to address them.

The divisions get reinforced by the audience. When the *New York Times* added conservatives to its editorial page mix, its readers were outraged. How can the *Times* give voice to this craziness?[87] And when Fox News commentators began to question the judgment of President Trump, the shows made a show of reporting the hate mail received by the commentators.[88]

No doubt, there are networks that build themselves to be cross-partisan. Or they try, at least for a while. No doubt there are moments in which the networks will commit to balance. But just as the processed food industry learns every time some enlightened executive decides that its products are poison, and that healthier foods would do good, and then the market teaches the industry that the market isn't interested in good, so too here: we want to feel at home, and as the meter measures the success of the network on the margin, it points in a direction driven not by truth or balance or fairness or understanding, but by attention and comfort and the familiar. We are tribes. We want to hang with our tribe—even when watching the news.[89]

Internet News

In at least one critical way (and at least just now), the Internet is different. But it is a difference that does not help. Television is one way. The Internet is not. We watch television. The Internet watches us. Everything we do on the Internet is captured and monetized. Everything we do is data, and data is gold. Not everything we do on TV is captured and monetized—or at least not yet. As a story in early 2019 reported, TV sets are increasingly cheap because the manufacturers are now selling the data about what we watch.[90] TV is still a relatively anonymous zone, but if the Internet is any lesson, it won't be for very long.

It took a long time for Americans to understand this basic fact about the Internet economy. Even in 2018, Senator Orrin Hatch had no clue about it, asking Facebook CEO Mark Zuckerberg, "So, how do you sustain a business model in which users don't pay for your service?"[91] For much of the early 2000s, many Americans believed that they were just getting great stuff for free, because the tech companies wanted to gain a huge market share. What they would do with that market share no one quite knew. But when they tried to do something, we could then, we believed with confidence, decide what we would do in response. If you've seen the movie *Independence Day,* the analogy will be clear: we presumed good faith, and watched them build huge infrastructure around us, trusting what we believed. Then we discovered: we were mistaken.

Early into this century, however, the technologists at Google and then elsewhere realized that they could capture data about the behavior of people on the Internet—"digital exhaust," as the behavioral data came to be called—and turn those data into gold. From *behavior* using the Internet, you could learn *facts* about the users. If you search for "hiking boots" and "White Mountain lodges," that's a pretty good indication that you're going to New Hampshire for a vacation and likely to go hiking while there. That fact is worth something—to the makers of hiking boots and the owners of lodges in New Hampshire at least. That fact is an indication that you might be interested in information about hiking boots or about the best places to sleep if you want an early-morning hike up Mount Washington.

No one saw this potential in the early 1990s. It wasn't what motivated Sergey Brin and Larry Page to build Google. At the time the Internet was born, the technology was not powerful enough to do the things that big data would eventually do. But when the tech companies tripped onto the gold that was flowing across the wires, they realized that this was the enormous surplus—the "behavioral surplus"—that would make Silicon Valley rich.

All of that is insanely great. Indeed, I want to exaggerate here so you don't miss my point. My argument is fundamentally different from the work of surveillance skeptics, like Shoshana Zuboff. Her magisterial book, *The Age of Surveillance Capitalism*, tells a terrifying story of the emergence of a new form of capitalism that trades fundamentally on surveillance. There is tons to learn from her analysis, and much to be anxious about. We do not begin to understand the scope of this surveillance, or how it is changing, fundamentally, our relation to each other.

Yet in the end, her criticism reaches too far. There is enormous social good that has been rendered by this extraordinary new capacity with data—good *and* extraordinary bad. We are nowhere close to realizing the full potential of that good. We also have no clue about how the bad should be regulated, or how it could be controlled.

Yet we should approach those questions through the specifics, not in general. We should be asking about the particular uses of data, not whether data is good, or gathering data is evil. No doubt the emergence of this platform of surveillance will change humanity. But humanity has always been changed. And as we face a population of close to 10 billion people by midcentury, we desperately need to understand how better to serve and regulate us with efficiency. We may well be losing the "will to will," as Zuboff repeatedly puts it, but we urgently need a better ability to feed the world and protect the weak. And to the extent these technologies drive efficiency, they could help us do that precisely.

This is a dangerous position to take. I get that. All the money in the world is on the side of defending the emerging status quo. That is reason enough to be skeptical of these emerging truths. Especially in an era of increasingly concentrated private power, the courage of scholars such as Zuboff deserves enormous respect. No single book does a better job in surveying the reality that just a tiny fraction of us even begins to understand. And certainly, I do not mean this tiny slice of one chapter to provide a critique of her work, or an alternative to thinking through the problems called "privacy."

Yet I believe that rather than thinking at the level of isms, we should think at the level of uses.[92] There are some uses of these data that we should consider just fine. So long as the data are not used to identify me directly, and so long as they are being used simply to connect the (unidentified) me with information that I might find useful, that use of data is a wonderful thing. It has produced enormous value in the market. And it has made it easy to market all sorts of new things to all sorts of people by all sorts of start-up creators.

Think again about Amazon with books or Netflix with movies: those technologies watch us. In the language of Zuboff, they are technologies of surveillance. They see what we watch or buy, and then they tell us about other things that we might want to watch or buy.

This use is a wonderful thing. That's not to say that antitrust law shouldn't have worried more extensively about how these two companies have evolved. That's a separate question.[93] My point so far is just that this technology of surveillance has created value that was not accessible before. Now that it is accessible, and because of the way Internet advertising is sold, it is accessible to practically anyone. If you invent a cool new hiking technology that makes hiking safer or more fun, it is trivially easy to target ads for that technology to the people who are most likely to want to buy it. My father doesn't need to see those ads. Neither does my middle kid, who doesn't like hiking at all. But for those who like it, the technology makes it easy to sell. It is a marketer's dream come true. If James Bryce had been triggered to think about it, he might well have called it "the final stage of marketing."

This goodness is true, I want to insist, controversially, regardless of the source of the data. When people began to recognize why Gmail was valuable to Google—because Google could "read" your email and know more about you—they freaked out.[94] "Google is reading my email!" But there are no humans at Google skimming billions of messages. It is machines. And while there is a potential for abuse—and that potential should be regulated—there is all the difference in the world between my neighbor (or the Stasi) reading my mail and Google "reading" my emails.

The same is true about Microsoft and Skype: When the public wondered why Microsoft was willing to pay $8.5 billion to buy Skype, it was quickly revealed that the company would use the Skype calls to train voice recognition algorithms.[95] "So wait, Microsoft is *listening* to my Skype-based telephone calls?" Yes, in a sense, but not in the sense that the FBI might be listening to your telephone calls. That again is not to say that we shouldn't be concerned about abuse, or even about the potential for abuse, given the architecture as it has developed. It is only to say that we have to be *real* about the threat we are describing when we use old words to talk about a new reality.

The intuitions that we bring along with terms like *watched, fol-*

lowed, read, listened, and *surveilled* have been developed in contexts very different from the digital one. Those differences don't cache out in good versus bad; they are just differences. But the differences cannot be ignored, or rendered invisible, as the normative force of terms from the twentieth century gets deployed against technologies of the twenty-first.

There's a parallel here with the fight about so-called intellectual property. A copyright may be your property, just as a car may be your property. But stealing the one is very different from stealing the other. Sloppy language sometimes obscures that difference. As U.S. attorney Carmen Ortiz said, as she threatened Aaron Swartz with a thirty-five-year jail term for downloading too many academic journal articles from the online database JSTOR, "stealing is stealing whether you use a computer command or a crowbar."[96] But that statement is just absurd. A crowbar does damage almost every time it is used to "steal"; a computer command rarely does. That's not to say that one is good, and the other is bad. It is simply to say that leveraging intuitions from the physical world to make judgments about the digital is rarely true or safe or justified.

The same is true about "surveillance capitalism." Rather than allowing the scary words *surveillance* or *spying* to drive us to "rekindle the sense of outrage," as Zuboff counsels, we should ask a more fundamental question: What precisely is the harm?[97] Some uses are plainly harmful. But some uses should be considered fine regardless. Specifically, if the use is not endogenous (in the sense that the use burdens the people creating the data, a dynamic we'll see more clearly below), and it is not tied back to an individual (in the sense that an individual is burdened by the fact that the data is collected), then, subject to concerns about security, that use should be fine—even if other uses that would not meet this standard are not fine.

My aim in these pages is thus not to condemn generally. Its criticism is more targeted. The objective here is not against all technology; it is instead to rally an understanding of a particular slice of that technology and the problem it creates for democracy. For whatever else is true about big data, *these* problems are urgent and real.

To see those problems, we need to see how the technology evolved. Once the technique of mining a behavioral surplus was born, a new kind of competition was born with it: the competition to better understand us. Sure, it may be that you can tell that I am planning a trip to hike in the White Mountains from the fact that I have conducted a search for hiking boots on Google. But not necessarily. Maybe someone else was using my machine. Maybe I'm handicapped but writing a novel about a hiker. Maybe I'm fantasizing about how I'd live my life, if only I could. The point is that there's lots of noise in the data of search. And that noise created a competitive drive to find a better way to know what anyone else might want.

That better way was Facebook. Launched initially as a tool to connect college students to college students, Facebook quickly became a platform for advertising as it became a dominant platform for people to share stuff about themselves. Facebook's initial ethic was identity; unlike MySpace or Friendster, Facebook would take some steps to ensure that you were who you said you were. That was intended initially to help police bad behavior. As philosophers since Plato have recognized, what you do when you are invisible is different from what you do when you know you're at least traceable. But whatever its intent, these added data were gold. As Sheryl Sandberg, chief operating officer of Facebook, put it, "We have better information than anyone else. We know gender, age, location, and it's real data as opposed to the stuff other people infer."[98]

Facebook thus added to what we could know about you. If you were tied to your identity, then what you did on Facebook produced more accurate data about you than what you did on Google (or at least Google before Gmail). And not just because of what you did, but because of what you could be induced to do. Facebook could get you to dance. And the more you danced, the more Facebook could know about you. This, Zuboff writes, was a shift "from using automated machine processes to know about your behavior to using machine processes to shape your behavior."[99]

This is a critical difference, even more critical as the engines for poking us become driven by AI. As the architects of Facebook (and the rest of the data Internet) recognized, there were ways to build the space to make users more committed, and ways to build the space to induce the users to reveal even more.

Facebook built a commitment to its platform through many techniques. Using the psychology of Las Vegas, it architected digital rewards within the environment of Facebook to give users random benefits; that random reward triggered a kind of slot-machine effect; each win would be a hit—literally, "a little dopamine hit," as its first president, Sean Parker, described it.[100] Those hits would then become addictive. You share your photos; an old flame gives them a like. "He still likes me!" You share a story, one hundred people you've never met share it again. "Wow, I'm famous!" It's the digital equivalent of high-fives—which then quite literally makes you high. At least until the effect wears off, and you need more. And so you share more, and more and more and more, and you engage more, and you watch what others do more.

Facebook wasn't the only digital platform working to addict—as Chris Nodder describes it (somewhat approvingly) in his how-to book, *Evil by Design*.[101] Indeed, the science of digital addiction was driven most effectively by gaming companies. Once an industry of backyard innovators, the "video gaming industry . . . transitioned . . . to an industry of multi-billion-dollar companies, hiring psychologists, neuroscientists and marketing experts to turn customers into addicts." The gaming economy today is bigger than the movies and music economies—*combined*. Borrowing the same techniques from the science of casinos, designers craft their games to trigger an addictive response. Random rewards and fake currency disassociate players, leading them to play longer and spend more. Surprise becomes a key: "An unexpected reward has much more power than one that is regular," Nora Volkow, head of the National Institute on Drug Abuse, noted. That "has been known for a very long time."[102] In 2018, the World Health Organization added video game disorder to its "International Classification of Diseases."[103]

But Facebook could do something that gaming companies could not. It is here that things got really weird. The data architects discovered many potential techniques of what former Google "design ethicist" Tristan Harris calls "brain-hacking." Building on the insights of Stanford professor B. J. Fogg, the industry began to architect the spaces that lived on the Internet "to combine psychology and persuasion concepts from the early twentieth century, like propaganda, with techniques from slot machines, like variable rewards, and tie them to the human social need for approval and validation in ways that few users can resist."[104]

The code of these environments constructs the environment. The code could thus leverage the natures of human psychology to make the humans occupying these environments better customers for their creators. As Roger McNamee, an early Facebook supporter now turned impassioned critic, describes it, "Autoplay and endless feeds eliminate cues to stop. Unpredictable, variable rewards stimulate behavioral addiction. Tagging, Like buttons, and notifications trigger social validation loops. As users, we do not stand a chance."[105]

There was a race, as McNamee puts it, quoting Harris, "to the bottom of the brain stem" "to the low-level emotions of the lizard brain, things like immediate rewards, outrage, and fear." For once "in an emotionally hijacked state," the users "become more reactive to further emotionally charged content."[106]

This is not just the speculations of a Facebook critic. In 2014, Facebook published an article in which it described an experiment in which it had manipulated the balance of positive and negative messages in Facebook news feeds, to test how the users would react. That study confirmed that Facebook could affect the emotion of its users, and then the willingness of its users to spread that emotion across its platform, by simply mixing the content of its news differently. And not just the content. "Brain-hacking" involves a long list of techniques, as Harris explains, to hijack attention to benefit the hijacker.[107]

This is something new. It's one thing (1) to collect data about people in public. It's another thing (2) to induce them to reveal data, in a space they consider private. (This is the endogeneity I referenced above.) And it's quite another thing again (3) to craft an environment that leverages insecurity for the purpose of inducing people to reveal as much about themselves as they possibly can.[108]

These three different cases raise different issues of privacy and justice. Case 1 is the least troubling and least new. Cases 2 and 3 are more, and the most troubling, respectively, because most new and most important. The nudge economy is just being born, and the ethics of nudge are complex.[109]

But put aside the question of how the data is collected—important and difficult but beyond the scope of this book. Focus instead on how the data that is collected gets used. What is the use that we can rightly complain about?

From Facebook's perspective, this issue is solely about its customers. Is it giving its customers what its customers want? If it is, then no harm, no foul. That's how Mark Zuckerberg defended his company in the *Wall Street Journal*. Our job is to serve, Zuckerberg all but said. What could possibly be wrong with that?[110]

That is a critically important perspective. Critically, though, it is not the only perspective. Besides the Facebook customers, there is the democracy that Facebook operates within—and affects profoundly. The question is therefore not just whether Facebook is giving its users what its users want, but whether in giving its users what they want it is also harming democracy.

This is not a new perspective. When Pokémon Go launched, it quickly became a massively addictive game for many, giving those many an almost obsessive pleasure in seeking out and capturing Pokémon in the wild. But as it gave its users what they wanted, many of those users were being led to do things that their neighbors didn't want. Placing a Pokémon in a park is one thing; placing it in a place where I have to trespass on someone else's property to get to it is something very different.[111] Pokémon had to recognize that harm and adjust to avoid it.

Or think about something as simple as straws: As anyone with kids recognizes, kids love straws. An establishment selling drinks has an obvious interest in giving its customers—at least the kids—straws. But as we now recognize, straws are an incredible burden on the environment. They are especially dangerous to certain wildlife. And so it is perfectly legitimate to ask not just whether McDonald's is serving its customers when it gives them straws. It is also perfectly right to ask—in serving its customers, is McDonald's imposing a burden on our society, too?

That is the question we should be asking about Facebook—and every other data company as well. Not just whether the data are being used in a way that customers want, but also whether the data are being used in ways that also burden or harm society. Is there, as Dirk Bergemann and Alessandro Bonatti put it, an "externality [to] social data"?[112]

There are clear cases here, both on the negative side and the positive. As I've said, when Amazon uses its data about the books I've read to recommend a new book to me, that use of my data benefits me. It benefits Amazon, too, of course. But unless one has something against books, it doesn't harm society or anyone else. Maybe we'd worry if Amazon only recommended books it had an interest in. Maybe we'd worry if Amazon only recommended liberal or conservative books. Maybe we'd worry if every fifth book it recommended was a story of how great Jeff Bezos was. Those are all certainly possible reasons to worry. But from the simple fact that Amazon uses my data to recommend things I should buy, we can't conclude that there's any real reason we need to worry about that use of data. Or the same with Netflix recommending a new television series. Or the same with Google giving me recommendations for hiking boots. In all these cases, the data companies are using my data to give me what I want, in a way that doesn't impose a burden on society in general. Of course, they need to pay their taxes. They need to make sure they are not polluting. They need to pay their workers according to the law of the land. There's lots these companies must do as well. But in using the data they collect about me in this way, they are not burdening me or society.

That's one clear case. Here's another clear case at the opposite end of this spectrum: Imagine researchers at Facebook discovered a simple way to identify a degenerative neurological condition, based solely on changes in the way that you type. They watch how you type. They know how old you are. They watch how your typing changes. And sometimes, from those changes, they can predict with high accuracy that you are likely to suffer from this degenerative neurological condition. Imagine the company then contacts insurance companies and offers to sell them those data. "If you pay us $X million, we will reveal to you which of our users are likely to have condition Y."[113]

No one should be okay with this. Here the company would be using the data it collected to make the life of its users worse, not better. No user would agree to this particular use. And thus, without even considering how this use affects society, we can say it should not be allowed.

Then there are cases in between: Imagine a use that benefits the individual but harms society. For example, imagine I'm a left-wing nut. (Imagine!) Imagine I love to read wildly approving articles about progressives, and wildly hateful articles about conservatives. Imagine we're coming up to an election, and I'm particularly keen to be triggered in ways that support my team and in ways that harm their team. And imagine finally that in this environment, Facebook feeds me precisely what I want. It greases the wheels of the stories that will get me going; it blocks or buries the stories that might balance or tamp down my passion. It gives the raving lefties an easy way to trigger me. It gives them an endless opportunity to rally me to the raving lefty's causes.

First, and to be clear: there is nothing *obviously* wrong with this sort of technology. Email companies do this. Political parties do this. Partisan newspapers do this. Whole television networks do this. The game of rallying one side or the other is the essence of politics. It is an activity that should be protected and celebrated, because it is the core of democratic speech. And it is an activity that should be well protected from governmental regulation because again, in a democracy, we don't want the government controlling political speech.

Yet even so, none of us should be completely sanguine about this dynamic on Facebook, or the Facebooks of the future. As I've described, this dynamic has no necessary connection to providing anyone what they need to make the judgments that we as citizens are called upon to make. The logic that drives the Facebook algorithms is not truth, or balance, or understanding, or importance. The logic is engagement for the purpose of selling ads. That purpose again is perfectly fine in a context that doesn't create an externality. But where it naturally and obviously and demonstrably drives people away from the understanding they need to make the judgments we require, it creates a problem for democratic society. If the technology "pollute[s] the public square," as McNamee puts it, that pollution should raise an obviously public question.[114]

That question is more pressing in part because of the way Facebook architects the communities within which its users live. This is the great contribution of Turkish academic Zeynep Tufekci's work about Internet platforms including Facebook.[115] These spaces confront us with other views as we sit with our own tribes. Our reaction takes account of these tribes. Our aim becomes our team, not the truth. Our focus is on us, and how far away we are from them. And as people learn better how to exploit these private groups, these groups become more consequential for understanding within society.

All of these concerns are independent of whether Facebook is rendering our democracy more vulnerable to Russia. Though there is plenty of good reason to believe that Facebook has rendered our political system vulnerable—and possibly hijacked in 2016—my argument here does not depend upon that. I'm sure Facebook could protect itself from the Russians. I'm sure the reaction to 2016 has given it ample incentive to do so. But whether they fix the Russian problem or not, the gap between the business model of Facebook and the citizenship model of a democracy remains huge, and maybe unbridgeable.[116]

This is the same problem that I described with cable news—but only worse. Here again there is a logic driven by incentives. The incentives are advertising. Here again that logic is producing a mix of speech that may disable the capacity for democratic self-governance. Here again that logic has no necessary connection to the truth of the content being distributed (hence, "fake news").[117] In both cases the consequences are the same. In both cases the reason for the consequences is the same. And in both cases those reasons are not tied to the systems *not* giving us what we want. To the contrary: in both cases the system is giving us *exactly* what we want. What we want is the problem.

We should be clear about this point, so we don't minimize how difficult this problem is. On my phone, I have an app called "Read Across." That app tilts the mix of news that I am exposed to, so that I am exposed to views outside my own bubble. I'm a progressive. Read Across exposes me to conservative views. Fox News appears in my feed, as does *The New Republic.*

I hate it. I know I should love it. I know I should use it. I know a good citizen would discipline himself to expose himself to views from the other side. I know that as a citizen, I should certainly "read across" the aisle. I know that is what democracy requires.

But I also know I don't want to. I know that in the day-to-day feed that I want to devote to national news, I want the news that I want. I want the views that I want. I don't want to be fed stuff that I don't want. I don't want to be made to feel un-American because I flip past the news I know I don't want to read.

I don't report this simply to confess. I report it to acknowledge something I take it we all experience as well. I think many on my side of the aisle would confess to the same; I know that many on the other side of the aisle would confess to the same, too. When news is entertainment, successful news is the news that gives the viewer what the viewer wants. And in a highly competitive world, that dynamic presses in an obvious direction: if your feed upsets me because there is too much Tucker Carlson, then I'll just switch to a different feed with less Carlson and more Rachel Maddow. It's a free country. That's what freedom is. And if the technologies of the Internet enable us to perfect that freedom, then perfected it will be—until, at least, we destroy the possibility for democracy.

Here again, it might even be worse than this. For these technologies not only enable us to choose the reality "we want." These technologies are creating the reality "we want." This is the deep and powerful point in Zuboff's great book. It is a point that we must reckon.

In the fall of 2017, ProPublica broke an incredible story about advertising on Facebook.[118] It turns out that in the incredible AI machine of Facebook advertising, Facebook was offering ads targeted to "Jew haters." To most reading that story, the idea seemed incredible. Did Facebook really have people who were trying to market to "Jew haters"? And of course, the answer to that question was no, it didn't. There was not a human with Facebook who had ever crafted the advertising categories to include "Jew hater." Instead, it was the machine. The AI engine in the Facebook advertising engine had crafted the category based on its observations about the people using Facebook. It could tell there were "Jew haters." So it created a tool to market to those people.

A category is not neutral. Naming something doesn't simply name it. By creating the machine for identifying this group, the technology created the opportunity for strengthening or expanding the group. Thus again there is a by-product, and even if we assume (as I do) it was unintended, we must account, as a culture, for its effect. And we should expect that as these companies embrace AI more fundamentally, to do everything from tweaking news feeds to crafting categories for advertising, the hive-like evolution will only grow.

This use of these data is thus different from the first generation of Google. When Google triggered advertising based on what I searched, it was not, in the same way, changing me. But when Facebook induces me to behave so that I reveal more, it does change me. Its relationship is not passive. It is engaging. And while its purpose is perfectly

American—making money—its means are wholly alien. This is not a market that gives the consumer what the consumer wants. It is a market that changes the consumer so it can know better what the consumer, so changed, "wants."

Yes, in some sense, this has been the complaint about consumer culture since the dawn of advertising.[119] But continuity does not negate difference: we need to be able to be sophisticated and learned about how similar stuff is, without being oblivious and obtuse to the effect of the differences. Whatever power Madison Avenue had in 1962, the power of Facebook is orders of magnitude different.

WITH BOTH TECHNOLOGIES, THEN, cable news and Internet news, relative to the world of compelled news—news that was not optional at least if someone was watching television—the incentives have changed. In a word, markets became competitive. The question becomes not just what is true or important, but what would commit our audience and keep them coming back. Like the food scientist tweaking salt/fat/sugar, the news scientist became focused on the right mix of partisan outrage and party loyalty. The politics of hate became a business model. And as the news became more and more focused on the relationship between what is covered and how the audience reacts, what is covered had no necessary connection to what was important or true.

Again, that's not to say that any network is opposed to the truth. Or that it is opposed to presenting the facts that are important or necessary for a democracy to work. It is rather to say that the truth or importance is contingent upon it creating followers. Just as Kraft Foods has no intrinsic interest in selling unhealthy food, Fox News has no intrinsic interest in selling falsehoods. But if unhealthy food, or unfair and unbalanced news is profitable, the competitive market makes it extremely hard for the sellers to resist.

This point is important, and bears repeating: there are those who want to see bad outcomes as only ever the product of bad people.

If Fox is biased, it's because an evil owner wants to bend the world to a biased view. If Coke is poison, it's because the owners of Coca-Cola hate America. If Facebook is destroying democracy, it's because Zuckerberg is the Manchurian CEO. Yet no such link is needed. In a competitive market, competitors must give the consumers what the consumers want. Enlightened executives at Coke might realize that it would be better if consumers drank less soda and more water. Or if the soda they drank had less sugar. But if consumers don't like it, they'll switch to something else. The good intentions of a corporative executive—within a competitive market—might be noble or inspiring. They are also short-lived. The competitive market will discipline companies to give the consumer what the consumer wants. And if the consumer demands crap, then crap it will be.

In the market for news, the externality is much greater. For if the consequence of giving the consumers of media what the consumers want—if that media about news, for example, is the equivalent of empty processed food calories—then we as a democracy suffer directly. If 40 percent of America lives in one partisan-fact-free bubble, and 40 percent in another, then the capacity of America to resolve questions of democratic import is weakened.

In part that's because of a difference in the nature of the good. If you don't watch *Better Call Saul*, that's too bad for you. It's not too bad for us. There's no comparable externality for culture. We all can live in our niches. It doesn't matter if what you consume is not what I consume. People might yearn for the day when we all could talk around the water cooler about the latest episode of some network television show. But what company has water coolers anymore? And who cares if only eight million Americans are watching NBC in prime time?[120] I understand talk about the romance of a "common cultural conversation." I just don't think we should sacrifice much to get it.

Yet with the news, the problem is different. If your consumption of news gives you a radically or critically different view of the world than I have, that's a real problem when you and I need to participate in a democratic decision that involves the nature of the world. If conservatives believe that climate science is bunk, that's going to make it harder for us liberals to get Congress to pass climate legislation. If liberals think GMO is bunk, that's going to make it harder for conservatives to get regulatory support for technologies that critically improve crops or organisms.[121]

This in the end is the most damning charge against this business model of advertising in our time. We are being nudged and crafted, rendered anxious and triggered, made happy, made lonely, made angry, made more partisan, *so that Facebook and the like can sell more ads.* Think about it: if we had destroyed democracy so we could end world hunger, if we had made it impossible to find common ground, so that we could cure cancer, or end climate change, then one might well wonder whether the sacrifice was worth it. But all of the sacrifice here *is so that some can sell more ads.* A "bet-the-farm commitment," as Shoshana Zuboff puts it, "for the sake of [advertising] revenues."[122] A business that literally did not exist in anything like its present form twenty years ago has now infected and corrupted critical domains of public life. Yes, I can find the Nike shoes I want much more easily. Yes, with a single click, they are on their way. And yes, in a million other ways, life has been made more interesting and more diverse. Yes, the Internet is not evil.

Until it is. Because besides all that, there is this: the platforms of modern media and communication may well be rendering us incapable as citizens. Democracy is made poor so that Facebook can be rich.

LET ME DRAW THE argument together.

In the days before broadcasting, culture and news was fragmented. We don't have a clear or comprehensive view. The romantics—like Al Gore[123]—like to talk about our framers and the nineteenth century as filled with well-read and informed souls. Maybe. But whatever they were well read about, it varied substantially from person to person, and community to community. We were an epistemologically fragmented nation, whether as fragmented or more fragmented than we are today.

Whatever fragmentation there was, however, was relatively invisible. There was no way to know what the "will of the people" was about tariff policy or the admission of California to the union, or whether there should be state-sponsored elementary schools. We know what the politicians said. We know they claimed to speak for the people. But we have no independent access to what America thought, because there was no scientific and regular method for sussing out the public's views.

Broadcasting changed fragmentation. As television became dominant, America became more uniform. We all watched the same shows. We all heard the same news. We moved from an epistemologically fragmented nation to a highly concentrated nation. Certain things we all knew, because those things we all saw on the television that we all watched.

At the same time, we could know what we all knew. The rise of polling tracks the rise of television. The more we know, the more we can show that we know. And the more that what we show sounds sensible, the more normatively significant "we the people" become. Put differently: just at the moment that we learn how to discover what the people believe, the people—in aggregate, as Page and Shapiro emphasize—have something interesting to say. And they have something interesting to say because they've been forced to watch a daily lesson teaching the news of the day. That lesson came from networks aiming right down the middle. It came from a journalist culture that valued—and could afford to practice—objective journalism. That's not complete journalism (race, economic inequality, sexual orientation are not topics that were well covered by this journalism). That's not necessarily true journalism (the story America was told about America's role in foreign nations was false). But it was a journalism that built a base upon which democracy could function. That base then got reflected in polls that measured just how much we all knew.

The post-broadcasting age shares attributes with both the pre-broadcasting and broadcasting ages. Like the pre-broadcasting age, we are now once again living within an epistemologically fragmented universe. There is no way accurately to measure whether we're more or less fragmented. There's no doubt, however, that we're more fragmented than in the broadcasting age. We all know stuff. But the stuff we all know is not known in common. Some people know that global warming is real. Some people know that GMOs are safe. The challenge for democracy is that those peoples are not the same—even though the world that they must govern is a world with each living together.

Likewise, the post-broadcasting age shares attributes with the broadcasting age. As with the broadcasting age, we are still polled. We still can know what everyone knows. We still can represent what "we the people" want. Our will is more easily known that at any time in human history. Anyone can buy any question from any number of polling services and report, "This is what the people believe."

Yet unlike in the broadcasting age, the knowledge that these polls reveal now is wildly more partial, and even more incomplete. The reflections of what we know are not coherent or consistent or compelling in the same way that they were. On many issues, we are fundamentally divided, in part because our values are different, but in the main because our understanding of the facts is radically different. What "we know" we don't know in common. And that fact affects fundamentally how we get represented.

Even worse, that fact affects how we get constructed. As I've emphasized, it would be one thing if the media were simply reflecting us as partisans. But what if the media—driven by the business model of advertising—is constructing us *as* partisans? I don't mean it's making the news up. I mean instead that in the subtle mix of forces that determine what gets covered and how, the interest in driving interest drives us to be seen as—and then made as—more partisan. The tropes for triggering partisan anger become obvious. The incentives to trigger, obvious, too. And thus is there a "we" that gets represented through this process of construction? Yet this "we" is both more partisan and, because of the pervasiveness of the polls, more present.

But should it? Should the "we" that gets represented in those polls matter? Should that representation be allowed to count for us?

INTEGRITY

Elena Kagan is a justice on the United States Supreme Court. She is also brilliant. There are many things she knows because she's studied them or read about them. But despite her knowing what she knows, there is a certain process to how we ask her to give her opinion about what she knows best. At least in the context of law. You don't walk up to Elena Kagan on the street and quiz her about admiralty law. Or if you did, she'd be perfectly entitled to reply, "Hey, I don't answer pop quizzes. If you want to get my view, or the Supreme Court's view, about admiralty law, get a case, bring it to the court, write some briefs, participate in oral arguments, and then, and only then, will we give you our view." The opinion of the Supreme Court is literally a document titled "Opinion of the Court." Absent such a document, there is no opinion to report.

And this is not just because they're the judges on the Supreme Court. A central part of the American justice system is the jury. Critical, and powerful, a jury can decide to condemn a criminal defendant to death or order a civil defendant to pay billions of dollars in damages. In reaching such verdicts, a jury goes through an elaborate and highly regulated process. Members are selected by first trying to segment out biased or incapable jurors; they are then presented with opening arguments, laying out the plan of the case from each side; evidence is then presented, under the careful supervision of a judge; the judge then gives the jury instructions about how to think about the evidence and law in the case; the jury then deliberates, in secret and alone, and if they agree in sufficient number, then they present their verdict to the judge, and to the public.

If, along that path, you entered the jury room and conducted a poll of the jury, you wouldn't have the "verdict" of the jury. You might or might not have sensible views reported to you by the jury. Those views might or might not be close to the ultimate views that the jury adopts. But we—at least we lawyers—understand that there is no "view of the jury" separate from a verdict, and that there is no verdict except as gets produced through this elaborate process of information and deliberation.

The same with the views of "the president." Though the recent past may make this hard to remember, presidents don't just blather. When a president reports the view of his or her (we can at least hope) administration, the president is reporting the conclusion of an elaborate and extensive process. The views of both sides on an issue are considered; the political consequences are weighed; the values of the president are appealed to; the costs of either decision are reckoned. And then at the end, the president speaks. Even when the president speaks "extemporaneously," such as at a press conference or on the road, the president has been briefed extensively about the issues he or she is likely to be asked about. And the same with members of Congress. And the heads of the departments. And the same (and especially so) with the governors of the Federal Reserve System.

In all these cases, public officials speak in a very particular way. They aren't quizzed. They can't be forced to express an opinion. Instead, the opinions that they utter are the conclusion of an elaborate process. And finally, and critically—in that process, they get staff. Their staff supports the decision. It helps them consider alternatives. It makes sure the official doesn't make a mistake.

In this sense, views of public officers are not just found. They are made. They're not simply discovered. They are constructed. They are not the product of a quiz. They are the product of an elaborate and extensively supported process.

In the history of republican thought, "citizen" has long been considered a public office, too.[124] Like a juror, president, judge, or representative, a citizen, too, is a kind of public officer. Yet what's striking about the citizen, as contrasted with the juror, president, judge, or representative, is that we believe we can know the views of the citizen through a pop quiz. The jury gives its views at the end of a process; the citizen gives her view on a telephone, while preparing dinner or to put the kids to bed. The president considers both sides of a question. The citizen doesn't even know there are two sides. The judge or representative is to deliberate with other judges or representatives. But the citizen is given no chance to deliberate. The phone rings. The questions are asked. The aim of the person answering the questions is either to get off the phone as quickly as possible or at least not to seem like an idiot—or worse, for a Democrat/Republican, to seem like a Republican/Democrat!

Most important, in this process the citizen gets no staff. The jury has the lawyers and the judge spoon-feeding the information they need to make their decisions; the president has an army of brilliant souls feeding every relevant fact and consideration; the judge has clerks as well as lawyers to frame her decisions; the representative has a modest number of staff and an endless army of lobbyists. All of these public officers get support before they are "represented." But the citizen gets no support before she is "represented."

It is a system designed to render us embarrassing.[125] So is there any doubt that public opinion polls make Americans look stupid? Is there any wonder that it seems crazy to anyone who knows anything that public policy would be driven by the "will of the people"? Professor Kirby Goidel speaks for many when he writes,

> **"We the people"** are simply not up to the task of self-governance; we are easily misled and controlled by corporate power and interest group campaigns. In truth, we never have been up to the task, but, for a variety of reasons, our failings are more evident, more troublesome, and more dangerous in contemporary politics.[126]

How does Goidel evince our ignorance? Through a series of public opinion polls that demonstrate we don't know squat about anything.[127]

The people are certainly ignorant—there is plenty we don't know. And we may be increasingly polarized in our ignorance—so that there are different things that different sides just don't know. But again, ignorance is not stupidity. And a system that imagines we can just quiz the public about matters of public import and produce through that process anything that should guide anyone—at least when there is no common understanding held by all—is not an ignorant system. *It* is a stupid system. There is no wonder we are embarrassing when we are represented like this. What is puzzling is not our ignorance. What is puzzling is that anyone believes this is how "we" should be understood to speak.

This point about us is urgent today, even if not so urgent in the past. In the age before polling, our ignorance just didn't matter as much. We had no way to find the "will of the people," except through an inherently edifying process of interpretation. In the age of broadcasting, it mattered, of course, but we were better informed. I don't mean we knew more—the Internet today gives us more access to more knowledge than at any time in human history. I mean instead that "we" had a common basis upon which to make judgments, and that common basis in fact more often than not overwhelmed differences in values. That common ground shows us to be "reasonable," at least as found by Page and Shapiro.

But when that common basis is removed, and partisan becomes the norm, then differences flourish. And as they flourish, we get rendered as ignorant. Or at least, "they" are ignorant; "we" know what's true. "They" think [global warming is fake/GMOs are dangerous]; "we" know they are just bonkers. The polling of a fragmented and polarized public then feeds democratic self-loathing. Pew found 56 percent of Americans have "little or no confidence in the political wisdom of the American people."[128] That's certainly the dynamic for the "exhausted majority," as one extraordinary study of tribalism in America characterized it.[129] It is true, as Markus Prior reports, that average knowledge about matters of public policy has not declined in the post-broadcast era. But as Prior notes, "average" means average. The news junkies know much more than the average person knew in the age of broadcasting; the rest of society knows much less.[130]

Yet rather than self-loathing, what this polling should feed is a little bit of "what the hell?!" Just as we'd say that a jury quizzed mid-deliberation does not "represent" the jury, or justices quizzed on the street do not represent the Supreme Court, or an offhand remark by a president just stepping off a transcontinental flight does not "represent" the presidency, or the quip of a member of Congress does not "represent" Congress, so, too, should we say that "we the people" as represented through George Gallup's technology in the age of fragmented and polarized media does not "represent" us. We should not be speaking as if it represents us. And we should demand better support before "we" are asked what "we" believe about matters of public import.

And thus, the point of this chapter: *they*—the people who speak in those polls, or in the million similar ways in which our ignorance gets manifested—*don't represent us*. They don't have the *integrity* to represent us. Integrity demands more than a representative sample. Integrity demands the opportunity to understand and deliberate, always and with everyone.

This might be a jarring point at first. It can be domesticated with just a little thought. In a statistical sense, of course, the "we" captured in Gallup's poll represents us. (Or maybe it does, or maybe it just did. There is plenty of skepticism about the science in modern polling that I point to in the notes.[131]) Yet as we've seen throughout this book, the idea of "representative" is not itself obvious, or self-defining. We need a normative argument for how anything gets represented. That argument can be successful only if it can trade on common judgment or common values. The point of this section is to trade on what I believe should be common values: Even in this hyperpartisan moment, and populism notwithstanding, no one should defend a "we" that is constructed from ignorance, or especially from tribal ignorance. The politicians aren't required to be so embarrassed—even if some seem quite eager to embarrass themselves. Neither should we be required to be so embarrassed.

Instead we all, whether Republican or not, should openly and loudly proclaim—hey, that "we" does not represent us.

CONSEQUENCES

The year I graduated from law school, the Berlin Wall fell. Two years later, I started teaching. From the start of my career as an academic, I was obsessed with how those newly independent nations would govern themselves. My first job was at the University of Chicago. That institution had the Center for the Study of Constitutionalism in Eastern Europe. I joined the center and spent many nights on cramped flights crisscrossing Eastern Europe and the former Soviet republics.

Georgia became a focus of my work. In December 1992, in Budapest, I met two leaders of the emerging Georgian democracy movement. They invited me to Tbilisi in March the following year. Flying through Vienna, I arrived in Tbilisi in the middle of the night. I was driven to a retreat used by the president of Georgia to host guests of the state. I slept for maybe four hours, and then was picked up by my host in a large black sedan. We were to attend a meeting of the leadership of the Georgian legal community. The meeting was intended to discuss the nature of any future Georgian constitution. I arrived late and entered a huge but beautiful conference room. Seventy senior lawyers and judges from Georgia sat around a long rectangular table. The chief judge of the supreme court sat at the head of the room, on a dais, almost like a king. When I entered, he welcomed me, in English. He then reverted to Georgian. A translator sat next to me, whispering his words into my ear. After some talk about the course of the program for the day, the translator uttered these words, which, though whispered, felt more like a scream: "We'll now hear a presentation by Professor Lessig of the

University of Chicago, describing the history of constitutional democracies, and comparing in particular the history of Germany and France, as it relates to the constitutional history of America."

No one had told me that I was to make any presentation at all. Had they asked me whether I wanted to make a presentation, I would have said my aim was to listen and learn, not lecture. But if they had insisted, I would have been happy to describe American constitutional law. That was my expertise. That is what I was teaching at Chicago. But I had never, at that point, studied or taught anything about German or French constitutional law. I had read an important book by a critically important American scholar that linked the post-communist constitutions to the story of Germany and France. But that was just a book read on a plane. It was nothing I knew anything about.

This was a real-life version of a familiar nightmare. Here I was called before the leading lawyers of a nation and given an exam about something I had not studied. The only advantage of the real-world version of this nightmare is that I had all my clothes on.

This is the experience of America, as *we* represent *us* today. We are systematically quizzed on questions that we have not prepared to answer. That experience, of course, is not as terrifying—only a very few are ever called, most can bluff through a telephone call, and many simply hang up. (When polling began, the response rates were more than 90 percent; now they are in the single digits.[132]) But the dynamic is the same, and the consequence is infinitely worse. We are presumed to know something we don't know. No doubt we could know it. We just don't. The system presumes something about what we know, and then we get rendered ridiculous when we show what we don't know. People listening to us wonder, why are we listening to them? People measuring the wisdom in our words come to believe there is no reason to link the future of anything to the craziness evinced through our words.

Yet there is an important difference between the embarrassment that I suffered and the embarrassment that is us today. As I walked to the front of that conference room, I knew what I didn't know. I knew

I could know it; I knew it was the sort of thing that I wanted to know. I had no doubt about my abilities. (I was young.) Instead, I had a recognition about my experience. I knew that experience did not qualify me for the talk I was being asked to give. I could understand why they believed I would be so qualified. Maybe I should have been so qualified. But I had no problem understanding the mistake as a mistake.

That is not as clear with us. When we're quizzed about trade policy, or about whether Congress should cut taxes, it feels like the sort of stuff citizens are just supposed to know. We don't have a clear guidance about what we're supposed to know. Or when. The question seems to presume it, and our ignorance thus feels like ignorance. We bluff or dodge or guess—and then that ignorance is represented as us. We feel stupid. We feel unprepared. We feel unsure about an enterprise that relies upon us—democracy.

And not just those of us unlucky enough to be polled. But all of us. We read a story that refers to a poll. In reading about what *they* (the sampled public) believe, we can't help but reflect, "How do they know that?" "Am I supposed to know that?" Or if you are someone who does know about the field or the subject, then the reaction is the opposite: "How could they be so stupid?" "God, are people dumb."

Or even worse, it is often identity, regardless of facts, that will drive the results. You don't know what you think about NAFTA or nuclear energy. But you know what right-thinking Democrats or Republicans think. So you report as your tribe would report; you stay loyal rather than look stupid. With the consequence that to each side looking at the other, "they" look insanely stupid, while "we" know what's what.

In this way, the consequence of the unrepresentative us may well weaken a commitment to democracy. Why trust us when even we can see just how little we know? That consequence in turn feeds an argument against democracy generally. Why build a system for governing a nation on top of the ignorant? Is that how Apple or Amazon does it? Is that how any sane organization does it? Why tie our nation to a mast of incompetence?

That weakened commitment then becomes a tool—for those who oppose democracy, and for those who would take advantage of it.

For those who would abuse it, it becomes just another lever to be manipulated in the game of public policy making. The random (or ignorant) get deployed to help one side or harm the other. Our ignorance becomes predictable. It becomes cheap to evince.

For those who would oppose democracy, it becomes just another argument for an alternative. Bestselling author Parag Khanna describes two models of governance in his 2017 book, *Technocracy in America*. In one, the government focuses on governing. In the other, it focuses on democracy. Not surprisingly, governments like the first, in Khanna's account, do more to deliver the services of government than governments like the second. Democracy is the chump in a world governed by smarter governments. We are the chumps for believing in it.

Either way, "rule by the people" takes a beating. The Putins smirk. Jefferson rolls in his grave.

PART II: FIXES

It is the style today to ridicule the monarchs of yesterday. No doubt, some were objectively ridiculous, or worse. King George III (king when the United States was born) was certainly mad. But it's not just him. It is the character of our time for a certain genre of film to see every monarch of yesterday as, in critical ways, just ridiculous or absurd.

I have no view about whether they were absurd or not. That's not my historical interest. But I do know enough to report an obvious fact: at the time these monarchs reigned, their subjects didn't think them ridiculous. Maybe the people next to them knew, but the public in general did not.

That ignorance was enabled by obscurity. The technologies of the time did not allow anyone to know anything about the monarchy beyond what they revealed. The law in Britain protected the royal family from gossip or worse. The king or queen was seen only at a distance, swaddled in the presumption that God's chosens must be something special.

As technology pierced that obscurity, monarchies were deeply threatened. Most collapsed. And the most extraordinary to survive—Britain—only did so because it brilliantly managed the transition from the silent invisible king to the selectively speaking king. That the actual monarchy in Britain passed through a stuttering king is just a metaphor for this story: the genius of Queen Elizabeth and the institution of the modern British monarchy was to devise a strategy for avoiding the judgment that they too were just ridiculous. Because as the brains behind the British monarchy recognized, it could not reign if it was viewed as absurd.

And so too with us and our democracy: As with the monarchy, our ignorance was obscured for most the history of democracy. As with the monarchy, technology has pierced that obscurity. As with the monarchy, the fact that we are ignorant has become unavoidable. As with the monarchy, if democracy is to survive, we must find a way beyond that ignorance. As with the monarchy, we will not be allowed to rule, if we, the people, are, or are viewed as, absurd.

The repair of us is the bigger burden of this Part in this book. We, the People, like the British Crown, must find a way to avoid being rendered absurd.

But fixing us is only part of the fix. I begin with the easier remedy: fixing them. How might we change the institutions of government to restore—or establish effectively for the first time—a government that represents us?

CHAPTER 3

Fixing Them

THERE IS A SINGLE PRINCIPLE THAT STANDS BEHIND EVERY REFORM that our democracy needs. That principle is *representativeness*. The law must structure—and the Constitution must require the law to structure—the institutions of our democracy to ensure as much equality in representation as possible. The Constitution does this explicitly with respect to the states. Article V requires that the "Equal Suffrage" of the states not be changed, at least without the state's consent. So too must we assure the "equal suffrage" of citizens, against all the structures or devices or tricks or institutions that might deny that equality.

Political equality, not economic or social equality. We can argue about how much economic or social equality our society has or should have. I believe it should certainly have much more. But the equality we can't argue about—the equality that is presumed within a republic—is political equality. As much as possible, given that perfection is never real, the system must make us equal as citizens.

Most of the changes that would make us equal could be made through statutes. The law could fix what ails us in a single act. But we should not stop with statutes. Instead, the principle behind these reforms should be embedded within the Constitution as well.

REPRESENTATIVE VOTES

Contributions are the monies given by people to political campaigns to support the candidacy of a politician. Separate from the contributions given to a political campaign is money spent to support a political candidate. For example, you and your kids might decide to make a sign to put on your front yard to support a candidate running for town meeting. That spending is not a contribution to the campaign. That spending is your (and your kids') free speech.

Americans engage in both kinds of speech. We have clear numbers for contributions to campaigns, both direct and indirect. We don't have clear numbers for the money spent to support candidates. Candidates for the House and Senate in 2018 raised about $2.8 billion.[1] Reports about the money given to independent political action committees is profoundly incomplete. OpenSecrets.org—by far the best site reporting these data—estimates independent expenditures on candidate campaigns topped $1.1 billion. That's higher than the total in 2012—a presidential election year. SuperPACs are among those that are spending political money "independently." In 2018, there were almost 2,400 SuperPACs; they raised about $1.6 billion and spent about $800 million. Since *Citizens United v. FEC* (2010), fifteen groups have been responsible for 75 percent of the "dark money" spent in elections. And in October 2015, *New York Times* reporter Nicholas Confessore calculated that half of the contributions in the presidential race came from 158 families.[2]

Thus far, these two kinds of spending are different constitutionally—and should be. That's not to say that at an extreme, they shouldn't be considered together. Indeed, I will consider that extreme below. But for the moment, let's separate contributions from expenditures, and ask the question, How far can the law reach in regulating contributions?

The Supreme Court has been fairly clear about the principle that answers this question, even if there is uncertainty at the margin. The only justification that a law could have for restricting the amount of money that an individual gives to a political candidate is "corruption." As the Supreme Court held in 1976, the government has an adequate interest "in preventing corruption and the appearance of corruption."[3] Beyond a justification grounded in "corruption," the Court has never upheld a restriction on the amount that one can give to a candidate running for office. Indeed, quite specifically, the Court has held that equality is not a justification for limiting the amount an individual can give to a political candidate. As the Court wrote, "the concept that government may restrict the speech of some elements of our society in order to enhance the relative voice of others is wholly foreign to the First Amendment. . . ."[4]

This authority makes it clear that Congress could not pass a law that set a maximum contribution of, say, fifty dollars, and justify that limit on the basis of citizen equality. If anything is clear in the Court's jurisprudence, it is that.

But what about from the candidate's perspective? What free speech rights does she have? Does a candidate have a First Amendment right to say, "I won't accept more than fifty dollars from anyone?" Does she have the right to insist that any contribution she receives be small enough so that anyone could, in principle at least, contribute that amount? Or that no one, in good faith, could believe that that money was affecting the representative?

The answer to that question is perfectly clear: Absolutely yes! While the government doesn't have the power to restrict contributions to achieve equality, individual candidates do have the power to insist that they don't want any contributor to count, or seem to count, more than anyone else.

That fact is the constitutional foundation for the most powerful reform that our democracy could see: a reform to change how candidates raise the money they use to fund their campaigns. Under this reform, candidates would no longer raise that money privately; they instead would raise it publicly, through funds made available to every citizen.

Those funds would be available through vouchers, or maybe better, following Rick Hasen, "coupons."[5] Every voter would receive $100 in "democracy coupons." (Call them "DCs.") They could then give those coupons to whatever candidate they like. The coupons would come in $20 increments. They could give all of them to one candidate, or split them among all the candidates for whom they could vote. They could only give to candidates for whom they can vote. But voters don't need to give any of their DCs to anyone. A candidate could accept a DC if he or she agreed to fund his or her campaign with coupons only, plus contributions maxed at $100 per contributor. Any coupons not used would go to the party the voter was registered to. If the voter is independent of a party, then the value of her unused coupons would go to improving the election system in her state.

Systems like this have been described for many years.[6] Congressman Ro Khanna, a California Democrat, proposed a similar idea for Congress in 2018. Khanna caps his "democracy dollars" at $50. Richard Painter, former ethics czar for George W. Bush, has proposed $100 vouchers, though his is not contingent upon a candidate forgoing other contributions. In early 2019, presidential candidate Andrew Yang endorsed a $100 voucher proposal. Though at the time of this writing, it is early in the presidential election season, I expect others will follow Yang.

Regardless of the precise form, the consequence of this change would be profound. In 2018, the total amount contributed to candidates running for the House and Senate was about $2.8 billion. At a hundred dollars a voter, to match that number we'd need less than one-fourth the people who voted to contribute. But voting is, for many, even harder than handing in a coupon. Quite plausibly, significantly more money would be raised through democracy coupons than through the private system of funding that we have now.

Yet what's important here is not the amount of money. What's important is how it is raised. It might be that candidates would spend the same amount of time raising money. But if they do, they will be spending their time raising money from ordinary citizens. Rather than fancy cocktail parties, they'll raise their money at block parties, or rallies. Rather than calling the very rich, they'll reach out through social media or local organizations to collect coupons from everyone. This is the experience of the one city in the United States that has adopted vouchers—Seattle.[7] If adopted nationally, candidates would thus affirm the value of equality through the restrictions they choose to live under through the voluntary system of democracy coupons.

Okay, but does that amount actually have to be equal? And does equality here do more harm than good?

This is the question raised by the profoundly important book by Eric Posner and Glen Weyl, *Radical Markets*. Posner and Weyl force us to rethink the market at the atomic level. Rather than presuming that property must be absolute, they argue that it is the ability to trade that should be absolute. Property, as they put it, is monopoly; monopoly is bad.

Their arguments are subtle and convincing in almost every context they deploy them. But one area in which they reach too far is with democracy. Posner and Weyl chant a refrain attacking the idea of "one person, one vote." The better alternative, they suggest, would be something closer to what Tom Perkins was describing—where votes are not equal, but rather rendered a function of something else. Their alternative is not as crude as Perkins's. Indeed, as we'll see in a minute, it is wickedly clever. But the net result, at least as they first articulated it, is that you could buy speech power. That is, you could have more speech power than I because you would have more resources than I. To which the obvious question is, how radical is that?

This is a reach too far, because nothing substantial in their argument actually turns upon rejecting one person, one vote. Certainly nothing convincing does. The legitimate objective of Posner and Wehl's innovation is to provide a way to track the intensity of a preferences. If I really really really want something, then that fact should count, on this account, more than you just barely wanting the opposite. That intuition drives them to their innovation. And no doubt, their innovation adds efficiency to the market of politics.

But every efficiency they seek to add could be added consistently with the ideal of equality.

Imagine rather than one hundred DCs, everyone received, as they put it, "speech credits" ("SCs"). Let's say, every America was granted 10,000 SCs. Those speech credits could then be converted into campaign contributions according to an important—if, for our purposes, obscure—formula. One credit gets converted into a $1 contribution. Four credits get converted into a $2 contribution. Sixteen credits get converted into $4. And so on: the formula is that dollars increase as the square root of the credits. If you want to give all your credits to a single candidate, that would be worth $100.[8]

The genius behind the formula is beyond the scope of this book. But what Posner and Weyl demonstrate convincingly is that this way of allocating speech credits overcomes the obvious inability of a purely equal system to track the real differences we each might have in the strength of our support for one candidate over another. There is plenty of math behind it, but this mechanism is a way to trace the intensity of support for one person over another, as a way to allow differences of intensity to register, even within a one-person, one-vote system.

In the purest case, the efficiency that Posner and Weyl want might best be advanced by permitting people to use whatever money they wanted to use to buy speech credits. But that idea conflicts with a deep and important republican norm—citizen equality. In the domain of politics, as political theorist Michael Walzer might put it, we are to be equal, even if in the domain of the market, we are not.[9] Instead, preserving the original equality—by giving every voter the same 10,000 SCs—coheres with that norm, while not losing much in efficiency of the innovation. Put differently, the efficiency gained from allocating a fixed and equal amount is likely already very close to the efficiency gained from allocating a nonfixed and unequal amount. Or again, any gain in efficiency from allowing the rich to buy more credits than the poor would be swamped by a deep sense of illegitimacy. Maybe geniuses like Posner and Weyl could think beyond the initial inequality. Most people are not geniuses.

I love the egalitarianism embedded within Posner and Weyl's system. I would prefer it to the simple DC system. But regardless of whether it is DC or SC, the point is just this: either change in the mode for funding elections would radically change the economy of influence for candidates. Either would end the tweedism of money in American politics, by changing the way candidates raise money, fundamentally.

What about a simpler solution? What about just giving candidates a chunk of money to spend on their campaigns? All candidates would get the same, at least after some qualifying process. No candidate would need to worry after receiving their check about raising money from anyone.

There is much to recommend in this simpler system. It is close to the system once used to fund presidential campaigns, and similar to the system for state elections in Connecticut and Maine. But conservatives don't like the idea of their tax money being used to subsidize speech they don't like (though I'll note that I don't like my tax money being used to kill, and no one seems to care much about that). Admittedly, the challenge of narrowing the subsidy to viable and deserving candidates is difficult. It could well be that a hybrid between the coupon system and a lump sum payment would be ideal. Maybe the payment goes to the party, and the coupons, whether DC or SC, are for the candidates.

Regardless of which is selected, however, or whether it is the hybrid that is chosen in the end or not, the key is how the change alters the economy of influence within *fundraising*. The objective is not to equalize speech. The objective is to change the dependency of candidates on the very few. And if the experience of New York City's system of a small-dollar matching system for funding the campaigns of city officials is indicative, the effect of this change would be to push representatives to represent their citizens more broadly.[10]

Okay, but what about the other spending? What about the amount individuals spend to support a candidate or to give to an organization that supports that candidate, independently of his or her campaign? What about the SuperPACs?

Subject to a pretty important exception that I'll get to in a moment, we should not—and the Supreme Court would not allow us to—try to equalize the spending of campaigns or equalize efforts by individuals to support a campaign. Such speech is at the core of free speech. Tweets made in support of a candidate, YouTube videos that endorse a candidate, editorials in favor of one party or candidate over another, yard signs, public protests, podcasts, Web pages, persistent echoes on Facebook or Instagram: no government should be in the business of equalizing this speech, if only (but importantly) because there could be no standard upon which to judge how much is equal to what. The Supreme Court might allocate equal time to both sides in an oral argument, but that context presumes a great deal of understanding. That understanding is not the ordinary context of ordinary political speech. The law should not purport to control how much we get to say about politics.

Yet what if the "we" is a corporation? Should the spending of a corporation be limited?

This is not a popular view with my tribe, but I don't think, in general, that difference matters. The constitutional question is not "who is speaking." The constitutional question is "what kind of speech is this." And if it is political speech, then the Constitution protects that speech as vigorously as it can. Even Justice Thurgood Marshall acknowledged as much in *Austin v. Michigan Chamber of Commerce* (1990): "the mere fact that [an entity] is a corporation does not remove its speech from the ambit of the First Amendment."[11] And so the mere fact that the *spending* comes from a corporation would not remove it from the protection of the First Amendment—as *Citizens United v. FEC* (2010) held.

But what about PACs? Political action committees can contribute to political campaigns. The committees raise their money within corporations or other associations. They are heavily regulated. They are capped in the amounts they're permitted to give. There's good evidence that these contributions are presently more moderate than are individual contributions—which makes the current rage among Democratic candidates to avoid PAC contributions more difficult to understand.[12] And while it seems clear that PAC contributions are often just tickets to access on Capitol Hill, if congressional campaigns were funded through either democracy coupons or speech credits, there might be little reason to block these sorts of contributions.

But what if a contribution to independent political action committees is in effect a contribution to the candidate? What if the level, or tacit coordination, makes it clear that the money is operating as a contribution—at least in the sense that we would expect it to affect the behavior of a candidate, so that the candidate could inspire the contribution? Should the government have the right to limit it then?

SuperPACs are political action committees that function independently of a political campaign—or so it is said. A contribution to a SuperPAC is thus a contribution to an entity that is not the campaign. On the principles that I've offered so far, such contributions would not be limited. The candidate can't limit them by refusing them, because they are not contributions made to the candidate. And the state can't limit them, the Supreme Court insists, unless they are a kind of "corruption."

They are not "corruption" in a familiar sense. If they are given independently of a political campaign (no doubt that's a big if), and hence, if they are given independently of a political candidate, they are not given *in exchange for* some kind of favor or official act. That kind of giving—what the law calls quid pro quo—is bribery. Bribery is corruption. But independent giving is, by definition, not given in exchange for something else. That's what makes it "independent." So again, *if* you believe it was truly independent, *then* it is not quid pro quo corruption.

But is quid pro quo corruption the only "corruption" that the Constitution should permit Congress to regulate?

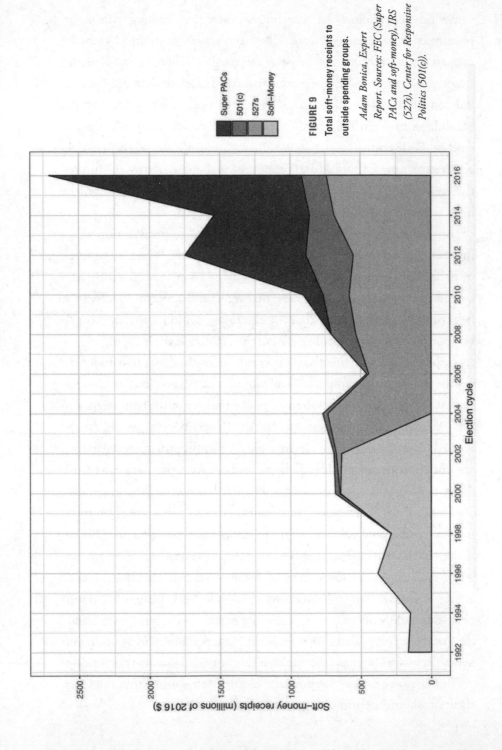

Super PACs
501(c)
527s
Soft-Money

FIGURE 9
Total soft-money receipts to outside spending groups.

Adam Bonica, Expert Report. Sources: FEC (Super PACs and soft-money), IRS (527s), Center for Responsive Politics (501(c)).

The answer to that question should plainly be "No." There is no principled reason why Congress should not be able to suppress other forms of corruption as well. Or, at the very least, Congress should be allowed to suppress the kinds of corruption that the framers of the First Amendment were keen to suppress. And if that's true, then it is clear that Congress should be able to suppress the kind of corruption that SuperPACs effect.

What kind of "corruption" is that?

I have felled many trees describing a corruption that is distinct from quid pro quo corruption, but that is within the scope of the kind of corruption that our framers were focused on.[13] That corruption is not individual, but institutional. It focuses not on the good or bad behavior of particular people. It focuses instead on the way a system supports or defeats the objectives of an institution.

This way of speaking of "corruption" is familiar to us, even if it's not the first idea that presents itself. We say a "hard disk is corrupted," which refers not to the particular wrongs of a programmer, but to the failure of the disk to represent what we intend it to represent. Or we might think that television news has been "corrupted" by the need to ensure ratings. As I said in chapter 2, that's not to say anyone has been bribed. But it is to recognize that we still (amazingly) have an idea of the purpose of television news, and a recognition that it is no longer serving that purpose if it is bending over backward to keep advertisers happy and the public ignorant.

This kind of corruption thus requires a clear sense of an institution's purpose. It requires as well a finding that some influence is defeating that purpose. If there is a purpose and that purpose is being defeated, then those together would constitute the "corruption" of that institution.

SuperPACs corrupt American democracy in exactly this sense. First, they have become hugely prominent in American political life. As this single graph by Stanford professor Adam Bonica screams, they have become central to the funding of American political campaigns.

In 2016, there was close to $1.8 billion in SuperPAC spending; independent expenditures that year comprised 40 percent of total spending on federal campaigns.[14]

That prominence, second, means that candidates are focused on—some might say, obsessed with—whether these SuperPACs will or will not support them. As law professor Richard Briffault put it, a large contribution to a SuperPAC "is at least as likely to affect the . . . decisions of elected officials as the relatively paltry amounts that candidates' personal campaign committees are allowed to receive."[15] That fact triggers focus. The focus manifests a kind of dependence. Given the prominence of SuperPACs in many political races, they have become a critical source supporting a campaign, and upon which our representatives are dependent.

But is that "dependence" consistent with the institution of a representative democracy? The answer here is plainly no: representatives in the House, originally, and presumably now the Senate as well, were to be "dependent on the people alone." By "the People," Madison instructed, the framers meant "not the rich more than the poor."[16] SuperPACs, however, create a dependence that is plainly on the rich more than the poor. And thus SuperPACs "corrupt" the intended dependence of at least the House, evincing what I have called "dependence corruption."[17]

This argument is deeply contingent. If there were such a thing as a SuperPAC, but there were only a handful that operated within any election cycle, one couldn't argue that they had created any improper dependence. Likewise with the spending of individuals or corporations: if independent spending were relatively small, then it would be hard to argue that it had created an improper dependence within Congress. No doubt it could be important to the election of one candidate or another, just as the endorsement from a local newspaper could be important. But for the spending or contributions (to the independent PAC) to be institutional corruption, it would need to be substantial enough for Congress reasonably to believe that it was systematically creating a dependence inconsistent with the "dependence on the people alone." SuperPACs, in my view, are a kind of "corruption" that Congress should have the power to regulate, and not to achieve equality in speech, but to ensure that representatives do not live under an improper dependence.

IN SUM, GIVEN THE Constitution as it has been read, it's clear that Congress could—and should—create a way to fund political campaigns that allows candidates to treat each citizen equally. That means it should be able to create a kind of public funding for campaigns. My favorite is a system of speech credits (SCs) or, alternatively, democracy coupons (DCs). Those credits or coupons could be supplemented by a grant to ensure that every viable campaign has a minimum amount to compete. The ability to participate in this system could be made contingent upon forgoing other kinds of contributions. In this way, the free speech rights of the candidates would leverage a system for funding campaigns that did not manifest a radical inequality among citizens.

Second, given the Constitution as I believe it should (and will be) read, Congress should also have the power to limit the size of contributions to so-called SuperPACs.

Finally, given the relatively small amount of money that is spent directly, but independently of campaigns, I don't believe there is a sufficiently strong predicate to restrict this kind of speech. It may be unseemly, and it may seem crass, but unless there is a reason to believe its effect is systemic, there is no reason to restrict what is plainly political speech.[18]

REPRESENTATIVE REPRESENTATIVES

A representative House would be a House of Representatives that was chosen under rules that maximized the opportunity of every citizen to matter to their representatives. Safe-seat gerrymandering is inconsistent with that principle. Not only does it make the minority in a particular district irrelevant to the election, but it even makes the more moderate members of the majority party less relevant, too. Primaries are contests dominated by the most politically engaged. The most politically engaged are the most politically extreme. Safe-seat gerrymandering gives those extremists more power than others.

You might resist this characterization by insisting that whatever power the extremists have, they have earned it. At least among the members of the majority party, the only reason that the extremists have more power is that they turn out to vote. If everyone turned out in same proportion, then no one in the majority party at least could complain that their vote was mattering less.

That moral story is certainly true. But it highlights the fact that this is not a morality play. We're not here to judge whether someone was right or wrong in choosing to vote or not. We're not selecting the rules based on our view of the goodness of some and the laziness of others. Our objective should rather be to maximize the opportunity of everyone to matter, given the nature of the people we are affecting.

The system that achieves this objective most plainly is one advanced by FairVote and embodied in the Fair Representation Act.[19] This system would create multimember districts for Congress, and then give every voter a chance to rank his or her choices for Congress within those multimember districts. The ordinary district would have five members of Congress. Each voter could rank up to five candidates running within that district. The winner would be chosen through a "ranked-choice voting" (RCV) system. If there are more than five candidates running, then the candidate getting the least votes gets dumped first. The second choices of the voters voting for that candidate then get allocated to the others. This process is repeated until there are only five candidates remaining. Those five candidates are then the five members representing that district.[20]

The consequence of this system would be to give a wider range of values a voice within our political system. And so long as your values represent at least 20 percent of a district, you've got a great shot at getting your values represented in Congress. There are conservative Democrats and liberal Republicans. Safe-seat gerrymandering with single-member districts drives both out of the system. Multimember districts with ranked-choice voting would give them a real chance to compete.

That's the ideal. Yet even without multimember districts, we can better craft districts that achieve representativeness. Congress has the power to require the states to adopt a nonpartisan system for drawing districts (Article I, Section 4). The consequence of that nonpartisan gerrymandering would be fewer safe seats and hence more electoral competition. That competition would give more Americans a voice, relative to the system we have now. It's not perfect, but it's better. It advances the idea of equal representation more effectively than our currently gerrymandered system does.

Even with nonpartisan districts, however, we still need a principle of majoritarianism. A core value of our framers' conception of democracy was a majority. Plurality, from this perspective, is failure, not victory. Increasing the competitiveness of districts, however, simply increases the chances that the representative of a district is not supported by the majority of the district. In a three-person race, for example, a candidate could be elected with less than 35 percent of the vote. And even if the third-party candidate has no shot at winning, her running could well flip the results from someone closer to a majority to one who is not.

The answer to this problem is precisely the answer that Maine gave—again, ranked-choice voting. In 2018, after almost eight years with a governor who was elected because of the effect of third-party candidates, Maine adopted a system that gave voters the opportunity to rank their choices for office. If an election results in a candidate winning with less than 50 percent of the vote, then the candidate receiving the fewest votes is dropped, and the second choice of the voters who voted for that dropped candidate get their votes. That process is repeated until one candidate gets a majority of the votes. The elected representative is therefore always someone with the support of at least 50 percent of the voters.

In Maine, that fact flipped the result from one party to another. In the Second Congressional District, there were three candidates vying to represent Maine. The incumbent, Republican Bruce Poliquin, received a slight plurality in the first-place votes (46.2 percent vs. 45.5 percent). But when the third-party candidate was then dropped from the tally, Democrat Jared Golden jumped ahead of the incumbent with 50.5 percent of the vote. Across the country in 2018, had every district used ranked-choice voting, five other districts would have triggered a ranked-choice vote, with four likely going Republican, and one we can't say for certain.

Six districts out of 435 may make the idea of RCV seem unnecessary. If such a small number of districts are not electing a representative said to represent the majority, what's the need for fancy new counting technologies? But that small number is a function of gerrymandering. It is also a product of the strong bias our system gives to the two dominant parties.

But if we fix gerrymandering, districts will be more competitive, and third parties will have a stronger interest in participating. That means there will be more multiparty contests. Which means without ranked-choice voting, there would be more plurality winners.

More candidates competing is a good thing, not bad. More parties competing would be a good thing, not bad. But their competition should not weaken the representativeness of a representative. Instead, the strong competition of third parties should drive candidates in both parties to try to satisfy the demands of those third parties, as the candidates vie to be the second-choice votes of those third-party candidates.

Ranked-choice voting thus both encourages more diversity *and* reinforces the idea of majoritarianism.

What about primaries? Shouldn't primaries also be eliminated, if we're to eliminate the unrepresentativeness of our representative democracy?

This is a closer question, though here I come down on the side of the status quo.[21] It's not because I like the unrepresentativeness of primaries, but instead because the biggest chunk of that unrepresentativeness comes not from what the state does, but from what the voter does. We don't vote, and hence the consequence is an unrepresentative representative. We don't not vote because the state makes it harder for moderates to vote; we don't vote because we can't be bothered.

That makes this inequality different from the vote suppression described in chapter 1, and even from the money primary described there as well. When it is harder to vote because I'm a Democrat, or because I'm a Republican, that's an inequality created by the rules. Or when I can't participate in the money primary because I don't have the money that Soros or the Kochs do, that's an inequality created by the system we've chosen to fund campaigns. But when someone doesn't vote as a moderate, so long as there's nothing blocking a conservative or a liberal, that's the consequence of a choice, not of the state. It's an inequality created by choice, not the state. And while we needn't moralize about that inequality, neither need we respond to it.

The question, however, is a difficult one. The inequality caused by safe-seat gerrymandering is also caused in part by people choosing not to participate. Why change the rules there but not with primaries? The answer in part is the same as Shigeo Hirano and James Snyder give—that the alternatives are not more appealing.[22] Perhaps a system of deliberative polls, as I'll describe more in chapter 4, would be better than primaries. I'd favor that innovation, for sure, but the public is far from accepting that alternative just now.

REPRESENTATIVE SENATE

The Senate is the hardest circle to square, because it comes to us as a conceptual mess. It's clear that the Senate was meant to represent the states—originally. It's clear that if that's what it is to represent, then giving each state two senators is consistent with the principle of equal representation. But if by giving citizens the power to elect senators, the system was intended to change who was being represented, then the fact that there are two senators from Wyoming and two senators from California radically violates the principle of equal representation.

The actual text of the Constitution tilts strongly in favor of viewing the Senate as representing the states. The Seventeenth Amendment notwithstanding, the Constitution not only expressly specifies the number of senators per state, but it prohibits any future amendment from changing that number in a way that denies any state its "Equal Suffrage" in the Senate. The Constitution could be amended to give every state ten Senators (or one); it could not be amended to give California ten while Wyoming gets only one—at least without Wyoming's consent.

There has been an army of scholars and constitutional reformers who have schemed about how to get around this requirement. Some suggest we amend the clause that says that you can't amend the "Equal Suffrage Clause." Some insist that every part of the Constitution is always amendable—that, after all, is the lesson of the Declaration of Independence: it is an "unalienable right," the Declaration declared, of a people to "alter or abolish" their Constitution, whatever the Constitution might say to the contrary. Some suggest we simply abolish the Senate. Some suggest we radically change the scope of the Senate's power. Some suggest we give the House the power to veto a Senate veto by passing any bill the Senate refuses to pass by some supermajority.

All of these changes would require a constitutional amendment. As my focus in this chapter is statutory, I leave these fantasies to the notes.[23] Instead, we should recognize that even if you believe—as I do—that it would be better for senators to represent citizens, not states, there are better ways to run the Senate to minimize the inequality that is created by the two-senator-per-state rule. And even as originally conceived, the Senate is not representing the states equally.

To see how, we must recognize first that most of the power and structure of the Senate comes from lore, not law. The rules and procedures are immensely complicated, including written, unwritten, and untested rules. Even career parliamentarians declare that they could not understand the Senate's practices through the written rules alone.[24]

But that means that the Senate can change its rules. First, it could pass a simple resolution changing its rules—though that would require at least two-thirds of the senators voting to support that change. Second, the Senate could issue new precedents through a reinterpretation of its rules. Through this procedure, the Senate could seize a "nuclear" or "constitutional" option, by which a majority establishes the precedent that a simple majority may change Senate rules. Richard Nixon did this in 1957 to enable the Senate to pass a Civil Rights Act.[25] It was contestable then, and the contest continues, but the precedent seems to be in Nixon's favor.[26] Recent fights over judicial confirmations confirm this precedent. Both Democrats (in 2013) and Republicans (in 2017) have changed the rules for ending debate on judicial nominees.

Rule changes could be many. In the balance of this section, I consider the most obvious.

Hold Reform

At the top of the list would be "hold" reform. The Senate operates essentially by unanimous consent: any objection to what the Senate is doing requires that there be a vote. One form of objection is a "hold"—basically an indication that a senator objects to some bill or nominee. Holds historically have been both secret and public. And while any hold can be overcome through a supermajority vote, they slow the process in the Senate dramatically.

One simple reform would either eliminate the hold (or require five to agree before it would have an effect), or to require that all holds be public. In 2011, the Senate passed (by a 92–4 vote) a resolution requiring the senators to either withdraw or make public their holds within "2 session days."[27] A simpler reform would just require publicity immediately.

Filibuster Reform

The filibuster allows any member of the Senate to continue a discussion or "unlimited debate" unless a sixty-member supermajority invokes "cloture." While nominally a procedure to force deliberation, the filibuster has become, in effect, an antidemocratic measure that requires the Senate to function by supermajority.

Numerous proposals to reform the filibuster have been advanced. The most obvious of these would simply kill the filibuster. Neither the Constitution nor the law protects the right of forty senators to reject a bill. To eliminate the filibuster, the Senate would only need a bare but willing majority to invoke the "nuclear option." So far, Senate leaders have refused to abolish the filibuster for ordinary legislation.[28]

Alternatively, the Senate could lower the cloture threshold. Cloture once required 67 votes; the Senate has already lowered the threshold to 60 votes. The Senate could lower the threshold even further—to 55 votes, for example. Or alternatively, it could weaken the filibuster without eliminating it.

The proposals here are many: The Senate could make the threshold decrease over time: for example, for every week a filibuster continues, the threshold could drop two votes. The Senate could require 41 votes to sustain a filibuster, rather than 60 to overcome it, to increase the costs of continuing a threshold (by requiring that filibustering senators remain in Washington). The Senate could require that someone actually speak on the Senate floor to continue a filibuster. The Senate could limit filibusters to certain stages of the legislative process (for example, during final deliberations but not motions to proceed). Finally, the Senate could "fast-track" more types of legislation than it already does with budget reconciliation and judicial nominees, to avoid the cost of the filibuster with these all together.

Each of these changes would bend the Senate back to a more majoritarian body (remembering that even if it were perfectly majoritarian, it would still represent Americans in a fundamentally unequal way). But even representing states, the system of the Senate could be made more equal.

Amendment Consideration

Currently Senate rules require it to consider at least ten amendments to each bill. The majority leader, however, can "fill the tree" (proposing his own amendments that may lack substance or serve only partisan interests) to effectively block any real amendments to the bill from the other side. As such, the majority leader can block minority amendments from an up-or-down vote.[29] Giving the minority at least half of the amendments to any bill could avoid this inequality. That change would not necessarily address the unrepresentativeness caused by population differences, but it would bolster the power of the minority to force compromise into the Senate.

Reforming the Seniority System

Seniority is a critical part of the power within the Senate. Traditionally allocated solely on the basis of years in service, it gave enormous power to the single-party South—and thus the continued ability of the South to block all civil rights legislation between Reconstruction until 1957.

The Senate could use the seniority system to partially neutralize the inequality in population, by allocating votes for leadership based on the population of the state. Each senator could have the same number of votes as her state has representatives. Larger states would therefore have more power, even though the equality of "suffrage" in the Senate would be maintained.

AS INNOVATIVE AS ALL these solutions are, in the end, however, I am skeptical. Madison knew that the Senate was a compromise with citizen republicanism. He knew it defeated the ideal of a representative democracy—assuming it is people who are being represented, not states. I'm with Madison, and I lament the corruption of representativeness caused by the Senate.

But I am not convinced it is fatal. If we achieved all the other reforms that I am describing in this chapter, achieving nothing in the Senate would not be a terrible loss. At the most, we should affirm again and again how anachronistic this body is, if only to build the support for the changes we should ultimately make. Those won't happen immediately. They would happen if the principle of representativeness were strengthened in every other aspect of our federal government.

REPRESENTATIVE PRESIDENT

Because of the rules of all but two states, the president of the United States does not represent America. All but two states allocate electors according to the winner-take-all method. That means that the only states that matter in a presidential election are the swing states. Those states don't represent America. The president elected by those states doesn't represent America, either.

There are three obvious ways to remedy this problem. The first is a likely nonstarter—to abolish the Electoral College. That's a nonstarter because such an amendment would require three-fourths of the states to be ratified. Despite the overwhelming popular support for a president of the United States elected by the citizens of the United States,

I predict there are easily thirteen states that would oppose such an amendment.

That leaves two solutions that the states themselves could adopt, and one of those that Congress, perhaps, could adopt for them.

The most obvious solution is at once both the most radical and the most conservative: an election effectively determined by a national popular vote, through a compact among the states to select electors from the party that wins the national popular vote.

This is the National Popular Vote Interstate Compact (NPVIC). First proposed by Professors Robert Bennett, and Vik and Akhil Amar, this solution envisions states selecting the electors who would vote for the winner of the national popular vote, at least if states representing 270 votes have so committed.[30] At the time of this writing, states representing more than 180 Electoral College votes have so committed. If that number gets to 270, then each of these states within the compact would select electors pledged to support the candidate who won the national popular vote. Thus, if that candidate was the Republican, California would select electors who would vote for the Republican. If that candidate was a Democrat, then Texas would select electors who would vote for the Democrat. (So far, California has joined the compact; Texas has not.)

This solution would obviously make every voter in the nation count equally. One voter in Wyoming would have the same vote as a voter in New York. Citizens would thus be equal, nationally. A president elected under this system would therefore be a president that represented (at least a plurality of) America.

Yet not everyone is enamored of this clever hack. Some fear it would create a flyover democracy: candidates would campaign in the big cities and ignore the rest of the country. Others believe it destroys a core feature of the framers' design—a preference for small states over large states.

I am not convinced that the NPVIC would produce a flyover

democracy.[31] A vote is a vote, and given the high cost of media in larger cities, it could well be cheaper to campaign for votes outside of them.[32] That's certainly what happens in the race for governor even in states with large cities. But it is true that a national popular vote would give no special benefit to small states, or rural states. And it is also true that a national popular vote could fundamentally upset the Jeffersonian model that I described in chapter 1. If there isn't ranked-choice voting at the state level, then the president could easily represent not a majority of Americans, but a plurality. In principle, ranked-choice voting should be able to solve this problem. However, elections are run state by state, and for ranked-choice voting to operate, the rankings would ideally have to cross state lines.

That fact may be enough to render the system vulnerable constitutionally. If the aim of the Twelfth Amendment was to get us to a "majority of the majority" —a majority of electors chosen by a majority in each state—for president, then national popular vote has no mechanism to assure the ultimate result gets even close to that ideal. Of all the arguments that could sink the NPVIC, this is the one I'd put my money on.

The second solution could do a bit better. If every state allocated electors proportionally, at least with fractional voting, then, as with the NPVIC, every state would, in principle, be in play. Your relevance to a presidential campaign would not then depend upon which state you happened to live within. All states would matter, since every state would have at least a fraction of an elector for a presidential candidate to fight to secure. But unlike with the NPVIC, proportional allocation would still give a preference to small states, as small states have more electors per capita. A thumb would thus remain on the scale, bending the system against one person, one vote, but in favor of the framers' original compromise with inequality.

There are two difficulties with this alternative. Assuming that electors do not cast fractional ballots—giving, say, two-thirds of their vote to one candidate, and one-third to another—proportional allocation could put even fewer states in play than WTA does. If a state has just three electors, then you'd need to shift a huge proportion of that state to gain one more elector. The consequence of that would be that most states would see very little presidential campaigning, because for most states, the campaigning just could not matter.[33]

The second difficulty is the first-mover problem: it's fine for California to agree to allocate its electors proportionally, but not unless Texas does so as well. If a blue state took the lead on its own, that would radically weaken the opportunity for a Democrat to be elected president. The same is true the other way around. Thus there's little reason to expect states to move to this more representative system one state at a time.

This second problem suggests why this question may well be appropriate for courts, as a matter of constitutional principle, rather than state legislatures. Winner-take-all (WTA) effectively denies the votes of those who are in the minority within a particular state. Their vote counts for nothing in electing the president of the United States, even though they are citizens of the United States. The Supreme Court could recognize this effective denial of equal protection (as well as the right to associate as protected by the First Amendment), and declare that WTA violates the Constitution.

But that conclusion then raises the question of remedy: What is the right alternative to WTA that best respects the principle of equal representation? If it is not the national popular vote, through the NPVIC, then the best alternative would be to allow electors to cast fractional votes. And while that remedy may seem too creative for a Court, if the Supreme Court declared the existing system unconstitutional, then Congress, exercising its power under section 5 of the Fourteenth Amendment, could direct the states to select electors committed to casting fractional votes.[34]

Could Congress or a Court do that? The challenge here comes from the need to synthesize two parts of our constitutional tradition—one part that allocated the selection of electors to the states, and the other part that made enforceable a principle of equality and free speech against the states. Fractional voting would be a slight innovation to enable both values to be preserved. No doubt, the idea is not in the text of Constitution. Under a strict reading of the Twelfth Amendment, it would be prohibited—but not necessarily.[35] And were it allowed, then it should be open to the Court, or Congress in light of a judgment about the constitutionality of the current system, to add this innovation to the way electoral votes get cast.

Proportional allocation, however, creates a real risk that the NPVIC does not. If states allocated their electors proportionally, and a strong third-party candidate entered the race, then there would be a significant chance that no candidate would achieve an Electoral College majority. The election then would be thrown into the House of Representatives, where, according to the Constitution, each state would get one vote. Yet whatever democratic principle guided that original design choice, as America has become more urban, equal state suffrage has become even more unequal.

Yet there's a simple solution to this structural problem that could get the best of both worlds. If states adopted RCV to determine the winner in their state, and then allocated Electoral College votes to the top two vote-getters from that state proportionally, that would both avoid sending the election to the House of Representatives (at least most of the time) *and* avoid disenfranchising the majority of America. Because of fractional voting, every state would still be in play, but the votes of citizens within every state would be counted to determine which candidate was actually supported by a majority in that state.

But how could ignoring the votes of third-party candidates when allocating electors be constitutional? And more important, how could someone (like me) who is making a federal case to challenge WTA advocate for a system that effectively dropped the votes of third-party candidates?

The answer again is the principle of one person, one vote. As a constitutional matter, the question is this: what interest does the state have in allocating its electors to ignore the third- (or fourth- or fifth-) placed candidates? The answer is equality: *given* the constitutional system for determining a president if there is no majority in the Electoral College, avoiding the inequality in that system would have a compelling equality justification behind it. We know the worst system for choosing a president—from the perspective of political equality—is the choice by the House of Representatives (where each state gets one vote). The interest in avoiding that result is substantial. That substantial interest should be enough to justify a state's choice not to allocate any electors to any candidate beyond the first two.

There are plenty of details to this proposal that I will bury in the notes.[36] This isn't an easy question, and crafting the result carefully is essential. But the only point we need just now is the obvious point about equality and presidential representativeness.

REPRESENTATIVE VOTERS

Because of rules created by states, it is harder for some to vote than for others. The most charitable interpretation of that consequence is political: the rules are different because the majority party is trying to screw the minority party. The less charitable is racial: the rules are different because white Americans are trying to screw black Americans (yet again).

Regardless of the reason, the difference is morally outrageous and democratically absurd. We should be able to craft mechanisms that would produce a sufficient incentive within the states to avoid inequality. We should, that is, counter the incentives for inequality with real monetary incentives that make inequality no longer pay.

This change could be achieved—in part at least—in a traditionally obvious way. The Voting Rights Act of 1965 was the most important law achieving political equality since the Fifteenth Amendment. As I've described, in 2013, in *Shelby County v. Holder*, the Supreme Court gutted the law on the premise that racism was no more—or more precisely, that Congress needed to evince the need for the law before the Court would allow the law to survive. Without doubt, one part of the remedy to these injustices could simply be the restoration of the Voting Rights Act.

In addition, we could make enormous progress with a federal requirement of automatic voter registration.[37]

Yet as I reflect on the pervasiveness of the strategies to disable some voters relative to others, I increasingly believe we need a much more fundamental solution. Rather than pervasive efforts that purport to suss out which inequality is a product of racism, and which is not, we need solutions that aim at eliminating any incentive the states may have for discriminating in the first place. And we should do that in a very American way: through money.

In a representative democracy, voters must be representative. One way to create a strong incentive to achieve that representativeness would be to penalize states that fail to achieve representativeness. Here's one idea that would get their attention: Federal spending within a state could be reduced by the proportion of eligible voters in the state who are not registered to vote. So if 90 percent of eligible voters were registered, then 10 percent of the federal spending in that state would be eliminated. Or if not eliminated, then directed to efforts that would ensure that 100 percent were registered.

This would radically change the economics of vote suppression. It could well flip the incentives of the state against any incentive to disqualify their own voters. Universal registration would thus pay the state—quite literally.

But registration is just one dimension of the problem of voters. The ease with which people can vote is another. If ID laws burden citizens differently, then a state could deploy an ID requirement to favor the voters it favors and burden the voters it does not.

Part of the problem with IDs, however, would be eliminated through the system established to distribute vouchers (what I'll use to refer to the democracy coupons or speech credits described earlier) to fund campaigns. If vouchers are to go to voters, then the system needs a way to know which residents are voters. That system could in turn pay states for certifying residents as voters. That payment could create a strong incentive for the state to increase the number who are certified to vote, and simultaneously, reduce the number excluded through an ID requirement. The same identification for the voucher would be made adequate for voting.

Yet even this might not be enough. That leads me to believe that the second part of these reforms must reach beyond the bureaucratic and enlist the entrepreneurial energy of ambulance chasers—aka lawyers.

Don't get me wrong. I make lawyers for a living. I am in endless awe of the good that at least some lawyers have done. There would be no tobacco regulation in America had lawyers not crafted a way to hold tobacco companies responsible for the death they have caused. The same with safety regulation in a hundred fields. The same with civil rights law since the fight against state-sponsored segregation.

But we who defend lawyers should be more open about the economy of influence that influences them. No doubt they go into the field to do good. But along the way, they get kids and mortgages and the desire for a vacation. Those acquisitions mean they must be paid. And we should recognize that fact and craft a system of legal enforcement that accepts that reality.

So imagine a new cause of action (basically, a right to sue) that could be brought on behalf of voters in a state. That action could have two parts. The first, and simpler, would fine any election official who wrongfully denies a voter the right to vote $1,000 per vote denied. That law would require that the fine be paid by the election official personally (though her defense could be paid for by the jurisdiction).

The second part is more systemic. It would give to individuals— and expressly empower organizations that aid individuals in securing the right to vote to defend this right—the right to an equal freedom to vote with others in the state. By "equal," the lawsuit would mean equally easy. The charge should be that for some the ability to vote has been rendered more simple than for others. The objective of the cause of action would be to tax the state whenever that inequality unreasonably conflicts with constitutional norms.

This proves to be a bizarrely complicated area of American law, and here again, I will bury the complexity in the notes.[38] But the nub of the idea is certainly possible, and its appeal should be obvious. The law would create the incentives to hold the state responsible, by giving the lawyers a substantial return if they succeed in proving inequality in the freedom to vote. And not within the ordinary courts of federal jurisdiction. Instead the law would establish a summary court, staffed by federal judges but removed from the ordinary structure of civil justice, that would be structured to process these complaints efficiently, armed with the experience and expertise to evaluate whether the claims had merit.

Here's a simple example to make the point clearer. In 2018, Republican Brian Kemp beat Democrat Stacey Abrams in the race for governor in Georgia. In the lead-up to the election, Kemp had been the secretary of state. That meant he oversaw the administration of the vote. In that capacity, he waged a war against—as his office put it—"voter fraud." The weapons in that war were a myriad of techniques for restricting the vote in Georgia. So, for example, Kemp placed 53,000 voter registrations "on hold," because using an "exact match" system, his office had found discrepancies between the registrations and other government records. (A missing hyphen in someone's last name, for example, would trigger the hold.) Seventy percent of those voters put "on hold" were African American.[39] In the three months leading up to the 2018 election, more than 85,000 voters were purged from the voting rolls. During 2017, almost 675,000 voters were purged. And between 2012 and 2016, Georgia had removed more than 1.5 million voters from the voting roles. The vast majority of those purged were African American and Democratic.[40]

Were the reforms that I'm describing in effect in Georgia in 2018,

Georgia would now face a substantial reduction in federal funding. Its officials would face a substantial risk of personal liability for the failure to protect the vote. And lawyers would have the opportunity to show that the state had allocated the freedom to vote in a way that made it harder for some than for others. Of course, the standard can't be absolute. But even with a relaxed standard, Georgia would have been substantially penalized. And if the penalty were substantial enough, then the good people of Georgia would work hard to ensure that the next time around, there aren't a gaggle of lawyers looking to collect the equal freedom-to-vote penalties. And the simplest way to do that would be to secure to every American, regardless of race or party, the equal freedom to vote.

The consequence of this intervention would be to radically change the incentives within the state. The state would have a real reason to ensure that all within the state had an equal freedom to vote. That equality would ensure that the government wasn't bending the system against some to benefit others. It would, in a word, help make the government more representative of all within the system.

Together

In each of these contexts, there is a single dimension of reform: representativeness. The aim with each reform is to set the rules so that they maximize the opportunity for each citizen to be represented equally. That's not to say that every view will have an equal force. The Nazis will lose, as will the Stalinists. But their loss should not be a function of the rules that the institutions of democracy adopt. Their loss should be a function of their views being the views of a minority.

Except for the problem of SuperPACs, what's striking about this range of reforms is that all of them require nothing more than an act of Congress. Each of these changes could be brought about by a law, not a constitutional amendment.

This is important not because constitutional change is unimportant.

They are important because it shows that these changes are possible. The great challenge for reform is not to convince America that change is needed. The challenge is to convince America that change could happen. There is a latent demand that will only manifest itself when it makes sense. It will only make sense when it is possible.

But these statutory reforms could be buttressed by constitutional change as well. This single value of representativeness should be made fundamental within our constitutional design. Our constitution should embrace and enforce a principle that requires that political power be allocated equally. Again, that doesn't mean every idea is equally liked. It doesn't mean every politician gets the same number of votes. A world of political equality will have winners and losers. The winners will have more political power than the losers. But they will have earned that power through a democratic process. That is the only way that unequal power should live.

CHAPTER 4

Fixing Us

IF WE'RE TO BE A DEMOCRACY, THERE'S A MINIMUM THAT WE ALL, AS citizens, must satisfy. That minimum—of understanding, or at least knowledge—is above where we are, or at least where the media leaves us today. It is way below where too many believe we need to be. The key is to distinguish what should be required of all of us, all the time, or at least, at an election, from what should be required of some of us, some of the time. The some-of-us bit is the more interesting; the all-of-us part is harder.

SOME OF US

Imagine a village called Jury, Alaska, and imagine that the people in Jury, Alaska, believe in "the jury." Both civil and criminal cases are tried before juries. Those juries determine an extraordinary range of important questions. They decide whether murderers will be executed. (Alaska has never had the death penalty, but neither has it had a town called "Jury.") They decide how much in damages a negligent doctor will have to pay an injured patient. They decide whether police officers will be punished for the use of excessive force.

The strange (and hypothetical) thing about (this hypothetical town of) Jury, Alaska, however, is that by law, except for the lawyers and the parties in the case, absolutely every adult in Jury sits on every jury. The courts webcast every trial. The lawyers post their evidence to a common website. And a daily tweet from the courthouse administrator informs the citizens of Jury when a new trial is started, and when their votes in any trial are required. Failing to vote is a crime, and each year, those failing to vote are fined.

When this system was started, it made some sense. Jury, Alaska, is a remote village. When founded in the 1930s, there was no television that could reach it, or any radio of any interest. Trials were held in the evening. And since there was nothing else to do—especially in the dead of winter—people would willingly watch the trials, and vote. The town thus created its own entertainment, in a sense. At first people would show up to the courthouse, en masse, for a potluck dinner. Eventually the town wired the courthouse with CCTV.

But over time, of course, technology improved. Today the Internet reaches Jury, Alaska. So too do satellite TV, cable TV, and best of all, Netflix. Nothing constrains the citizens of Jury to watch JurycourtTV. Some do, some don't. "It's a free village," the citizens insist.

The citizens of Jury defend their system with the principle of democracy. Every citizen of Jury is an equal citizen, citizens of Jury say. Every citizen, they insist, ought to have an equal role in determining how justice in Jury will be meted out. So every citizen is therefore entitled to the vote on every jury. Any true democracy, the citizens of jury insist, would grant nothing less.

So then imagine a citizen from Jury visited a courthouse in Lancaster, Pennsylvania. In Lancaster, the 60,000 or so citizens also have courts. They also have juries. But only a small number of Lancaster citizens ever serve on those juries. Jury pools are randomly summoned, based on the voting rolls in the city. From that random pool, a dozen plus alternates are selected for any particular criminal trial.

A citizen of Jury, Alaska, might challenge a judge in Lancaster:

"How can you call yourself a democracy, when by law you exclude 99.9997 percent of citizens from service on a jury? Why do citizens give away their franchise so easily? Why don't more defend their right to participate equally in the allocation of justice?"

None of us would have any trouble defending Lancaster against Jury. Yes, in a sense, the jury system (in every place except Jury) denies the right of ordinary citizens to participate always. But that denial makes sense. Justice requires that the deciders know something before they decide. It requires that we exclude those who we know have no reason or opportunity or interest to know or know in the right way. Justice requires—in a sense that we need to make more general—that the system reckon its own epistemology. What do we know about what those within the system will know? Is what they will know enough? And if it is not enough, how could we fix it?

WE ARE NEVER GOING back to the 1960s. We are never going back to the age of Walter Cronkite. It will never be the case in at least America again when (practically) all of us see (practically) the same news, presented in the same relatively middle-of-the-road way, practically every single day. We are never going to have a public regularly and reliably educated en masse to understand issues of national import. We are never going to live in Jürgen Habermas's "ideal speech situation."[1]

And more important, whatever common story we see will never again be a story unconnected to spin. Partisanship has become part of the business model again. It is not going to disappear anytime soon.

Nothing could be more obvious. Yet it is striking how little in democratic theory tries to come to terms with this obvious fact. We continue to console ourselves with the idea that journalists might be objective, or schools might better educate our kids about civics. But all that misses the fundamental point: The weird quarter century in the history of humanity when most were focused on the same set of stories—and most viewed those stories as the product of truth, not spin—was a weird quarter century that will never happen again. There will be no rerun of the 1970s. That age is over.

The question now is how to build a democracy that does not assume that we all, at any particular time, know anything, and that accepts that what's told to us is told to us with partisan spin. How do we govern ourselves when we, in fact, know squat about even the most important issues? How do we run a democracy when the people are inherently ignorant, and we the ignorant live in tribes?

There is an answer to that question, a solution to that puzzle. The answer is not to imagine a world in which we are all wonkish enough to know what's true or right or even just with every issue. The answer is to imagine a true or right or just democracy that relies—in the main—on the few, and not the many. Like the jury, we may all be entitled to serve. But like the jury, we need a democracy that at any one time relies on just a few.

That statement sounds scandalous. How can it be that a democracy should rely on the few, and ignore the many? How could it be that a democratic theorist would argue that a democracy should rely on the few and not the many? How is this anything other than simple elitism? A Harvard professor counseling that we ignore the rabble and focus on the chosen?

The answer to those obvious objections will take work. But the hint to its answer is the central idea of this book—*representative*. If the many can't be relied upon, then can we craft a representative few who can? Could those few speak for the many? Could they be, in effect, our jury—not as in Jury, Alaska, but as in the kind of jury we all already know?

I TRUNDLED OUT OF BED just before 7 A.M., local time, disoriented and exhausted. Jet lag. I had flown from Europe through Moscow on the way to Ulaanbaator, Mongolia. I had not slept enough in weeks. I grabbed a coffee and stepped out on a beautifully sunny morning. It was the end of April, but it was still cold. I had about a mile to walk.

The parliament building in the Mongolian capitol is a huge and beautiful structure, built in 2006 to replace a hideous "governmental palace" that itself had been built in 1951 (and then complemented with a Lenin-wannabe mausoleum added in 1952 to honor Mongolia's closest parallel to Lenin, Damdiny Sükhbaatar). At the center of the main entrance is a massive statue of Genghis Khan. As I stood just below that statute, close to seven hundred Mongolians organized themselves for a picture. Most were dressed in traditional formal wear—beautifully colored deel. Many looked like any average businessman or businesswoman from any Western European city. Some were old. Some were not. In fact, as I would later learn, the seven hundred were an almost perfect representation of Mongolia itself. The group was about half of the original 1,568 who had been randomly selected by the National Statistical Office; the mix was designed to be representative. If, as John Adams had promised, a legislature "should be in miniature, an exact portrait of the people at large," this was an ideal Adamsonian legislature.

These seven hundred Mongolians had been summoned to the capital pursuant to a kind of citizen-draft. Mongolian law required that the parliament conduct a "deliberative poll" before it considers any amendment to the Mongolian constitution. These Mongolians had been summoned to participate in that poll. More than half had been on a bus for more than two nights; just under half came from the capital. And over the next two and a half days, these seven hundred citizens would meet in small groups and together to debate a set of proposed amendments to their 1992 constitution.[2]

Mongolia is different from the United States in many ways. Its per capita GDP is about $15,000, one-fourth the United States'. Thirty percent of its population lives below the poverty line, twice the percentage in the United States.[3] Inequality is greater in the United States (measured by the "Gini index" it is 45 versus 34[4]). Eighty percent of Americans use the Internet; less than 25 percent of Mongolians do.[5]

I'm pretty sure most Americans would balk at the idea of riding a bus two days to get to Washington, D.C. I'm pretty certain they would demand nicer hotels than the Mongolians I observed over the course of a weekend did.

But I doubt that Americans are any more educated about the contours of their constitution than the Mongolians are about theirs. I doubt that they would bring to the conversation any broader comparative perspective. And I'm quite sure that the Americans would be just as committed and engaged as I saw the Mongolians become. Though, yes, the Mongolians are different, in the only relevant sense, they are just as Americans would be, if Americans were asked the very same question of them.

Over the course of that weekend, I became a committed advocate, not for Mongolia, but for deliberative polling. I entered the weekend skeptical that ordinary Mongolians could even begin to understand issues of constitutional design; I left the country convinced that they had not only understood them, but that they had resolved them with wisdom.

"Deliberative polling" was developed by Stanford professor James Fishkin. The process involves gathering a random and representative sample of a public and giving them the opportunity to deliberate about some particular issue. The sample is briefed before the deliberation, through materials developed by representatives from all sides of the issue; they are polled on the question at the start of the deliberation; they then deliberate together in large and small groups; they have the opportunity to ask questions; and then at the end, they are polled again. The movement from the first poll to the last is the measure of the deliberative public's view. In the scores of deliberative polls that Fishkin has conducted over the past thirty years, that progress is almost uniformly edifying.[6]

Mongolia is the first country—ever—to mandate a deliberative poll before a constitutional amendment could be considered. The results of the poll are not binding; they are just persuasive. But between the proposals suggested (by the Mongolian politicians) and the proposals agreed upon (by the seven hundred), it's hard not to be persuaded by the judgment of the seven hundred.

Mongolia is not the only country to experiment with reflective, citizen-driven policy judgment. Indeed, two of the most interesting followed immediately after the 2008 financial crisis—Iceland and Ireland.

Iceland's project was the more ambitious. Many in Icelandic society believed that the crisis had been caused in part by the absence of a constitution. So Iceland launched an incredible citizen-driven process to effectively crowdsource a constitution. After a randomly selected forum of a thousand Icelanders met to identify the values that any Icelandic constitution should embody, the government conducted an election to select twenty-five to serve on a drafting committee. Over four months, that twenty-five crafted a new constitution. They posted their drafts to Facebook and revised them based on the comments they received. In 2012 the draft was submitted to the nation in a referendum. More than two-thirds of those voting expressed the desire that the Icelandic Parliament adopt a new constitution "based on [that] draft."[7]

Ireland's reform was less fundamental and perhaps even more innovative. Also inspired by the 2008 financial crisis, the government instituted a process to convene a "citizens convention" to consider a host of issues, some fundamental and some less so. That convention recruited 100 participants: 33 from the Irish parliament, and 66 randomly selected citizens, and one prominent national figure as the chair. For a period of fourteen months, they met once a month to deliberate and resolve the question within their mandate.[8]

Many criticized the Irish experiment because the numbers were so small. Sixty-six citizens can't be said to represent a population of 4.7 million fairly. But the process was transformative, both for the participants and the nation. And because some of the participants were members of Parliament, the proposals were considered and engaged. The convention resolved to end the prohibition on abortion—but did not adopt a constitutional right to terminate a pregnancy. In a subsequent Citizens Assembly, the convention determined to expand the right to marry to include same-sex couples.[9] (Remember, this is Ireland, where 78 percent are Catholic!)

This is democracy, as Fishkin puts it in the title to his most recent book about deliberative polling, "when the people are thinking."[10] But it's more than thinking. It is democracy when the people know something, and then have a chance, together, to deliberate about what they know. It is democracy like a jury is democracy—where people also know something and have a chance to deliberate. But it is better than a jury, since whether one hundred or seven hundred, the aim is to be representative of the society as a whole. "Deliberative polling" is a method to overcome the informational environmental flaws of modern society, to construct a public that can understand well enough to make a judgment that is informed enough. It is just one of a family of techniques for radically improving the capacity of citizens to contribute to governing, and to help build trust in the results.[11]

THE ICELANDERS, IRISH, OR MONGOLIANS ARE NOT a model for how democracy should happen always and everywhere. The point of the story is not to sketch a replacement for representative democracy. The point is to mark whether and when we can be confident about the views of a democratic public. What are the conditions under which such views emerge? How are they bred? How nourished?

Those conditions are rare. And thus our demand for these conditions must be rare, too. There's no way we could imagine everyone within any democracy—Mongolia or America—understanding enough about the intricacies of constitutional design to opine about one system over another. That understanding is not and could not be latent.

But the Mongolian, Icelandic, and Irish cases in particular, and deliberative democracy in general, show us that we can construct the contexts where we can speak more sensibly. And as our resistance to Jury, Alaska, shows, latent within our own political culture is precisely the recognition that while some of us can do it sometimes, it makes no sense to imagine all of us doing it always. It's fair and sensible to ask a regular jury whether some defendant is guilty. It's not fair to ask all the citizens of Lancaster. And it's fair and sensible to ask the participants within the Mongolian deliberative poll whether there should be a new chamber in the Mongolian parliament. It is not fair to ask the citizens of Mongolia generally.

If we're to begin to repair the potential for democracy, we must begin here—with this distinction, so understood. There are questions that are appropriate for some of us, at some particular time. Those questions are not appropriate for all of us at every particular time. If those inappropriate questions get asked of all of us, we need to learn to ignore the answer. Or at least, to bracket it. Or at the very least, set it against the same question asked of some of us in the right way.

This is where we must engage our democratic imagination. Political scientist Larry Bartels and others have expressed deep skepticism about democracy, specifically, whether democracy is "realistic." Citizens, Bartels tells us, have "attitudes but not preferences."[12] But what if contexts crafted like this could elevate attitudes into meaningful and democratic perspectives? If we can't imagine a world in which we all, all the time, are educated enough about what should be—so that when a representative sample of us gets selected, that sample knows enough in a nonpolarized way to answer the questions it is asked sensibly—we can still at least imagine institutions and practices that give us something just as good, or maybe even better than anything we have ever had before. We know enough, I want to argue, to know that "we the people" can be rendered well, even if "we the people" rendered in the ordinary way today are not rendered well.

It may have been rendered better before. It was rendered better when it lived within the frame of nonpolarized, common understandings. Now that common understanding is gone, we have but two meaningful choices. We could either give up on the idea that the views of the people matter, or we could commit to constructing those views in ways that we could defend. We could, that is, either concede the antidemocrat's point, or we could repair the cause of the rightful skepticism that the world now brings to the very idea of "the will of the people."

That repair would require first a certain kind of understanding and acceptance. Just as we accept a jury's determination that cigarette manufacturers must pay $145 billion to consumers because of a class action lawsuit,[13] or that Boston bomber Dzhokhar Tsarnaev must be executed, we as a people would need to come to accept the results of these, let's call them, "civic juries." By "accept" I do not mean necessarily in some formal sense. There's no reason to insist that civic juries have legal authority, at least initially, any more than public opinion polls have legal authority. Instead, take "accept" in the narrow sense of recognizing that they speak, in an important sense, for us better, and that they have a normative significance that is greater than the significance of George Gallup's machine.

Ordinary juries in America show us that as a people, we can accept the idea of some speaking for all. Deliberative polls show us that some of us can understand enough to make sensible and persuasive judgments. Civic juries, as deliberative polls considering important issues of public policy, could then become institutions that enable us to accept the views of some as ours.

I am frankly not sure we can get there. The first steps seem obvious. Whether they would be enough to move the public's understanding and acceptance is less clear. Yet given the certain bankruptcy of the systems we now embrace, it seems at least clear that we should take these steps and see where they get us.

Civic Juries

Though there's tons to be anxious about when we think about how digital technologies affect understanding, there are certainly aspects that are incredibly valuable. One of those is the consequence of exposure to different thinking. Against the standard view that the Internet isolates us into our own bubbles, there is important research that suggests that in fact the Internet is exposing people to perspectives they otherwise would never have had.[14]

That exposure doesn't necessarily help. Especially for smart people, seeing there's another side to the argument doesn't convince them that they're wrong; it more likely simply triggers a more aggressive effort to rationalize why they are right.[15]

But for some people, seeing a credible and disinterested view on the other side at least moderates the confidence they have in their own view. They don't flip to the other side. They don't believe that they are themselves wrong. But they're less likely to bet on whether they're right. They'll continue to brandish the flag, but if something depends upon it, they're less likely to go to war.

This dynamic suggests the first and most obvious role for civic juries—simply to identify where "we" are wrong. Imagine a well-funded institution that could roam the public opinion space and test views of "we the people" as reported by the Gallup-like machines against the views of "we the people" are reported by civic juries. This is not a cheap or easy thing to do. The costs of a deliberative poll are significant. And they can't happen overnight. But there are issues that citizens have views about that remain stable over time. And one critical question that this imagined institution could address is how those views contrast with the views of a civic jury. Do we, informed and reflective, have the same views as we, collectively, over time? And if we don't, then where are the gaps? What are the issues where a better understanding is necessary?

The agenda of any such institution must be developed with care. No doubt there is blindness on the right and on the left. And there are mistakes made by "us" as reported by Gallup that are the mistakes of liberals and the mistakes of conservatives. But if the only mistakes that were discovered were the mistakes of one side, then the institution making that discovery would be rendered political. If it "just turned out" that only conservatives were crazy, or only liberals were nuts, then the institution making that discovery would itself get swept into a partisan spin. To avoid that spin, the director needs an almost Chief Justice John Marshall–like intuition about how the truth will be heard, so that speaking the truth doesn't destroy trust in the speaker.[16]

She also needs some sense of salience or significance. She needs some way to get the perspective of the civic jury recognized. In the post-broadcasting era, there's no sure path to universal exposure. There's no guarantee that the truth will rise to the top. But there are mechanisms that would make this perspective at least relevant. And here again, Mongolia hints at a way forward.

Shadow Conventions

There is an Article V convention movement in America. It provides a perfect opportunity for the civic jury.

"Article V" refers to the part of our constitution governing amendments of the Constitution. An "Article V convention" is a procedure for proposing amendments that has never happened in the history of America. Under this procedure, if two-thirds of the states demand it, then Congress "shall call a Convention for proposing Amendments." If the convention succeeds in proposing amendments, then Congress gets to decide how those proposed amendments should be ratified. Congress can either send the amendments to state legislatures or to state conventions. In either case, the Constitution requires that three-fourths of the states agree with the amendment before it is "ratified."

There is all sorts of malarkey spouted about this provision in our Constitution. It used to be the John Birch Society and then Phyllis Schlafly who organized the right against a convention. Now it is the left that insists that a convention would be the end of our constitution as we know it.

I find the arguments against the convention literally embarrassing. I can't begin to believe that especially the people I respect so much would utter such utter nonsense. I've written two books each with a chapter defending the idea of an Article V convention. And I remain convinced that the only way we're going to see meaningful constitutional change is through a convention.[17]

But Mongolia suggests an idea for how we might better encourage thought about a convention, while also constraining the work of a convention. Following the example of Mongolia, Congress should pass a law that requires that before any Article V convention is convened, there should be a shadow convention, or a "constitutional jury," by ordinary citizens, run simultaneously and charged with considering the questions that the Article V convention will address.

These constitutional juries could work like this: The law would convene five simultaneous national citizens' conventions in five cities across the country. Each of these conventions would include five hundred randomly selected and representative Americans. Those citizens would be obligated to attend—though their expenses would be paid; their jobs would, by law, be protected; their salaries for the week would be reimbursed to their employer; they would receive a generous stipend; and the costs of any extraordinary domestic expenses (child care, or the care of parents) would be borne by the government. Think of it as a very generous draft, not to military service, but to civic service. These 2,500 citizens would be called to serve for a single week, to give their considered views about the question that triggered the conventions.

Each national convention would convene on the same Monday night. Delegates would travel to arrive by Monday afternoon. They would first convene together that evening. Then for the next three days, the conventions would consider the question presented to them.

Before they arrived, the delegates would be given an introduction to the questions. That introduction would be developed by a team to present both sides of the issue. The job of that team, or advisory board, would be to ensure that the claims made on either side are based in fact. And once those claims are vetted, then a production team would turn the arguments both for and against into a video. Each delegate would be obligated to watch the video. Each delegate would have the chance to earn a supplemental stipend if he or she answers questions at the end of the video accurately. The aim of the videos would be to give the delegates a sense of the field. They would not aim to resolve the issues one way or the other.

When the delegates are first selected, they would be polled on the issue they will deliberate upon. They would be polled again after they complete the video preparation. They would be polled when they assemble. And then they would be polled one final time at the end of the week. Those polls would capture any evolution in the views of the delegates. They would help the public understand how and why any evolution happened. They would also help researchers isolate the aspects that people responded to, and the aspects they didn't quite get.

On each day of deliberation, the work of the delegates would bounce between small groups and large groups. The issue would be quickly introduced, as each delegate would have been exposed to the introductory videos and materials. They would then break into small groups to discuss their own views. At no point during the day would anyone poll anyone about where people stood. They would instead identify questions and share with their fellow delegates the reasons that pull them one way or another.

Each convention would be extensively documented, by documentarians and political and social scientists. But, perhaps most controversially, while they are happening, the delegates would be sequestered. No news about the proceedings would be reported during the proceedings. And no contact with the delegates would be permitted during the time they are deliberating. Once each convention was finished, everything could be known. But while they are happening, none could know how the debates were going, or whom they needed to sway one way or the other.

The obvious reason for this sequestering is that there could be highly motivated individuals on all sides of these debates. And as the solutions could have profound consequences for the future of America's democracy, there would be many who would be fiercely committed to pushing the conventions in one way or another.

But during deliberations, those persuasions are not appropriate. There will be time enough for politicking, both specially interested and publicly interested, once the deliberation is done. But as with a jury deciding whether to convict a defendant of murder, or whether to hold an oil company liable for a massive oil spill, while the deliberation occurs, persuasion from the outside would be forbidden. And by architecting the deliberations to happen simultaneously, any interaction effect by the different conventions could be minimized.

At the end of the week, the results of the conventions would be presented to Congress. Congress would then be obligated to consider the results and make a determination about whether to act upon them or not.

These conventions would cost money. Not, in the scale of things, lots of money, but some. And they would have to be conducted with absolute integrity. No doubt, regardless of the results, the conventions would be attacked. But there are obvious steps they could take to mitigate the potential for that attack.

Here's one such step: the constitutional jury should only ever consider either questions on which there is cross-partisan agreement or a brace of questions, one from the left and one from the right. For example, in the convention movement in America today, there are proponents for conventions that appeal to people on both the right and the left. On the right, there are people pushing for a balanced budget convention, and a convention to limit the power of the federal government. On the left, there are people pushing for a convention to address the issues that this book has been devoted to—issues of representational integrity.

The constitutional jury could consider both issues. That is, the five simultaneous conventions could spend time considering both the questions of the balanced budget proposals, and questions of representational integrity. That combination would give each side a reason to give the process room to work. Of course, results might disappoint. But that is unavoidable.

The consequence of these constitutional juries would not be an amendment to the Constitution. No one could pretend that these conventions have any legal power, since their very creation would declare that their conclusion has no legal force. But what they would have is normative force. And for all the reasons outlined in this book, they should have greater normative force than an equivalent Gallup poll about similar questions.

The normative field governing the questions of whether there should be Article V conventions, and what those conventions should cover, would thus be complemented by the civic juries. There would still be the politicians (and groups such as the Koch brothers pushing for an Article V convention). There would still be embarrassingly ignorant views of the public (gathered in Gallup-like polls) and the pundits. But added to that field would be a different "we the people": one we should understand to be more representative of us, because representing us in our best possible light.

Shadow Congresses

If the constitutional jury worked, we could take things one step further. I don't believe in direct democracy. And I don't believe we should weaken the institutions of representative democracy. But we could imagine complementing those institutions with an institution that could add a perspective of "we the people" to the mix that exists now.

To see that potential, however, we need to introduce some history. This idea will seem a bit nuts, until we recognize that within the history of democracy it is as common as mud.

From the beginning, theorists of democracy have understood that there are two very different ways for a democracy to select its representatives. Elections are one way. Random selection—or "sortition"—is another. And as historian David Van Reybrouck has argued, for much of the history of theorizing about democracy, at least before the eighteenth century, most believed that elections would lead naturally to aristocracy, while random selection would not. "Aristotle," van Reybrouck writes, "put it frankly: . . . 'the appointment of magistrates by lot is democratical, and the election of them oligarchical.'"[18] Montesquieu repeated Aristotle's view: "Voting by *lot* is in the nature of democracy; voting by *choice* is in the nature of aristocracy."[19]

But when at the end of the eighteenth century, the two great experiments with large-scale democracy were launched—one in France and one in America—neither embraced sortition for selecting representatives.[20] Instead both embedded elections at their core. Theorists of democracy thus quickly forgot that for hundreds of years, democratic systems had followed a different way. Very quickly, the presumption became that elections are the sine qua non of a democracy.

Yet it had not always been so. As Van Reybrouck describes, and as Oliver Dowlen explains as well in his wonderful pamphlet, *Sorted: Civil Lotteries and the Future of Public Participation*, there are many examples—from ancient Greece to much of the history of Florentine Italy—of governments that were filled with people who selected randomly. The Greeks invented a device that would do the random selection. Their commitment to sortition survived for more than two hundred years. A Venetian lottery system survived for more than five hundred years. And even in Britain, the town of Great Yarmouth had a scheme that lasted for more than three hundred years, until it was replaced in 1835.[21]

Each of these examples presents a solution to an obvious problem. Each needed humans to exercise judgment. Each wanted to select humans who were, in a critical sense, disinterested. None of these societies had a rich sense of probability theory. (Probability theory is probably born in the sixteenth century and matured in the seventeenth century.)[22] But each had an obvious intuition that a random selection would avoid selecting people having the wrong reason to serve. Service would not be self-interested. Service would be service.

Elections could not promise the same result. People who run have an interest in running. Sometimes that interest is public regarding, but not always. And the fear of those who fear elections is that the few who would choose to run are precisely the people we don't want making the decisions.

I rehearse Van Reybrouck's arguments here not to argue that we should eliminate elections and choose representatives by random selection. (Indeed, neither does Van Reybrouck.) Instead, the point of the history is to force to the foreground a point that is too often lost: that we have *forever* delegated to subsets of us the power of government, and that such delegation has *very often* been a very good thing. It would be insane to require all of us to "sit" on every jury. "We" in these cases never means "all of us." "We" in these cases only ever means some of us. And the critical question that we should always be able to ask is not "why some," but "why this method of selecting some."

This is, after all, the question that George Gallup had to answer from the very start of his project, too. Building on the teaching of statistics, Gallup had to convince a nonmathematical public that there was a good reason to believe that what one thousand randomly selecting Americans believed was actually a measure of what all of America believed.

Elections of course are different from public opinion polls. They can be better. They can be worse. To the extent that the voters know something, they can be better. To the extent the voters are unrepresentative, they can be worse. But the key is to recognize how sortition was deployed to compensate for both potential weaknesses. A properly sorted public could be both representative *and* informed. And the lesson of history is that we should consider whether and where a sorted public might be better than an electing public—both to ensure better judgments and ensure a more representative mix.

So against the background of that history, consider this structural innovation: Imagine that either the president, or a vote by both houses of Congress, could convene a shadow Congress, or "congressional jury."[23] Not in general, and not for an unspecified purpose. But when the president or both houses of Congress believes the national debate needs it, they can convene the congressional jury to consider a particular question.

The congressional jury would be like the shadow conventions, though there would be just one. It would be crafted in the same participant-protective way. The aim would be to ensure that all could participate, regardless of the position they were in in their life. All would be able to participate; all would be required to participate.

Now, again, there's no reason to make the work of the congressional jury binding on anyone. We don't need to imagine it exercising power—the way a jury does. At least not initially. But what it could do is to break certain political stalemates. It could, in other words, give the politicians a way out.

So for example, consider a congressional jury convened to consider the regulation of guns. Right now, there is wildly strong support for sensible gun safety regulation. There is very little chance that representative bodies will enact it. The political consequences are thought to be too risky. So nothing happens, except more die from guns.

A congressional jury could consider gun safety regulation. If it supported it—after considering the facts, and both sides of the question—that could give moral weight to the movement supporting legislation. A congressman could announce himself morally bound. He could weigh the deliberations and acknowledge their wisdom. The process, in short, could catalyze a solution, where there is little chance for a solution now.

There's an interesting precedent for this way of proceeding. When the nation became resolved to end the experiment with Prohibition, the politicians knew that decision would trigger the ire of leading prohibitionists. To protect that decision, Congress, for the first time in American history, set the mode of ratification for an amendment to be state conventions rather than state legislatures. The conventions were insulated from political consequence. They could do what the public thought was right, and not fear the punishment of a minority that held strongly opposed views. That's the same function the congressional jury could serve, allowing Congress to escape the political consequences of decisions that organized special interests would strongly oppose.

There are ways to improve the views of some of us; we should use those views to inform what our representatives do, not all the time, not on every issue, and not in a way that could be easily exploited politically, but at certain times, when the views of "we the people" should matter. If a convention is going to consider amendments to the Constitution, let a shadow convention do so as well. If the president or Congress believes it is stuck, let a shadow Congress give it a way out. In both cases, the objective is the same: to add something that could add value to the democratic mix within the republic we have inherited.

Both cases build upon a faith that we the people, properly informed, do have moral and democratic significance. I have that faith. We should rank that faith as the litmus test for democracy today. One should be skeptical of the public's view when one sees there's no reason to believe the public has the access or the opportunity to have an informed and balanced (read: nonpolarized) view. But if one is not willing to defer to the judgment of a public that has been informed, and that has had the chance to deliberate, then one is simply not a democrat. And if one is a democrat, and therefore willing to defer, then we should build the institutions that give us something to defer to, because there is an endless supply of stuff that gives us no reason to defer at all.

THE SOME-OF-US PROBLEM IS both about what we should not expect everyone to understand, and about how we could at least constitute some-of-us to understand it, at least to the end of informing representatives. It requires that we develop an ability to say collectively, "Why would you ever think we would know that?" It depends upon the capacity to distinguish between what we know we won't collectively know, and what we should know.

The part we should all know is the all-of-us problem. How do we raise the understanding of all of us, not to the level of policy wonks, but to a level that democracy needs?

Here again, I am not certain it is possible. But the next steps are clear.

ALL OF US

If we are what we eat, then we are, as a society, in real trouble. Our diet is terrible. We eat too fast. What we eat is too processed. What we miss is nutrition without the empty calories.

The slow food movement is a response to something in the nature of humans and the nature of nutrition. It is a strategy to enable us to resist what we know would be most tempting, but what we have learned is empty or harmful.[24]

The strategy relies on an understanding about how humans work. Given that understanding, the movement says: slow down, and cook. If you cook your food, your food will be healthy, and you will eat an appropriate amount. This is not because it's not possible to cook bad or unhealthy food. It's just not easy. Processed food is incredibly difficult to make, at least in an edible form. And most of us, in our own kitchens, don't begin to have the chemicals or talent to replicate the magic in Buffalo wings.

To solve the democratic problem with all-of-us, we need an analogous "slow democracy movement."[25] This movement would rely on a similar strategy. It too would be a response to something in the nature of humans and knowledge. It, too, would be a strategy for resisting what we know would be most tempting but what we have learned is both empty and harmful. And it, too, would rely upon an understanding about how humans work. Given that understanding, the slow democracy movement says that we should do politics in particular contexts, not because those contexts can't be hacked or will never be poisonous, but because it's just harder to hack them or make them poisonous.

We know that humans can be triggered through emotion and anger. The biggest and richest companies in the world now profit from that knowledge. These companies leverage our insecurity to get us to act, because in our actions we reveal what we want or would buy. From Facebook to Google to Twitter, the technology triggers us to open up, so markets can better sell.

You don't have to believe that these technologies are evil to believe they're not great for democratic understanding—just like we don't have to condemn Domino's pizza just to eat healthy food. Instead, we just need to see the ways in which these technologies steer us away from the understanding we need as citizens.

"The understanding we need as citizens": In the last section I described at length the techniques we could adopt to develop a deep understanding of the people about some public issue. I described the civic juries, and the idea of a shadow convention and shadow Congress that might overcome the gaps in knowledge and understanding that so clearly mark us.

But those institutions will never completely remove our responsibilities as citizens. We can't outsource our job as voters to some deliberative poll (or not completely—I'll describe a bit of outsourcing below). We can't call ourselves a democracy if we don't have *any* understanding of the issues that our representatives must resolve.

So as well as imagining new institutions that could craft or discover a will of the people worth following, we need to reimagine the old institutions, too. Elections are going to be with us forever—and should be. And that means that as citizens we need to know enough to know which leaders should lead us. We need the institutions to ensure we know enough to choose well.

We don't have those institutions today. The bastardized version of broadcast news that cable television has become does not inform, it inflames. The complement on the Internet doesn't correct the error, it exaggerates it. If democracy is going to survive, it will not survive in reliance on these forms of media alone. We will never ban them—nor should the government have the power to ban them. But we must add to them with a different understanding that is richer and more complete—and hence, the basis upon which democratic choice is possible.

What are the changes that would strengthen the understanding of all of us on the basic question that democracy can rightly ask of us— who should represent us? I consider each of these changes to be part of a slow democracy movement, and in the balance of this chapter, I propose a number of changes that could better make us the citizens we need to be.

I don't pretend to know whether these changes are enough, or whether added together, they would change enough of anything. We don't have a metric for measuring democratic understanding. We need one. Urgently. I therefore offer these as first steps, without any sense about how many more after these we will need.

Doing Less

We can start by recognizing our limits: We need to understand what we as a people can and cannot do. We need to craft our institutions in light of our democratic capacities. And we need to reject vigorously ideas about us that we know are not true.

This is not our practice today. We are a people who regularly lie and feel fine about it. You're thinking that you don't lie. Let me remind you how many times you have "affirmed" that you have read the terms of service to some website or product or service, and that you have understood it. We live life constantly acknowledging what we know we can't affirm. We don't even notice it anymore.

It hasn't always been like this. As a kid, I was an obsessive truth teller. I refused to do what I knew was wrong. I don't think I was ever forced to say what I knew wasn't true, as a condition for doing what I (legitimately) wanted to do. Now I am required to do that all the time. It is corrosive and demeaning. Yet this is our life.

One place where I have always recognized that demeaning deception is voting. Every election, I walk into my polling place (now in Brookline, Massachusetts) and vote, ignorantly. Not on all questions or all offices, and not as ignorantly as I did in California (where the referenda were *absurd*). But on at least some offices and some questions, the god's honest truth is, I have no idea. I know the federal offices. I have a good sense of the state offices. My wife is a member of town meeting. But selectmen? Trustees of the public library? Constable? At least it's not as bad as in other jurisdictions: Clerks of court? Mosquito Control District board members? Register of wills? Judges of orphan courts? Dog catchers? There are more than 500,000 elected officials in the United States, almost 1 for every 500 adult citizens.[26] (I grew up in Pennsylvania, where they had the office of "prothonotary." One of my best friends became the prothonotary. I still have no idea what that office even is.) Is it even surprising that Pew finds just 39 percent of Americans say, "Voters are knowledgeable about candidates and issues."[27]

We know we don't know anything about most of these offices, because we can observe that 90 percent of the campaigning is simply a sign with someone's name. The assumption is that name recognition gets you 90 percent of the way to a vote. Yet how could it be that a system that decides critical offices on the basis of whose name is more easily remembered makes sense? Does any major corporation hire people based on name recognition? Does any university? Or nonprofit?

There are some scholars who work hard to demonstrate that this ignorance doesn't really matter. That if a small number know something, then the rest of us can't really screw it up.[28] But this is an strange rationalization for a system that can't really do what it needs to do—which is to select great people for important offices. We, the people, should recognize that we, as voters, will never understand enough to make that kind of judgment for a very wide range of public offices. And once we recognize that, we should reform our system in light of what we know.

Since the time of Lord Bryce, commentators have noted the absurdly long ballot that is the American political system.[29] As historian Charles Beard wrote:

> The glaring absurdity of this system can best be illustrated by concrete examples, which bring home the details of the voters' task. I have before me the ballot for the thirteenth and thirty-fourth wards of the sixth congressional district of Chicago in 1906. It is two feet and two inches by eighteen and one-half inches; and it contains 334 names distributed with more or less evenness as candidates for the following offices:
>
> State treasurer, state superintendent of public instruction, trustees of the University of Illinois, representatives in Congress, state senator, representatives in the state Assembly, sheriff, county treasurer, county clerk, clerk of the probate court, clerk of the criminal court, clerk of the circuit court, county superintendent of schools, judge of the county court, judge of the probate court, members of the board of assessors, member of the board of review, president of the board of county commissioners, county commissioners (ten to be elected on general ticket), trustees of the sanitary district of Chicago (three to be elected), clerk of the municipal court, bailiff of the municipal court, chief justice of the municipal court, judges of the municipal court (nine to be elected), judges of the municipal court for the four-year term (nine to be elected), judges of the municipal court for the two-year term (nine to be elected).[30]

No doubt, in the days of patronage, these jobs helped grease the wheel of democratic politics. Maybe they were necessary to make that form of democracy work. But there is no reason today to make most of these offices elected offices. And there is every reason to remove them from the ballots that citizens are asked to cast. We should not be asking ourselves the questions that we know most will have no reason or capacity to answer.

Capacity. That's a dangerous word, I know, especially when used by a presumptive member of the information elite. But again, I don't mean "capacity" in the sense of intelligence. I have no doubt that any citizen *could* reckon the facts necessary to make a judgment about who should be sheriff or prothonotary. I mean capacity in a different sense—the knowledge we should ordinarily or reasonably expect people to have in the ordinary course of their democratic life. I have no problem believing that citizens have the capacity to know who their congressman or senator or president should be. And for some local races, I would say the same. My only claim is that we should not *presume* capacity when we know it is not there, and will not be there, regardless. The rational ignorance described by Anthony Downs may in certain contexts be overcome. But we should be clear about when that cure is likely.

I don't have an answer for all cases. I do have a view about many. What we need in a democracy are people we can hold responsible for how our government works. That suggests we elect fewer people, and that those fewer are responsible for selecting the others that a government requires.

Or if we're to continue with elections for some office, then we could at least add a layer of citizen advice into the process to help guide the ultimate results. In 2006, one of the two major parties in Marousi, Greece (the suburb of Athens that hosted the 2004 Olympics), used a deliberative poll to select its candidate for mayor. We could do the same, if not selecting the candidate, then at least advising the public about which candidate the civic jury would select. Certainly—and obviously—that choice would be more informed than the choice that is made on a ballot. And if the citizen jury were properly representative, it would certainly be more representative of the public than anything produced through an election.

Elections are rarely anything but flawed, and multiplying the number of offices subject to election is rarely anything but corruption. Humility should guide us to narrowing the places in which the people must choose to those where we have good reason to believe the people *can* choose. Not "can" in the sense of can recognize a name, but "can" in the sense of can meaningfully consider the alternatives. And where there is an office that must, in its nature, be elected—a representative or a president—then humility should guide us to complement the process with guidance from an "us" that we all should respect.

When We Choose

Like many universities, Harvard has a quadrangle. Dormitories, ancient and beautiful, ring the quad, leaving an ample yard in the middle and pathways crisscrossing the yard. In the spring, students sit on the grass and read or listen to music. Many hang out with friends. Some try to recruit others to join clubs or causes.

Imagine for a minute that these were the only places in which it was possible to reach the students. Imagine calculus and history and physics had to be taught to the students as the students hung out on the lawns. Imagine the professors stood in the windows of the buildings surrounding the lawns and had to yell to get attention. Imagine they had to take turns—you couldn't have advanced calculus and ancient Roman history screamed at the same time—so that there was a round robin of screaming, as professors tried to convey the essence of what was needed before the attention shifted somewhere else.

Obviously, this architecture for conveying information would constrain the kind of information that could be conveyed. If all you had was the equivalent of a tweet, that would limit, dramatically, the sort of ideas you could discuss. No doubt, some ideas could be communicated in five-second bites, but not all ideas, and certainly not the most important or most difficult. The architecture for education would not be useless, but it would not succeed in most of what education tries to accomplish.

There are a million ways in which this picture is not a picture of democracy. Democracy is not the education of the people by professors. It is not a set curriculum taught year after year.

Yet consider for a second the way which this picture is very much like our democracy today. Political speech in America today is nonconsensual communication. Not all of it: when you sit down with your friends to talk about who you're going to support in the next election, that's consensual communication. It's people choosing to talk about something, and that something is politics.

But most political advertising happens in a context that is not consensual. You're watching *Monday Night Football* and the game gets interrupted by commercials. If you're in a swing state or a purple district and it's near election time, then you can be quite certain that most of the ads during that break will be political. Yet there is no reason to assume that the people watching that football game want to watch that ad. The ad is the price they pay for watching the game. Most people pay that price reluctantly.

That reluctance in turn affects the strategy of the ad. On the margin, it makes negative ads more effective than positive ads. If you've interrupted my game, and you start telling me about your great ideas for health care, my anger—whether conscious or not—is going to be directed at you. But if your ad talks about how terrible your opponent is, then that negative message will register and may even be reinforced by the nonconsensual nature of the communication. Describe your opponent as a liar, and even if the person hearing the ad thinks "God, do I hate political ads," the ad is likely to have an effect. Somewhere at the back of the mind of the person hearing the ad, the opponent is weakened. And over time, the effect is either to disgust the viewer enough to disengage from the election, or, ideally, to disgust the viewer enough to support your candidate.[31]

Either result is a victory for the advertiser. As much as politicians complain about the low turnout of American voters, the truth is, they love it. The disgusted are not controllable. They're not predictable. They can't be easily counted. It's easier to build a strategy for victory if you can keep them at home. So turning them off is not a failure. It is instead one less uncertain vote in the election.[32]

And obviously, if the negative ad turns the voter in your favor, that's an even bigger victory. One more vote for you, one less for your opponent. Either way, you win with negative ads—which explains why in 2016, close to 50 percent of the ads in key races in the House, and more than 50 percent in key races in the Senate, were negative.[33] And in 2016 especially they were extremely ugly.

The business model of American politics—at least in the space of nonconsensual political communication—is thus ugly. Sure, every campaign starts off idealistically. Every candidate promises never to go negative. But as campaigns get close, the politicians learn an important lesson. They get rewarded the uglier they make it. And so it should be no surprise that negative advertising will increase, and as it does, more people will tune out.

Of course, not every voter will tune out. There is a small slice of America who will show up, regardless of the advertising. The politically engaged can't be kept away, so the politically engaged are the ones who pick our representatives.

And that itself becomes a problem. Because what we know about the politically engaged is that they too don't represent us. They show up, but they are the extremists. On both the right and the left, the politically engaged are far removed from the ordinary citizen.[34] But the politicians must respond to them, if the politicians are to be elected by them. And so they do: as those who show up become more extreme, representatives become more extreme, and our politics becomes more extreme. That is to say, our politics becomes less and less like us.

This point is related to one I made about the incentives of advertising in chapter 2, but it is different. There is a *where* to speech: where it happens affects what gets said. When we push speech into a nonconsensual space and that nonconsensual space becomes dominant, then that changes the character of what can be said.

There's almost nothing we can do—we, in America—about this dynamic through law. At least, there's nothing we could do to restrict the nature or character of the political speech that happens in these nonconsensual spaces through law. The First Amendment is a pretty absolute bar against the government burdening one kind of speech over the other. There couldn't be a negative-ad tax, or an effort to restrict ads because they were negative. It's most possible to imagine restricting short ads.[35]

But rather than restricting ads, why not try enhancing them? Rather than forcing less, why not pay for more? We need more spaces in which the expectation is that the audience will do the work that understanding requires. That they will, in other words, focus enough to see more than the slogan.

Imagine we did this by paying people to watch political ads. Imagine you would watch an ad—preferably a longer ad—and then answer some questions. If you answer the questions correctly, you get paid. Every voter would get a number of chances to get it right to get paid. But the very act of choosing to listen would change the character of what could be said. If I stepped into your room to hear you persuade me to vote for you, and you spent all your time trashing your opponent, that would register. More directly than ten-second negative ads do today, it would affect how I thought about you.

These changes wouldn't end the negative ad, but they could make it sufficiently less valuable. If the return from the alternative was greater than the return from the negative ad, the negative ad would fade. And if the return from engaged and serious—I don't mean boring; I predict these ads would be wonderful and hilarious—consensual political speech increased, then it could easily drive out the demand for the nonconsensual political speech.

With Space to Think

As I've hinted, for about six weeks beginning in August 2015, I was spending endless time on cable news shows. By the end of that time, I had a sense of what was needed in that context. That is, what was needed from me if I was to succeed in that context. That's not to say I was good at it. But I got it. I understood what would be required for my words to be heard: punchy and short; preferably a quip that fit on Twitter; preferably something that triggers what people already think; preferably something that captured the essence of an argument in a title.

This sensibility came from an environment in which no subject got more than five, maybe ten minutes of cable TV time. Cable news shows are platforms for advertising. The news gets ten minutes tops before it turns back to the ads. Those ads add up. According to the *Wall Street Journal*, the average commercial time on cable TV per hour was 15.8 minutes in 2014, up from 14.5 in 2009.[36]

In obvious ways, this format constrains what can be said. It's fine for some things. It's perfectly appropriate for recounting the rundown from the day's football games. It's fine for reporting the weather, or the movies that are trending at the theater. It's fine, that is, for any content that needs nothing more than showing, rather than explaining. It is perfect for the stuff that simply asks the audience to agree, or that enrages the audience by disagreeing.

Yet often, at least we could hope, political speech requires something more. Often it requires not just affirmation or outrage. Often it requires understanding or explanation. Often it requires living space—a space for the idea to develop or mature.

Without really recognizing it, I tripped into such a context when I was asked to be a guest on the podcast *Mixed Mental Arts*, with Bryan Callen and Hunter Maats. After we finished a conversation that went on for about an hour, I asked, "So how are you going to distribute this? Will you excerpt ten minutes? Or a collection of quips?" My host was puzzled. "The whole thing—start to finish." And I realized I had entered a whole new world.

Podcasting is not new, but its recent growth is quite phenomenal. By 2017, *Forbes* estimated that 67 million people were listening to podcasts on a monthly basis—about the same number following Twitter. That means one in four Americans over the age of twelve. The platform has grown 45 percent since 2015, 180 percent since 2009.

But what's most striking is the long form. The average podcast is forty-five minutes long. And astonishingly, according to Edison Research, 85 percent of people listen to the end.[37]

The podcast is consensual. It doesn't interrupt your day. It's not a pop-up on a Web page. It doesn't grab you as you go to get lunch and pull you aside. It is not the thing you have to watch to be able to watch the game.

It's something you choose to listen to—as you choose to read a book or watch a movie. But because of the change in technology, you can do this while you're doing lots of other things, too. While commuting, or jogging, or waiting for a delayed flight to take off.

And because you can listen as you want, you can listen for as long as you want. The conversation continues, like the best of a dinner conversation, for hours at a time. When I remarked on this fact while on the Joe Rogan podcast, he observed we had been speaking for two hours and fifteen minutes. I couldn't believe it. I was a believer.

The podcasters today live in a data-shallow universe. Podcasters know, of course, how many download their podcasts, and how many listen. But they don't know precisely which parts of the conversation are the most interesting. There is no dial testing in a podcast. The host is simply telling a story, and as that story unfolds, he or she develops it. Rogan was convinced he wouldn't change how he did it regardless of the format, or the data he was given. Maybe that's true. Maybe that's true about Rogan. But if technology gave the podcaster a constant opportunity to understand how the words were mattering, that would change what was said. If there were a minute-by-minute report about how many were watching, you could be damn sure that at least some podcasters would follow the dial.

This is another example of a phenomenon described well by Tim Wu in his fantastic book, *The Attention Merchants*. When broadcast television was born, the network executives took seriously their obligation to cover the news. So they covered the news, while making extraordinary profits in entertainment earned by their extraordinary market share. But when Nielsen started providing the networks with reports on audience sizes, those numbers started disciplining the networks and network executives. News turned out to be expensive—and not because of the cost. Rather, the expense was also the effect on the market share—interesting and important attracted less than funny and compelling. The networks started reacting to this data. The mix and character of the news changed.

The podcast doesn't suffer from this dynamic—just now. It therefore provides a critically valuable channel through which to convey the ideas needed for democracy. As it does so, it constructs we the people differently from how ordinary television does just now. From the perspective of the slow democracy movement, it constructs us better.

And Laugh

Politics is never about getting us all to sing kumbaya. It is always about rallying *us* against *them*. But there is a way that comedy can do this that keeps that fight honest. The jokes only work if they can tap into something that is true or understood. Comedy works by being one step ahead of what we all are coming to see and by pulling us along.

Comedy Central is, of course, central in this story for us right now. People on the right might see it as unfairly critical to people on the right. No doubt there is that unfairness. But what's striking to anyone who watches the best of these shows is just how nonpartisan the attacks can be. Democrats are ridiculed just as Republicans are ridiculed, even when they are being praised.

How such comedy works is a brilliantly complicated question. In every totalitarian or authoritarian society, comedy flourishes, because it is the one space where the truth can be told without consequence, because the truth is only revealed indirectly. But I believe political comedy flourishes in our society because it feeds a political desire in an entertaining way. Not with a lecture, but with a joke. And not a joke guaranteed not to disturb, but a joke by a comedian who has earned the right to get in our face.

It is striking that the most successful comedy network reads liberal, while the most successful news network (not just now, but over the past decade) is conservative. Even *The Colbert Report* was a liberal playing a conservative to mock conservatives. Maybe this is the product of decades of essentially conservative government. The Democrats have controlled all three branches just four years since 1981 (the Republicans have controlled it for eight years and have controlled the presidency for twenty). Maybe if there had been more years of Democrats, there would be a whole generation of conservative comedians.

But the critical point is that here, too, understanding gets conveyed, and not in a balanced or "fair" way, but in a way that motivates. Each side needs this, and if Comedy Central is the left's version of Fox News, then we can certainly say that the right needs its own Comedy Central (even if we would not say that the left needs its own version of Fox News, whether it has one, MSNBC, or not). Both sides need a way to take the mic from the other side, while also checking the hypocrisy of their own side. Exploding the opportunities of comedy—and embracing its importance—is thus another course in the slow democracy movement.

Practicing Empathy

In 2011, Showtime launched the television series *Homeland*, initially starring Claire Danes and Damian Lewis. The plot surrounded Lewis as Sergeant Brody, a just-released prisoner of war in Iraq. Unclear to the audience initially, it turns out Brody has been turned against America. Danes, as CIA agent Carrie Mathison—brilliant and compelling— suspects it before anyone else does. But as is her apparent nature, she complicates that understanding by becoming sexually involved with Brody. Over the course of the first three seasons, Brody returns home as a hero, gets elected to Congress, almost assassinates the president, flees the country, kills the Iranian intelligence chief, and is then executed by Iran.[38]

The striking fact about this extraordinarily compelling series is its complexity. The show pulls in every direction. No one is left wondering whether terrorism is good, but everyone is left understanding better the complex story that produces terrorists. The consequence of watching that series is a different understanding—of American foreign policy, of terrorism, of the Middle East, of the human aspect of that endless struggle.

That's not to say that the story is fair or balanced or true. I share the views of many that the image of Islam crafted through this story is thin and incomplete and wrong. I also cringe with many at the self-satisfied certainty of even the most compelling characters.[39]

But the point is not that the story speaks truth. It is that the story meets America where America is, and moves the audience as it develops. America begins with a radically skewed and incomplete understanding of "The War for the Greater Middle East," as historian Andrew Bacevich describes it in one of his many extraordinary accounts of that deep and unjust American blunder.[40] It begins with a ridiculously romanticized view of its own Death Star–like engagements throughout the region. No doubt the very creators of the series are themselves responsible for some of that ignorance—in describing the new series as the "standout TV drama" in 2011, *The New Yorker* described it as "an apology for *24.*"[41] But whether responsible or not, the reality is that we start with a nation that fundamentally views the injustice of these wars as justice, and the cause of America as right. And over the course of the many seasons of the show, it moves that ignorant audience to a deeper, if still partial, understanding.

And astonishingly so. Because if you had set as a project the idea of teaching these ideas to the millions who watched that show, it would have been literally impossible. Even Walter Cronkite could not have conveyed the depth of understanding that Carrie Matheson does. No professor in a college classroom could; no public lecture series in towns across America could. No place or person at all could do what that series did for the millions who watched it.

This is a form of art that is increasingly critical—and available—to democracy today. Think about the series *House of Cards*—dramatically as compelling (at least in the first seasons), even if substantively less obscure. When *House of Cards* launched, Netflix released every episode in the first season at the same time. What that meant was that it had essentially released a thirteen-hour movie. That length meant that the story could be that much more involved, or complex, or real. Like ordinary life, we could come to understand the characters of that story, and the facts that constrain them, much more completely than ever before.

Of course, it has always been the case that the great lessons of morality and politics have been taught through literature, not philosophy. Society understood itself through the novel, not the political tract. Whether Jane Austen, Edith Wharton, or Upton Sinclair, it was in the richness of stories that society came to understand what it was, and then from that understanding resolved to become something different. Professors and pundits are just who we say matters; who we know matters is something quite different.

The difference today is just that these narratives get carried to video. Novels are great, but their reach is small. Television reaches orders of magnitude differently. (Not always: there have been more than 500 million Harry Potter books sold; at whatever reading rate, that easily beats the best of television.) And as television embraces the ethic of shows like *Homeland,* it becomes an increasingly important part of democratic culture. The truths that we can take for granted are different. What America understood about terrorism and the Middle East on September 12, 2001, is fundamentally different from what we understand today, and not because of Fox or MSNBC, not because of universities or fancy lectures series, not because of pundits or professors writing books. We understand differently because we have read deeper into the story. And within the very best of this creativity lives an important ethic.

What is that ethic? Obviously it cannot lecture. It cannot moralize. It is not a sermon. It is not a history lesson. It must be a story that captures and compels. But if it is to contribute, then it must be more than empty calories. It must have an informational nutrition that leaves the audience satisfied *and* better informed. It must carry us into a story in a way that leaves us understanding differently, not just more facts, but more humanity. I should know not only why the other see as they do. I should know them.

In describing a strategy to respond to the weakness in American democracy, Professor Kirby Goidel advises that journalists

> ditch the objectivity norm . . . and tell stories with powerful narratives, depth, and complexity. Provide audiences with developed, intellectually honest perspective, not raw information. Seek the truth based on the best available evidence and expert judgment rather than focusing on the narrow "gotcha" journalism of fact-checking.[42]

That different form of journalism, Goidel argues, will "do more to engage and mobilize" than the practices we inherit from our parents.

There is an important point here. We take it for granted that knowledge must be delivered to us in a particular way. But my whole aim in this book is to emphasize just how contingent, historically, any particular way is. We've inherited a wildly rosy picture of our past. But our past was different from what happened before it. Democratic society was not born with Walter Cronkite. And the model of learning or understanding for democracy was not created by the *Wall Street Journal* or *NBC Nightly News*. We need to stop imagining fitting ourselves into models of understanding that are foreign, and think instead about fitting what we need to know into the way we want to experience life now.

And thus does the gap between fiction and documentary shrink (while the demand for documentary skyrockets[43]). We have a taste for something more. And this incredible market of creativity begins to satisfy that demand.

The measure here is not neutrality. The measure is depth and understanding. What's extraordinary about *Homeland* is that we don't really even know the politics of those at the core of the story. Or if they were ever revealed, they quickly faded to the background. Instead, this story about the critical political decisions that our nation has made can be told without the central fact of politics making any important appearance at all. Narrative is not political, it is human. And understanding comes from stories told by humans, not lectures by professors at Yale (or even Harvard).

And so has it always been. When I was a student studying philosophy at Cambridge University, the then most prominent bad boy of the Anglo-American philosophical tradition, Richard Rorty, came to present a paper. Rorty's essential argument, as a philosopher, was that philosophy was useless, that the truths or justice or insight that the Queen of Science pretended to teach were fake. The queen was wearing no clothes, Rorty insisted. And those of us training in philosophy, he argued, had to have the courage to acknowledge that truth and move on.

This was a long time ago. Apartheid was still the rule in South Africa. And just after Rorty finished his introduction to the paper we were to discuss, one of the leading local philosophers, young and romantic in his passion, took the floor for the first question. On and on he droned about how much philosophy had to teach the world; how truth and justice were essential; how only with such knowledge could we actually make the world better; end suffering; deliver justice; end apartheid in South Africa. There was a flourish at the end of his speech. His passion was just icing on a cake of the most articulate and brilliant prose, the sort that the obsessive and perverse English educational system produced in spades. The room broke out in applause, and we philosophers and philosopher-wannabes felt vindicated in our fight against this traitor to our field.

Rorty waited for the room to quiet down. Then he waited for about a minute more, as the room sat silent in anticipation. And then he said just this: "If I wanted to convince a white South African about the injustice of apartheid, I would give him a novel by Alan Paton, not Kant's Critique of Pure Reason. That's the point. And that is everything."

He stopped. That was it. A colleague had harangued him for maybe ten minutes. He responded in a couple of sentences. After ten seconds, some applauded. Some spoke out loud in outrage. A number of fellows and professors got up and left. And then the seminar continued, just like any other seminar in the history of Cambridge.

What Rorty was teaching about philosophy we must learn about politics more generally. Our aim should not be to force the public to read Kant. Or Rawls. Or Al Gore. Our aim should be an ecology of stories that develop a deeper and more complete understanding of the politics of America, if not the world. Change happens in these stories, not in the courtrooms, and certainly not on the floor of Congress. And it happens when we find ways to tell stories that connect with the values that we have.

The history of the struggle for gay rights in America is the clearest example of this lesson. When the courts and the politicians first tried to adjudicate the struggles that emerged once gay and lesbian activists pressed their civil rights cause to the fore, it was embarrassing. Literally embarrassing. John F. Kennedy's one appointment to the Supreme Court, Justice Byron White, wrote his most embarrassing opinion of his thirty-one years on the Court, upholding a law that regulated sodomy (*Bowers v. Hardwicke* [1986]). In Colorado, a referendum to forbid civil rights laws from applying to gays and lesbians passed overwhelmingly—53 percent to 47 percent.[44] In California—*California*—an amendment to ban same-sex marriage passed almost as overwhelmingly—52 percent to 48 percent.[45]

But in the culture space, a different dynamic was developing, as a different story was being told. Early in the arc of this narrative, there were explicitly political films about the burdens of being gay. In 1993, Tom Hanks broke a critical barrier when he played a gay lawyer who was dying of AIDS.[46] Very quickly, LGBTQ characters moved from the outside to the center—and then to the normal. The cultural narrative was not about gays and lesbians as special or different. It was about humans as humans, characters in shows who experienced the same love and hate and good and bad as anyone.

As that cultural narrative matured, it embarrassed the political and especially legal fights, because it quickly collapsed the foundation for the harassment and hatred within the law. Ten years after the Supreme Court had called it "facetious at best" to claim that the Constitution protected homosexuals who wanted to engage in sodomy, a conservative justice on the Supreme Court, Anthony Kennedy, wrote an opinion striking down Colorado's ban on civil rights laws benefiting gays. Seventeen years after that, the Court reversed *Bowers*.[47] A dozen years after that, it struck down laws that banned gay marriage.[48]

Many on the right believed that this judicial activism would trigger a new and emboldened politics against the courts. It didn't. The backlash fizzled. Very few could even recognize the justifications for denying to some the freedom to affirm their love and commitment for someone else. It was no accident that the lawyers who successfully challenged the California referendum against same-sex marriage were two of the most famous, and famously politically opposed, lawyers in America—Ted Olson, who had won *Bush v. Gore* for the Republicans, and David Boies, who had lost that same case for the Democrats.

Many look at this history and insist that it teaches us where politics must happen. "We need a movie to press campaign finance reform." "If only there were a movie about economic inequality." But I think the real lesson is about how understanding happens today. The narrative that touched the lives of LGBTQ Americans *while telling an ordinary and compelling story* conveys understanding, not membership in the American Civil Liberties Union. It changes the way people *see,* not what they *argue.* These stories show, they don't tell. And through the discipline of telling stories that captured attention and passion, they help us *feel* something we hadn't *understood* before.

In the long history of humanity, stories have always been how knowledge is conveyed. They are also how lies and bigotry and hatred are conveyed. (Think *Birth of a Nation,* from 1915.) My point is not that their virtue is guaranteed. My point instead is simply that this is how we humans come to know. There are small slices of life when we can be taught. There are moments when we seek out lessons ourselves. But in the main, how we come to understand the world will turn on the stories that get told to us. And how.

As the ecology of communication continues to evolve, as the rich diversity of content continues to mature, we can't direct. We can only hope and hint. The government can't tell the creators what they should create. But we all individually can reward creators for the kind of work they give us. Just as healthy eating begins with people making choices, so too does healthy understanding begin with people making choices. We need to seek out and celebrate the stories that enrich our understanding. We need to walk past the stories that simply confirm the ignorance we already possess.

If there is hope for all-of-us, it is here. Complex stories alone can't fix democracy. Any hope depends upon our fixing *them,* and I'd say, first. But if fixing them has the consequence that I believe it would, it will lessen the pressure on us to be the crazies the politicians need us to be. And when that pressure releases, it will give us space for the effect of complex stories. Seeing *them* differently will help us see *ourselves* differently, and in seeing, learn.

THERE IS AN UNDERSTANDING that we as citizens need. We need to look to where that understanding could reasonably come from. When people my age or older start lecturing that we need better civics classes in high school, we need to be more aggressive in our rejection of that pipe dream of reform. First, civics classes never taught the injustice of Jim Crow. And second, the understanding of a citizen at sixteen is not the habit of understanding that citizens generally need now.

Instead, the understanding we need will come through practices that respect certain norms. Wikipedia, for example, works only because the editors are constantly enforcing a norm of neutrality and evidence. That's never easy but it is essential, because on balance it produces a resource that tries as much as possible to remain grounded in truth.

The creators of culture must find a similar set of norms, not in substance but in form. The constant question must be, What understanding does this convey, for all sides and all people? These norms can be established by a surprisingly small number of people: 25 percent can trigger large-scale social change.[49] That's not to say that we need an HBO series to help us understand pedophiles. But *Big Love* certainly did change the understanding about polygamists. Great culture here will be like great culture at any moment in human history—constrained by the needs and loves of humans at the time, subject to the steel walls of reality.

We won't ever banish Fox News or Breitbart. Neither *Morning Joe* nor Rachel Maddow. The talking heads on daytime cable will continue to blather. The constant drumbeat of Twitter-deep understanding is never going away.

But we can discipline ourselves to tune it out. We can choose to tune it out. And more important, we can look for understanding in many different places. The obligation of citizenship is understanding, not a reading list. The politicians know what they want you to see. That is not the measure of what you should watch.

In Contexts We Can Trust

When you walk into your doctor's office, you expect something. Even if you can't describe precisely what you expect, you expect something. You expect that she or he will treat you, keeping your interests in front. If your doctor tells you that you need an expensive drug therapy, you expect that's because you actually need that. If you later learned that your doctor had recommended the expensive therapy over a cheaper generic therapy solely because she got a ten-thousand-dollar payment from the drug company, you'd be rightly angry.

That's because doctors—and lawyers, and certain financial advisors and a few others—have a specific relationship to their clients. The law calls it a "fiduciary relationship." A fiduciary is obligated—by law—not to act against the interests of her client. And if there is a conflict in the interests of the client and the fiduciary, the fiduciary must act in the client's interest. He or she, that is, must sacrifice his or her own interest to benefit the client. That means, in the hypothetical I just gave, that the doctor must recommend the generic treatment, even though it "costs" (in the sense of forgoing a gain) him or her ten thousand dollars.

Law professors Jack Balkin and Jonathan Zittrain have proposed that we extend fiduciary law to those who gather data about us online. They propose using the law, in other words, to create an online context that we could trust, so that as we go about online, we don't need to worry at every step about whether what we're doing is going to come back and haunt us. Or worry that a corporation with a friendly face is just a systematic online con.[50]

This is an enormously important conceptual step, even if its boundaries remain unclear. In my view, the most critical part of the insight is its rejection of the idea that the measure of justice is consent. Privacy law and online practices have assumed that if the lawyers can bury the permission in a click-wrap terms of service, then all bets are off. It's the duty of the consumer, this view has it, to read the policies. And if you don't like the policies, then go someplace else.

That idea is just nuts. There is no way that we could negotiate our life online reading, let alone understanding, the muck called "terms of service." (Researchers at Carnegie Mellon calculated it would take seventy-six days to read all of the privacy policies one encounters in a year.[51]) And even if we could, it is an extraordinary social waste to imagine a system that requires us constantly to police exactly what our cable company is trying to get away with. (The same researchers put the cost of such reading at $781 billion annually.) Terms of service routinely give the author the right to modify the terms, subject to your ability to opt out. It is a bizarre from of crazy that would even have imagined that this level of consumer protection is the right level online—or anywhere.

	BENEFITS SOCIETY	HARMS SOCIETY
BENEFITS USER	Amazon books	Ad-driven news feeds
HARMS USER	Identifying predators	Exploiting addicts

This is not the book to map out a full theory of privacy and how it ought to be regulated. But with the distinctions I offered in chapter 2, mapped within this matrix, we can make a stab at understanding how these digital spaces must be reformed if trust is to be bred.

The clear cases remain clear. When Amazon infers I would like Jack Balkin's latest book, it's a good thing that it tells me that—even if Amazon also benefits from me buying that book. And if Facebook or Microsoft or anyone else were to take facts about me and infer that I had some sort of disease, and then sell that inference to an insurance company, that's a bad thing—because that platform is benefiting at my expense.

Between these clear cases, fiduciary law would have some hard cases as well. Consider the amazing mapping app Waze. Building upon user reports, and tracked data about driving conditions, Waze recommends a way for you to get from point A to point B. If the path it recommends is clearly the fastest, then that's obviously unproblematically okay. Equally clear, as Balkin and Zittrain write, would be if Waze took me on a detour past a fast-food restaurant, slowing me down, simply because Waze got paid by the restaurant. That's an example of a conflict between the client and the fiduciary; fiduciary law says that conflict must be resolved to favor the client.

But what if Waze takes me along a slower path, past a poké bowl shop, because it knows I like poké bowls, and it's lunchtime? Should the fact that Waze gets paid if I stop make that a violation of its fiduciary obligation?

Or even harder: what if Waze takes me on a slight detour to evaluate whether that's in fact a faster path than it currently predicts? Here, I'm being experimented on, but for the benefit of both Waze and all the other drivers like me. Can I be asked to sacrifice for the collective, even if I'm also sacrificing for Waze?

Those are hard questions. They are nothing compared to the puzzle at the center of this chapter: what's the obligation of the platform when serving me stuff it knows I want individually, but which we know is harmful to society generally—simply because it benefits the platform specifically?

There are some clear parallels in real life. If you drive to a bar, we all understand why it's okay to tell the bar owner to stop serving you after some number of drinks. You may ask for another—so it's something you want—and the owner of the bar might want to sell you another—to make more money—but the public has a real interest in stopping you from drinking and driving. So your private preference, even added to the bar owner's mercenary desire, is outweighed by the public's need.

Or imagine the bar used a certain food—like nuts or salty chips—to drive people to order more drinks than they otherwise would. Specifically, it discovered that without the nuts, people drank moderately, but with the nuts, they drank excessively. In this case, we could imagine either controlling the drinks or controlling the nuts—both get us moderate drinking.

Then consider one final twist: Imagine the owner of the bar is a pharmacologist, who has studied precisely how to spike drinks so that people want to drink much more than they otherwise would. Nuts are a kind of spike, no doubt, but the spike is more obvious, more transparent, maybe more clearly something the customer should regulate himself. Drugs are another matter. If the bar owner is spiking a drink with a substance he knows will make the customer drink more, then once again, fiduciary law would forbid the bar owner from using that substance to induce the client to buy even more.

These cases about a bar are different for an important reason we'll see in a moment. But we should be clear right away that the problem of Facebook is a million times harder to solve than the problem of drinking and driving. Because unlike drinking, you have a constitutional right to speak. And unlike regulations of alcohol levels while driving, the First Amendment plainly bans the government from regulating speech except when there's a compelling interest. Whether we could imagine any such interest or not, as the First Amendment has been interpreted, it is extremely unlikely that the Supreme Court would uphold any regulation aiming to force Facebook to change the way it encourages people to engage on questions of politics.

So in the balance of this section, I'm going to imagine we're talking about a jurisdiction not governed by the First Amendment—specifically, Britain.

The reason is that in 2016, Britain too suffered a critical political catastrophe maybe more clearly driven by social media than the American election was. In June 2016, the nation voted to leave the European Union (EU), stunning an elite who had thought the idea just nuts.

Analysis after that election strongly linked the results to the effect of social media.[52] The online campaign against remaining in the EU was passionate—and manipulated. Thousands of pounds in advertising was spent to drive the results against remaining. Those ads were grounded in lies and misinformation. They were paid for by entities that were crafted for that election alone. In the end, it was hard to avoid the conclusion that Facebook had caused Brexit, in just the sense that its pattern of media had changed the votes of enough citizens in Britain to bring about the referendum's result.

The Brexit story fits the bar analogy to a t. Facebook is the bar. People are coming to the bar to hang out and talk. At first, the drinks facilitate the talk. Eventually the drinks inhibit understanding. According to the critics of Facebook, its secret sauce was in effect spiking the conversation. Advertisers took advantage of that spiking. The spiking quickly got out of control. On June 24, the day after the vote, much of Britain woke up and couldn't quite remember what had happened the night before.

Against the background of American First Amendment law, there's nothing in the story of Facebook and Brexit that the government could have remedied. The complaint, boiled down as a First Amendment analysis would see it, is that some speech was more powerful than other speech. The cure for that problem, to the First Amendment maven, is just more speech. I'm of the view that this view misses something. But I'm also of the view that we will only ever convince American courts that it is missing something if we can see the effect of other nations regulating these problems differently—at least if those regulations work.

So imagine there is a new vote on Brexit—which, at this writing, still seems possible. What could the British government do to protect the process the second time around?

The conceptually clear response would be to ban the spiking of drinks—which in this context would mean selling any ads attached to Brexit-related messaging. Yet this proposal would be attacked as being both too little and too much:

Too little, because the strategy of fake news and division is often executed far from the political issue you're trying to affect. In the United States, for example, the Russians didn't buy anti-Clinton ads; they bought ads intending to sow division on the left (to suppress the vote on the left) and on the right (to spike participation on the right). A rule that banned ads about the political issue at stake would completely miss this strategy—and hence maybe the most important technique used by the corrupting forces.

Too much, because the strategy would block the ads of legitimate speakers, if we can make that distinction, as well as illegitimate. It would block the Labour Party as well as the Russians. Even without a First Amendment, it should be clear why that result is contrary to democracy.

These two concerns would be addressed by a tweak to the anti-spiking rule. The rule could ban all advertising for a short period around the elections, but then permit exceptions for recognized and previously registered entities, both political and non. So political parties would get a pass as well as Boots or Marks & Spencer. But ads by anyone else would be banned for a period—say a month—before the vote by the public.

In the United States, it is just slightly less difficult to limit ads as it is to regulate the content of the ads. But outside the United States, that distinction is more available. And we can see quite directly why it would be less of a free speech concern for the government to ban ads regardless of content than for it to ban ads because of the content. It makes sense for government to avoid the consequences of intoxication; it does not make sense for the government to be allowed to pick which messages it believes are crazy and which are not.

What the world needs now is for governments everywhere to experiment with these differently structured responses. Britain would be perfectly free (so long as the EU courts don't step in) to ban Facebook ads, or to ban ads by unregistered political or economic actors, within the period leading up to the election. The world would learn a great deal if it tried that strategy on a new Brexit vote, and if it then required Facebook to produce the data to evince how that strategy mattered. We don't know yet whether it would matter, or whether it would matter enough. But we do know that our democracies are extremely vulnerable, given the incentives of "surveillance capitalism," and of entities keen to twist democracy against the democrats. Democracies everywhere should be experimenting with ways to build those protections, because governments everywhere (and especially in Europe) should recognize just how tenuous the experiment of democracy remains.

If those experiments happened, and proved successful, we might imagine them having an effect even here. Because even in the United States, we have a long tradition of protecting the balloting process from the corrosive effect of political speech. As you approach a ballot in almost every jurisdiction, you cross a line. Once across that line, political speech is banned. You can't have posters. You can't hand out leaflets. You can't proselytize. You can't give speeches. Every core First Amendment activity is suppressible, once you cross that line. Because in the tradition of American democracy, we have learned that speech in certain contexts can do more harm than good.[53]

Banning ads, of course, won't end the ability of people to speak about politics on Facebook, or even to share stories they find interesting. It won't make "fake news" go away; it won't turn suspicious and skeptical souls into believers. But it would change the business model of intervention by reducing the return fundamentally. Instead of buying ads, you'd have to persuade many people to follow your crazy idea. That persuasion would be more difficult, but not impossible. And if you succeeded, then your success would be more clearly the product of democracy than a success achieved through spiking the drinks of a voting population.

American law would permit the government to impose a fiduciary duty on platforms—especially through the technique Balkin and Zittrain suggest, where platforms opt into that regime to avoid conflicting and burdensome state regulation. We should certainly take that first step and begin the process of deciding which uses of data are consistent with a fiduciary duty, and which are not. We should take this step, whether or not we take the other steps that many right-thinking souls believe we must take with platform industries—such as antitrust breakups, or significant taxation of the business model. My suggestion of some reforms is not a rejection of others, too, just as my mapping one corner of the concerns around surveillance capitalism is not an endorsement of the status quo elsewhere.

But by moving in this way, even with just baby steps, we should recognize again just how stark the landscape has become. With both broadcasting and the Internet, commercial ends do not create a context we can trust. That makes it urgent for us to find the interventions that might restore that trust.

SINCE THE BEGINNING OF time, elites have whined about the people. "The people are ignorant." "The people can't be trusted." "We need to build institutions to protect us from the people."

During some of that time, those words could be uttered directly. During most of our recent times, those ideas are only ever conveyed indirectly. Sometimes they are gussied up with fancy political science to show our inconsistencies or ignorance. Sometimes they are only hinted at, with a roll of the eyes.

I have no doubt about the potential of "we, the people." If we could build institutions and practices that don't render us ridiculous, we could learn once again just how powerful an idea democracy is.

Those institutions must take account of the technology of the time: Broadcasting is over. Now what? And those practices must take account of the nature of people: We can learn, all of us can, if the lessons are framed in a way that we want to hear. We can learn, all of us can, if they are offered in a context we can trust.

If we're to craft a representative we—one that we're proud to say represents us—then we must change both how we come to understand and how we are represented after we understand. As I've described in this section, we can summarize those changes in a single line: We should be doing less, when we choose, with space to think, and laugh, and practice empathy, in contexts we can trust.

Those changes are all possible. They are also necessary. Whether they are possible for us—both because of our constitution and the powers that would resist them—is unclear. We must act as if they are.

CHAPTER 5

What "Fixed" Would Get Us

THE REFORMS I'VE DESCRIBED WOULD REMOVE REPRESENTATION-distorting muck within the systems we have evolved. It would give us a clearer and more reliable way to understand what we the people believe or want or desire. But those two consequences do not mean that we should increase the frequency or intensity of democracy. To the contrary, those two consequences should reconfirm the critical value of *representative* democracy, and the ideal that our representatives should represent us.

It is a luxury that we should demand more vigorously. If you hired a lawyer to represent you in some transaction, such as buying a house, negotiating an employment contract, or settling a dispute about an accident, what you'd want is someone to represent you. You'd want the experience and judgment to represent you. No doubt the lawyer needs to understand you and what you want. She needs to stay committed to the idea that she is representing *you* (and not angling for a job with the firm representing the person you are suing). But in that representing, she needs to do her job. A constant list of question back to you is not "doing your job." To the contrary: "Hey, that's what I pay *you* for."

It is that sense of representation that we must also cultivate within democratic society. We must first ensure that representatives actually represent us—in the sense that who we are has affected who they are.

But once that representative is selected, we want her to do her job. We want her to understand us, and then act as strongly as she can within the system of our democracy to advance the interests that we—as Americans—have.

In that process, however, we have to have a clear sense of the project of democracy. Democracy is that system we have crafted to give people who disagree with each other a way to live together. It is the mechanism for resolving that disagreement. What that means is that our representatives are not just our paid shoppers. We don't just give them the equivalent of a list and expect they are going to return from Washington with the groceries we've demanded. No doubt they should return with as much as they can, given the constraint of governing the nation we need to govern. But that constraint means we won't all get what we all want. That constraint must also mean that every compromise that a representative makes cannot be rendered as a compromise of principle.

And here we begin to focus on a very different sense of the term *representative*.

So far in this book I have used the term to mean "equally representative." That the rules, for example, get crafted so that every citizen has an equal opportunity to have her views count. This sense of the term emphasizes the ongoing control by citizens over their government. In the language of our framers, it is the "dependence" of our governors upon us. In its extreme, it imagines us having a perpetual ability to register our views—of course, equally and proportionally—and have those views count. This is the world envisioned by scads of apps and websites, all designed to give us, the people, a million ways to make our views known.

But this is *not* the democracy that I am advocating for. To the contrary, in a very specific sense, I want less representativeness. Following the foundational work of Harvard professor Jane Mansbridge, I believe we need representatives who are selected (by us), not sanctioned (by us). And we need to think about the process of choosing our representatives based on whom we would trust to represent us well. The promise we should make is not that we will monitor them day to day. Instead, we are asking them to represent us, and we will reelect them based on the character of that representation.[1]

The opposite model imagines us constantly monitoring our representatives and sanctioning them when they don't do what we want. That's what, for example, lobbyists do. It's what special interest groups in Washington, D.C., do. They spend their time watching and responding. They, in other words, sanction.

Yet in that process of sanctioning, they weaken the opportunity for representative democracy to function effectively. If a representative must work with others to craft solutions for the nation as a whole, then there will be times when we, in our district, will lose. There will be times when she can't do something that we want. But if she is to think about her job in the right way, we need her to think about her job, not vote by vote, but through the integrity of her representation.

Because governing is difficult. There are critical choices that a government must make. Those choices involve trade-offs. Should we benefit this group or that? Should we benefit today or tomorrow? In answering those questions, our representatives must embrace a critical norm. The question should always be simply: what is in the interests of our nation, or as I (Lessig) would wish, in the interests of the world?

The selection model is better from this perspective because of the representatives it would select. As Mansbridge describes, certain occupations—and we could hope that representative would be one—"attract agents whose intrinsic motivations include what might be called public spirit." This is true not exclusively, but ideally, primarily. No one expects a doctor to work for free, but no one wants a doctor who's in it just for the money.

Yet "public spirit" is vulnerable. Certain factors scare it away. Cynicism, for example: if I know everyone's cynical about my motivations, I'm less likely to care about being public spirited. Or extrinsic incentives, for another example: if I'm being paid or rewarded for specific outcomes, I'm less likely to care about being public spirited. Or finally, monitoring: if you're constantly watching me, you're saying you don't trust me; if you say you don't trust me, I'm less likely to care about being public spirited. Call me a liar and I'll behave like a liar. Treat me as if I am just a self-interested politician and guess what: that's exactly who I'll become.

In each of these ways, as Mansbridge describes, "public spirit" can be crowded out. Institutional designers keen to preserve public spirit should therefore avoid these factors to the extent that is possible,[2] so that representatives can remain focused on a public, and not just on their own private interest.

Practically everything in Washington today works against this ideal of selection. The city is filled with monitors: they're called lobbyists, and since the Legislative Reorganization Act of 1970 made practically everything our representatives do transparent, they've had an endless source of input to feed into their sanctioning machine.[3] And lobbyists are not the only source of monitors: public interest and advocacy groups rally their members based on good votes and bad votes. Scorecards rally funders based on who is doing what we want, and who is not. That funding becomes a kind of extrinsic incentive that makes it easier for the representative to ignore the public spirit. And the cynicism that is spread throughout the nation then gets concentrated in the district: only chumps work for the public; everyone else works to get reelected.

This perverse dynamic is made especially so by the way we fund campaigns. Greenback tweedism selects candidates based on their responsiveness to funders. Yet the funders are the most enabled monitors of what candidates as representatives actually do. The business model of representation driven by the way we fund campaigns today is a thus perfect hydraulic away from the selection model of representation to the sanction model. And as the democracy seems and is more and more corrupt, it makes the selection model no longer even applicable. As Mansbridge writes, the selection model "works only when honest, competent, and mission-oriented individuals whose policy orientations are aligned reasonably well with those of the citizenry are available and willing to take up the representative role."[4]

That is not so with a corrupt democracy.

It's not easy to imagine creating the conditions for selection. But a first step is simply to name the ideal. The specifics of design are hopelessly underspecified. They beg a million other questions. But the point of the norm is not to resolve specific issues. The point is to channel conversation in a certain way. The constraint of the assembly should be to speak about the interests of all, even if the representatives in that assembly are there because of the interests of some. Only that framework will make the hard challenge of good government possible.

This is the insight that motivates the work of scholars such as Frances McCall Rosenbluth and Ian Shapiro. As they argue powerfully in their book *Responsible Parties,* we need democracies to focus on the problem of society generally. And we get that, they believe, through electoral systems that concentrate power in just two parties. The struggle of those parties will be to articulate policies that attract a majority to its side. But in attracting a majority, the parties ensure that all within the party continue to benefit. The consequence of that structure of critical incentives, Rosenbluth and Shapiro argue, is a system that tilts to the long-term interests of a society and avoids capture by short-term factions. We don't sell the future to pay for the present, because the parties are competing for a benefit in the future, and not just in the present. Two parties force each of them to struggle to represent not a plurality but a majority. In a democracy, that is a struggle well worth supporting. Shapiro and Rosenbluth's work complements the earlier grounding work by Nancy Rosenblum, arguing strongly for an ethics and passion for political parties.[5]

I am not certain Rosenbluth and Shapiro are right about the need for just two parties to achieve the ideals of majoritarianism. But whether they are right or not, their work aims in the same critical direction: how do we build a democracy that can represent us? And that question must be answered by a critical shift in the focus of representatives. In the process of getting elected, the challenge is to demonstrate that "I will represent you." But in the process of governing, the representatives must ask the question, "How do we all represent us?"

This is a perspective that any family member knows. You might have a strong desire for pizza. But you know your brother hates pizza. So in deciding where to go to dinner, you understand the question is not, "How do I make sure we get pizza." You understand the question has got to be, "How do we pick a restaurant that we all can enjoy." Maybe that means you take turns. Maybe that means you never have pizza (but neither do you have his favorite, at least if you don't like his favorite). "What should we do as a family" is different from "what do the individual members of a family want individually." It is always and inherently so.

That's the same difference at the level of the representative body. The question can never be "what do I or my people want" exclusively. The question must also be "what can we agree to collectively."

If you're a Tea Party Republican, you can be proud of your views. You can believe your views are correct. And you should certainly work hard to persuade others of your views in the elections that select representatives. But we know your views represent just a fraction of America. And so we know that if you leverage whatever power the accidental division of politics gives you to force your view on America, then you are not serving the end of democracy.

The same is true on the left. There are many fine and true beliefs held by so-called "Democratic socialists." Many of them are also held by a majority of Americans. But we know that some of them are not. And if the accidental division of politics gave the Democratic socialist faction the power to force one of those policies on the nation as a whole, then they, too, would not be serving the end of democracy. The question of governance is the question of how we govern all of us, together.

In that process, there is a role for public opinion. But that role should be primarily, and most forcefully, during elections. "We the people" speak through the representatives we select—members of Congress and the president. In that voting, we express something significant that the elected representatives must then respect. The election establishes the moral authority behind some views. It removes the moral authority behind others. It should constrain the willfulness of those within the government, given what we, through our votes, have said.

Here again, President Trump is a clear lesson. Consider his demand at the end of 2018 that Congress fund a wall along the border of Mexico. President Trump was elected president under the Electoral College that had evolved. He was not (as Bill Clinton and Woodrow Wilson were) a plurality president. He is a president selected because of the quirks of the Electoral College. At no point were his views the views of a majority of the voters. He demanded a wall, which he promised Mexico would pay for. That demand did not earn him the votes from even a plurality of American voters. The candidate who received that plurality did not get selected president. But that his views lost is a critically important democratic fact that should constrain how he could, morally, behave.

In the first two years of his presidency, his party controlled both houses of Congress. They pressed the vision of a wall. As it became clear that Mexico was not going to pay for it (Surprise! Surprise!), that vision evolved. By 2018, the idea of a wall paid for by Americans was a clear and powerful image that drove the election. The Republicans tried to leverage the fear from a "caravan" of "illegal immigrants" into an electoral victory that would promise to build a wall. They failed in that objective. The nation had the highest turnout in a midterm election since 1914. It was the largest turnover of incumbents since 1974. The Democrats had the largest sweep in more than a generation, gaining forty-one seats, with the largest midterm margin of all time.[6] Though the Republicans kept the Senate, after the election the Democrats had a seventeen-seat majority in the House.

That fact weakened any democratic pedigree that the president might have claimed for his wall. Whatever weak argument he had before, it was even weaker now. The president had teed up the question of the wall to the American voters. He had tried to trigger electoral support based on the fear of immigrants. He failed in that quest, miserably.

That failure should have consequences. At a minimum, it should mean that he would not have the democratic authority to leverage his enormous power as president to force the funding of the wall. The question of governance is not, What can I get? The question of governance is, What does America want? And even if a committed minority wanted the wall, it is clear that America as a whole did not.

These electoral moments are the most important inputs that we as citizens should have into the work of our government. They won't be the only. Instead, we know from the reality of media and polling that there will be a constant complement to elections, in the form of the views of "we the people" as represented in these polls.

These views, too, need a critical balance. Specifically, we need a way to add to these views the views of the public represented well. That means something other than a simple public opinion poll. It means specifically something like a deliberative poll. There needs to be a mechanism to give the politicians a way to register our views on some critical issue—not easily and not frequently, but whenever that view becomes important to know.

But even with the best system for triggering civic juries, we should resist triggering juries frequently. We should resist the idea that we ourselves could become the representatives. Again, that is what we pay them for.

Not enough, mind you. I know that sounds crazy to most people, but we don't pay our representatives enough. A congressman makes as much as one of my students makes in her first year as a lawyer on Wall Street. I believe firmly that we should be paying government officials much, much more.[7] Even more important, I believe we should be supporting them much, much more. Congress needs a radical increase in its informational independence. Not by accident, Congress evolved a system where most of the facts that representatives rely upon come from interested lobbyists or partisan think tanks. What the institution of Congress needs desperately is the ability for members to know the truth, by relying upon institutions like the Library of Congress or the Congressional Research Service, staffed with professionals whose aim is the truth. We are not using our representatives as representatives. We are not supporting them as they need to be supported. Yet this is what we need them for—to represent us. We need to develop the democratic self-awareness that teaches that the test of a good representative is not a simple graded voting record by some special interest group.

Separating more clearly the project of getting elected from the project of governing might help. As it is, that distinction is almost nonexistent. From the moment a member is elected, she is focused almost exclusively on reelection. There is no time for governance any-more. There is only the time for elections. In 2018, my mother, a Republican, wanted—for the first time—to vote for a Democrat for Congress (in her safe-seat Republican district). Amazingly, that con-gressman won. Literally, the night of his victory, he started sending emails to his supporters raising money for 2020. I get why. I wonder whether he gets why this is so crazy.

But if we could repair that system of debilitating incentives, then we might encourage a distinction in these dispositional attitudes. As a can-didate for Congress, I should announce clearly and honestly my values. I should declare what the values are that I will carry to Washington. You should assure yourself that those values are your values, too. You should be confident that I will operate with integrity in pursuing them.

Yet once they are in office, we all should recognize that the question is different. The left has succeeded to this degree in electing representa-tives; the right has succeeded to that degree in electing representatives. The question now is not how each side can grandstand. The question now is how we can govern. Sometimes there are questions that a rep-resentative has no choice about how she'll answer. Those questions are fundamental to her values or her election. A pro-life representative elected by pro-life constituents simply cannot negotiate the question of life. That's not on the table, given the nature of the value. But the tax rate for millionaires, the level of government spending for highways or the Internet, the extent to which we give foreign aid: a representative needs to be able to come to an understanding about these questions that allows the body as a whole to govern.

For *governance* is precisely what we cannot do right now. Our Congress has been led to a point where it simply cannot govern. The norms of that institution are so bent by the necessity to fundraise, the ideals of that institution are so polluted by the notion that compromise is sin, that that institution cannot achieve even the most basic of reforms.

Fixing this is ultimately the most critical, if difficult, challenge we have. It is in part about fixing them. It is in part about fixing us. They must work differently. But they will work differently only if we learn to allow them to work as the functioning institution that a democracy needs.

Let the fights within elections be fierce and engaged. Let all sides speak loudly and clearly about their vision for the future. But the election deals the cards, and once the election is over, the focus must shift: We've said what we want; now the question is how we, together, might govern.

Conclusion

KATIE FAHEY WAS A TWENTYSOMETHING MICHIGANDER WHO WAS puzzled by Michigan's response to the 2016 election. Initially a Clinton supporter, she was surprised when the state voted for Bernie Sanders. And then, she was surprised again when a state that had gone for Obama in 2012 (54 percent versus 45 percent) voted for Donald Trump. "What's going on?" she asked herself. And then, as she described to me afterward, she tried to answer her own question.

> "Okay, what do Bernie Sanders and Donald Trump have in common that maybe Hillary Clinton didn't have." I really do think it was kind of like this: Bernie Sanders was all about the political revolution, and Donald Trump was about "drain the swamp." I saw it on so many bumper stickers across Michigan. Those messages to me were actually pretty similar: . . . "The system is broken, and I will fix it."[1]

That idealism, however, faded quite quickly soon after the election. No longer were voters talking about fixing a broken system; instead the Net was quickly inundated with hate and despair. "We were having such a different conversation before the winner/loser part." That led Katie to ask: "What if we could keep these conversations going between the next four years, and not just go back to life as usual, where we're only going to talk about politics during the presidential election?"

Just before racing off to work one morning in November 2016, Katie posted a message on her Facebook page: "I'd like to take on gerrymandering in Michigan, if you're interested in doing this as well, please let me know. :)"

She didn't give it much thought—"I'm going to throw it out into the universe and see what happens"—and she didn't expect much of a response.

Yet that single post may have been the most consequential single political post of any on Facebook in the past half-decade. When she came home from work, she was surprised by the number who had responded with interest. "Hey, I saw your post. This is an issue I've cared about for a long time. Tell me what to do, how to sign up." The messages started piling up. Katie called a friend. "There's a lot of people who actually want to do this. Could we do it?" Her friend and co-worker, Kelly Schalter, was clear: "I think we have to try."

So she began organizing part-time. By April she had quit her job and turned to this task exclusively. The team created committees and started recruiting volunteers. They had a videoconference—the first had 70 people, 67 of whom turned off their video—so then they had telephone conferences instead. They organized town halls across Michigan, 33 in 33 days. Thousands volunteered to help first frame the problem and the solution, and then to help craft a strategy to get it enacted.

Like twenty-five other states, Michigan has a referendum process to allow citizens to enact any law, including an amendment to the Michigan Constitution.[2] To get the measure on the ballot requires first a proposal that is approved by the state, and then the valid signatures of 315,654 citizens (that's 10 percent of the votes cast for governor in the prior election). The language was to be approved within forty-eight hours; in the end, it took fifty-three days. On August 17, 2017, the campaign was allowed to begin collecting signatures. From every corner of Michigan, literally every county, 3,883 volunteers from Katie's "Voters not Politicians" collected more than 425,000 signatures in 110 days. On December 18, 2017, they turned the petitions in to the secretary of state. The secretary reported a 93 percent verification rate—meaning 93 percent of the signatures were valid and authorized. That was an astonishing rate for any such initiative; ordinarily, even 78 percent would have been considered exceptionally high. Katie's single Facebook post had triggered a proposal that would be on the Michigan ballot in November 2018.

If, at least, the judges didn't screw it up. All through the lead-up to the verification of the signatures, the opposition (mainly, Michigan politicians) indicated that they would stop the initiative in the courts. That flabbergasted Katie. "I'm like, you don't even have the language you say that you're against, but okay. And so the filing against us comes pretty quickly after we do the signatures." In April, "Citizens Protecting Michigan's Constitution" filed a lawsuit to stop the initiative. On June 7, the Court of Appeals upheld the initiative. That ruling was appealed to the Michigan Supreme Court. On July 6, the court agreed to hear the case. Two weeks later, they heard arguments. Two weeks after that, on the last day of July, the court allowed the initiative to be on the ballot.[3]

The argument of the opponents, as Katie saw it, was that the "people of Michigan are not to be trusted to amend the constitution in this way. It's too complicated." The attorney general, who would end up running for governor, sent his deputy to argue before the Michigan court: Can we really trust the people to be able to make important decisions for our government? "I was like, 'Oh, gosh, that is so not the 2016 tone or messaging that you, that Trump and Bernie had.'" For Bernie and for Trump, it was all about the people. But now in the Michigan appellate court, it was all about the politicians.

The actual idea that these troublemakers had put forward was pretty ingenious. Rather than a drafting committee composed of political insiders, the proposal envisioned a citizens committee. That committee had to be diverse—both politically, and importantly to those in the process, geographically. Half would be randomly drawn from people who had applied to be on the committee, half from ordinary registered voters. In total there would be thirteen members of the commission: four Republicans, four Democrats and five independents. Those citizens would work in public, drawing districts that aimed to be fair and representative. Rather than politicians selecting their voters, these citizens would give voters the chance to pick their politicians.

The campaign to persuade Michigan began in earnest in August. Almost a year after they had begun the process to allow Michiganders the opportunity to speak, they could now, with three months remaining until the election, begin the campaign to get people to support the initiative. The fight to that point had been expensive enough—though the organization was run by volunteers, the lawyers who would defend the referendum charged more than $750,000. All told, the cost up until the moment the campaign to win votes could begin was easily more than a million dollars. Voters Not Politicians had crowd funded that money. By the end of the campaign, more than 14,000 people had contributed close to $2 million.

But then the real spending would begin. The group crafted a clever informational video that began to run six weeks before the election.[4] Millions were contributed by large donors keen to see reform happen here. The team (literally thousands) was hopeful that the fight would be won. And then fifteen days before the election, an opposition campaign dropped $4 million in ads against the proposition. So blatantly false were some of these ads that the campaign was able to get some of them taken down. And so completely tone deaf was some of the opposition that you might have thought it was planted. (Some Michigan Republicans defended gerrymandering because it "protects incumbents."[5]) But as the election approached, no one had a clear sense of whether the lies would work.

They didn't. In the end, 61 percent of voters supported the reform. That result mirrored the results in four other states (Missouri, Colorado, Ohio, and Utah) that had similar ballot initiatives. It was a stunning victory by a first-time organizer who had managed to inspire thousands across the state to step up to demand real reform.

How?

Because conventional wisdom, among the experts at least is that, as one friend put it to me, "people don't give a shit about process." What the voter wants is health care, or a higher minimum wage, or tax cuts. How he gets what he gets is not important.

That conventional view has long—and powerfully—been resisted. Elizabeth Theiss-Morse and John R. Hibbing's fantastic book, *Stealth Democracy,* makes a powerful and empirical case that, in fact, the *only* thing people really care about is process.[6] What people judge, Theiss-Morse and Hibbing insist, is the fairness of what happened, not so much what happened. And their frustration with politics owes not to them losing, but to them believing that the system is just rigged.

That view is consistent with my own experience as well. For the last dozen or so years, I have been on the road talking about the corruption of our democracy and struggling to understand how we could build the movements it would take to fix it. Never have I found people who thought the issue was secondary—actually not never: Once I had spoken to a reporter covering Hillary Clinton's campaign who asked, "What if you don't think fixing the system is that important?" That was, unfortunately, the Clinton vibe too. But the general sense that all of us want change seems overwhelming to me. I was therefore very keen to understand how Katie had tapped into it.

It was just two months after Katie's incredible victory when I got to speak with her. She was clear about the important elements. From the very beginning, the movement had rules. Never was the issue rendered partisan. This was not—nor would it be pressed as—a Democratic or Republican issue. This was an issue about democracy.

Second, from the beginning, the movement was inclusive. "We really did try," as she explained to me, "to accept anybody where they were at, and with the skills that they had." They "crowd sourced skills."

Obviously, I didn't know how to write constitutional language, didn't know how to do bookkeeping, whatever. But we found people who had those skills—people who were willing to donate their time in that way, to then build this campaign cohesively together. I noticed that a lot of people felt like, "Oh, I've never volunteered on a political campaign before, so of course I can't participate, or of course I'm not sure if I should even be here." . . . But by changing that, and recognizing that the political system is an industry, too, and people have very good professional skills that they have used in their day jobs, that even though [the roles] aren't completely equivalent, [they] can be pretty close to taking a lot of those lessons, and actually applying them to be "useful."

This part was critical.

If we would have done it differently, not as many people would have been engaged. Because they do feel like outsiders in that way, and it's uncomfortable to be forced into such a brand-new experience. By using that [process], not only could we have people feel comfortable, but we also got a lot of creativity, and innovation, and people sticking with it for two years, because . . . they could feel like they were really valued. . . . That was really critical.

Third, the issue was energized by the opposition. When the politicians and insiders stepped up to stop the movement, that just fed the force and purpose of the thousands who had joined. "Voters, not politicians" was a slogan. The politicians made it real.

And finally, there is the hope.

It might sound like common sense, but nobody is happy with the state of politics. I can't say that enough. . . . [W]e don't give other people enough credit, and so we just assume, "Oh, we're the only ones who care." I felt that way. I'm so guilty of feeling that way. But nobody is happy with the state of politics. . . . Not everybody, but

I'll just use that word, everybody wants to change the world. People want purpose. So if you can combine the frustration of, "I don't like the status quo," and "I know that this impacts me," and "I want to do something about it," there is so much potential that comes together to empower people to actually do it.

IN 2010, Paul Richard LePage, a sixty-two-year-old businessman from Waterville, Maine, and a Tea Party Republican, ran for governor. Four other people in Maine ran as well. LePage won the race, with 37.6 percent of the vote. He would go on to win reelection in 2014 in a three-person race, with a plurality of 48.2 percent of the vote. Never having been elected by a majority of the state of Maine, LePage was ultimately a very unpopular governor. In April 2018, he had a 53 percent disapproval rating, making him one of the four most unpopular governors in the United States.

Cara Brown McCormick is a political consultant. In 2014 she had been a consultant for almost twenty years. In 2012 she had been a researcher for Angus King, Maine's independent senator. And as the election in 2014 began, she started working with others to challenge LePage. Eliot Cutler was running as an independent—a seventy-two-year-old lawyer who narrowly lost to LePage in 2010. Michael Michaud, a fifty-something-year-old former congressman, ran as the Democrat. Cara was struggling to understand how best to defeat LePage. "The entire campaign was like beating your head against the wall," she told me, "because the whole thing was about who was going to spoil the race for whom."

This struggle led Cara to look for a fix to this, as she would describe it to me, "antidemocratic system." She began speaking with an economist who was also an independent state senator from Yarmouth, Dick Woodbury. Woodbury had authored legislation while in the senate to introduce ranked-choice voting (RCV) into Maine law. In 2014, he decided not to run for reelection. Cara convinced him to help pass an initiative to bring RCV to Maine. Together, they recruited an extraordinary campaign manager to make it happen, Kyle Bailey.

Maine law required that they collect 61,153 signatures before their initiative could appear on the ballot. They began collecting at the end of October 2014 and set election day in November as their primary day for getting signatures. The team put out a call to all their volunteers. The volunteers met the team organizers on the turnpike. Most of the petitions got distributed up and down the state the weekend before the election. It wasn't easy. This was Maine, it was the winter, and they were suffering their first major snowstorm. But on election day they collected 30,000 signatures—40 percent of the total needed. Cara herself collected 900. As she recounts the day, "And I knew. I had 900 separate conversations, and I absolutely knew that it was going to work on that day. Because every single person whom I spoke to signed my petition. Every single person."

That unanimity was not hard to understand. As the people in Maine were entering their polling places in November 2014—deciding whether an extremely controversial and even then unpopular governor would be reelected—they were feeling, as Cara describes, "like they had to vote for their fear."

> They weren't feeling like they could actually cast a vote for the person they liked the most, without the fear of electing the person that they liked the least. And so it crystallized for them, for the voters, and they signed the petition to try to bring . . . about [a change] in two years.

The committee succeeded in getting the signatures. They succeeded in getting the referendum on the ballot. And on November 8, 2016, they succeeded in winning the election with the second-largest vote for any referendum in the history of Maine.

The law went into effect on January 7, 2017. Four days later, Cara began to realize that the politicians were going to repeal it. "That was a mistake on my part," she told me two years later. "It had never occurred to any of us that they would completely try to wipe the law off the books. But that's exactly what happened." Ten months later, the Maine legislature would vote to repeal the results of the Maine referendum. "They thought that the people didn't know what they had voted for," Cara told me. "They thought it was much too confusing." And anyway, the system was way too complicated to be implemented, the supporters were told. Matthew Dunlap, the secretary of state, said it would take his office "one hundred years" to be able to implement it.

The legislature delayed and repealed the RCV initiative in a special session in the middle of the night. Cara was in the gallery. When the vote was taken, she immediately sent a press release, announcing the launch of a People's Veto movement. Under Maine law, a referendum can veto the decision of a legislature. If they could get the signatures (again!) and prevail on the ballot (again), they could restore the system that the voters had already directly approved.[7]

They had eighty-eight days to collect 61,123 signatures. Again, it was Maine. Again, it was winter. Operating out of a tiny office, with 1,800 volunteers, they launched the campaign to try. On February 2, 2018, the team turned in 80,000 signatures. The state determined they had qualified, and the People's Veto was on the June 12, 2018, ballot. By a 54 percent to 46 percent margin, the voters approved the People's Veto. RCV would then be used for every office it could, constitutionally, on November 6, 2018.[8]

How had they done it? Again, as in Michigan, here was a geeky technical procedural question of democracy that had somehow motivated thousands of people to get out in the snow and rally citizens against their politicians.

How is not very different from Michigan. First, the campaign disciplined itself never to be partisan. There was, as Cara described, an "absolute ethos of nonpartisanship. . . . We were very disciplined in that regard, because the system needed to change despite the actors in the system."

Second, it was, in a similar way, crowdsourced. The team was filled with volunteers. The campaign "got everybody in the same room together, all working to solve a problem of democracy." That multiplied the energy. And it helped everyone see how the solution they were fighting for was a solution that would help everyone.

Weirdly, RCV actually solves two problems that might at first seem very different. The first is the problem Ralph Nader came to represent—that the system was forcing people to pick "the lesser of two evils," and that it was crowding out less mainstream candidates for fear that they might spoil the result for everyone else.

But the second problem is the LePage problem—elected officials who don't actually represent the majority. If you simply made it easier for everyone to be on the ballot, that would increase the chances that the person who won was not supported by the majority. But if you could rank your choices, then anyone could run, yet in the end you'd have an elected official who was actually supported by a majority. As one of the Maine volunteers put it, "it elects someone that we can all live with"—after encouraging anyone with a good idea to step forward and try.[9]

The third lesson also parallels Michigan—the more the insiders fought the change, the more energy the rebels could muster. As Cara described it,

> When the people who were in power tried to stop it in this really anti-democratic, really brazen way—when they trampled on top of the democracy and trampled on top of the results of a free and fair election with a bunch of ridiculous arguments that weren't true— . . . instead of making us weaker, they made us stronger. Way stronger. Our numbers multiplied because they opposed us.
>
> . . . [F]or some people it became not even about ranked choice voting. It became: do the people have the power to choose the way we elect our leaders in a democracy? Once you have that argument, then you started to get real buy-in.

And finally, the fourth lesson is the power of a different kind of politics. The campaign never attacked anyone. "You're trying to promote something that will bring out the best in people," Cara told me, "so you can't attack people when you're doing it." They needed to practice the politics they wanted the politicians to live—because they knew that if they, too, seemed like politicians, that would be kryptonite for their movement. They were above politics. They used politics to make politics better.

NEW JERSEY TODAY IS a very Democratic state. It has a Democratic governor and a Democratic lieutenant governor. Its Senate is Democratic (26/14). Its House is Democratic (54/26). Both United States senators are Democratic. *Eleven* of its 12 members in Congress are Democratic. And Hillary Clinton won the state with more than 55 percent of the vote, beating Donald Trump by almost a half a million votes.

Democrats are rightly sensitive to the games that Republicans play to rig the system across America to benefit Republicans. As I've described throughout this book, through gerrymandering and voter suppression, the Republican Party has embraced a pretty ignoble purpose, as it seeks victory by making it harder for the other side to compete.

Some Democrats see those wrongs as a justification for Democrats to do the same. If they're going to cheat, then we get to cheat. It's only fair.

And in the fall 2018, that's at least how many viewed the actions of the Democratic New Jersey legislature when it proposed a pretty fundamental constitutional change aimed at cementing a partisan advantage.

Activists across New Jersey had long been engaged in the fight for a system of fair representation—in New Jersey and elsewhere. Princeton University has an extraordinary professor of neuroscience and molecular biology, Samuel Wang, who has also made himself an expert in election science. In the early 2000s, he launched a center at Princeton that would become the Princeton Gerrymandering Project. Devoted to "bridging the gap between mathematics and the law to achieve fair representation through redistricting reform," the team (four full-time employees and a number of volunteers) provides scientific analysis of proposed electoral reforms and resources to citizens eager to engage.[10]

One of the most important groups nationally that has been engaged in this fight has been the League of Women Voters. Founded a century ago, the League has made nonpartisan electoral reform a fundamental part of its identity. In New Jersey, the League had launched the "Fair Districts New Jersey" campaign in early 2018, with the aim to reform the state's redistricting process. The campaign's lead organizer was Helen Kioukis.

The Fair Districts project had been monitoring the New Jersey legislature. They had been holding public meetings across the state to inform voters about the campaign and recruit supporters. And so when, on the Monday before Thanksgiving, Democrats in the New Jersey legislature surprised everyone by announcing their intent to amend the New Jersey Constitution to alter the redistricting process, the League was ready. "We got an action alert out to our full membership list the very next morning," she described to me a couple of months afterward. And with that email, she began an intensive, grassroots lobbying campaign.

Much of the general education had already been done. But this bill was weird, and weirdly complex. As the Princeton Gerrymandering Project confirmed, it was a reform that made little sense in a state like New Jersey. On the surface, it looked to "give Democrats a lasting advantage," Sam Wang explained to me. But it had "a weird loophole . . . that one could [use to] manipulate incumbency and other factors to give an advantage to either party." Wang doubts the loophole was intended. "We concluded," as he explained, "that it was faulty in terms of achieving a good government goal, and we started saying so."

Helen took those words and, through the organization she had helped craft, amplified them. Very quickly, the perception grew that New Jersey was trying to rig its system even more to ensure an even more secure Democratic Party. "The League sent out a warning," Ben Williams of the Princeton Gerrymandering Project described it, "Paul Revere it if you will, and everyone took up action in defense of fair redistricting."

"Everyone" means more than sixty separate organizations. The word spread from one to another, and very quickly, an army of the willing had been assembled to fight the insiders. The League of Women Voters itself, as Wang characterizes it, feels like it "come[s] from a different age of non-partisanship." But when this threat was presented, they "came out of the woodwork" to stop it.

Helen organized a virtual town hall to explain the plan. The overwhelming reaction of everyone was to say just how bizarrely complicated it was. As Helen put it to me,

> I heard from many people who reached out to me saying things like, "You know I've read this like 10 times and I still don't get it." So to that I would say, "Well that's an issue in and of itself. If . . . you as someone who considers yourself an informed and engaged and active voter have read this proposal 10 times and you still don't understand it, that's problematic.'"

The complexity alone troubled people. But even worse was the idea of the legislature pushing this amendment through in the weeks between Thanksgiving and Christmas.

The essence of the reform was partisan. That's how politicians view districting. That's how the proposal dealt with districting. Built into the formula was a factor that would reflect the partisan divide in the state.

But the citizens didn't see "partisan" as a category that merited restricting consideration. As the League saw it, the "driving forces of redistricting [should] be public input, protection of communities of color, protections of communities of interest, and census data that shows us where the demographic shifts are. Not the use of partisan data or election histories." The activists wanted "neutral standards" that didn't aim to embed partisan division. "If you are manipulating those boundary lines to secure a victory for a certain party in each district then that's not the will of the people."

They therefore launched their attack against what they called "the Partisan Gerrymandering Bill"—even though it benefited the party most of the activists were affiliated with. They did this because to the League, and to these activists, questions of democracy were "beyond party."

The League had learned about the proposal being fast-tracked through the legislature on November 19. The first committee meeting was scheduled for the twenty-sixth. Immediately after they learned of the proposal emerging from the committee, activists started rallying citizens across the state to come to the public hearings and to show their opposition it. On the day of hearings, the activists learned that rather than schedule the hearings between the House and the Senate together, as they had recently done, for example, with a marijuana legalization proposal, the legislature scheduled the two hearings at the same time in different parts of the state capitol. "The fact that they did that also really, really angered everyone," Helen told me, "because it was just a blatant attempt to further divide our voices and to try and make our numbers not feel as big as they really were."

The hearings didn't go well—for the proponents of the legislation. Not a single person beyond its sponsors testified in favor of the bill. An endless stream of opponents testified against. One sponsor explained that the "problem" that the citizens had with the bill was simple ignorance. "People just need to read this bill," he insisted. But of course, he was lecturing the wrong crowd. These people *had* read the bill—carefully and repeatedly. And the suggestion that their opposition was nothing more than ignorance didn't rally the troops to support the bill. As Helen summarized it, that

> was quite insulting and condescending. Because we all had. . . . Trenton is not an easy place to get to. [I]t can take as long as three hours depending on where you are. . . . So the people who took the time to prepare a brief testimony, to travel, to take a day off or to take time away from whatever holiday preparations they had to do—you know all kinds of things people are dealing with in their lives— . . . to come to Trenton to speak in opposition and then to hear someone say to you, "Well you're just not understanding . . . either you haven't read it or if you have you're not understanding it, you're not understanding the language." It was a very condescending response . . . to make.

Not surprisingly, condescension backfired. "It got people to speak much more passionately," Helen told me, "and with more anger than they would have had." And very quickly, this insiders bill, designed to cement the power of the insiders, the Democrats, in a Democratic state, became a point of principle for the more than hundred citizens who had descended on Trenton, and then millions more as the story was told. These were politicians acting as politicians, when the citizens of New Jersey wanted them to act as citizens.

On December 15—two days before the proposal was scheduled for a full vote in the Legislature— to the surprise of everyone, the bill was pulled. Helen was having dinner with her husband at her mom's house. She was ignoring her phone, trying to find quiet time with her family. But as the notifications multiplied and it was "beeping over and over," she knew something was happening. She checked her phone. People had sent her screen shots of the announcement of the Senate president that the bill would be withdrawn. In less than a month, they had stopped a bill that all had expected the politicians would affirm. "It was a very, very exciting night."

As she reflected on the experience on the phone with me, her story struck a familiar tone. First, as in Michigan and Maine, the movement was militantly nonpartisan. Not a single person testified that "the Republicans have been doing this for years and it's time we fight fire with fire." Instead, as she recounted to me, the people were just "longing for basic fairness." That fairness was not to be reckoned in partisan terms.

Second, the movement was fueled by insider arrogance. As the citizens confronted politicians who were convinced their opposition was grounded in ignorance (or naivete), that only reinforced the citizens' commitment. There could not have been a member of the legislature who understood the bill as well as the Princeton Gerrymandering Project, or the League activists did. That fact became obvious to all.

And third, as in Michigan and Maine, the surprising citizen power came from a genuinely grassroots effort at organizing support. No one group tried to own the mobilization. Each shared its information and collaborated together. The first time this idea was floated, earlier in the year, only the Princeton project was there to testify about the arcane formula in the amendments. When it came back a few weeks later, just after Thanksgiving, scores of groups had taken the issue up. No one owned that movement—except the citizens of New Jersey. As Will Adler, a computational analyst with the Princeton project, put it,

> We talk a lot about how the legislature can just drop something in the middle of the night and vote on it a few hours later. The legislatures have a lot of power in terms of being able to advance things quickly. With this, it was really cool to see that citizens can actually rev up the protest machine at pretty much the same scale. That was a surprising thing to see. And very cool stuff.

THERE IS ORDINARY POLITICS and there is constitutional, or as I will call it, platform politics. Ordinary politics is the fight between Republicans and Democrats. It is the stuff of professionals. It is the battle among those who make their career serving us as us. It is the world of Washington, D.C.

Platform politics is different. It speaks differently. It aspires differently. The aim of platform politics is to craft the system within which ordinary politics happens. It sets the rules that the politicians must follow. It is the adult on the playground, the referee holding the whistle.

These three stories are stories of platform politics. The leaders in each are not politicians. They may or they may not aspire to become politicians. None of them entered the battle they won as a stepping-stone to something else. Instead, each of them stepped up as citizens because they believed their democracy was broken, and because they believed that they could do one thing to help fix it.

They did this despite believing that victory was unlikely. None of these citizens launched their campaign with a plan that promised a win. There was no guarantee of victory. They acted with love, not calculation—with love for their country, and the ideals they thought it embraced.

It may be because they were women. American history is filled with examples of great women fighting the impossible battles of constitutional politics—from Myra Bradwell demanding the right for women to serve as lawyers in the 1870s, to Doris Haddock walking across the country at the age of ninety to end the corrupting influence of money in politics just twenty years ago.

But I think the key to these victories is less specific to sex, and quite general and generative.

Each of these fights had a similar character. Each committed itself to remaining nonpartisan. Each leveraged enormous grassroots energy because it was so framed and constrained. And each was bolstered by the outrageous presumption of insiders in American politics, insiders who conveyed to these citizens that citizens were irrelevant. Insiders who announced, never directly but always distinctly, that we the people, as Cara put it, "just didn't get it."

Ordinary politics is not this politics. On the left in America, there are leaders. Those leaders are partisan. Alexandria Ocasio-Cortez (AOC) and Elizabeth Warren are not cross-partisan peace makers. They are completely committed to defeating Republicans—and to defeating the Democrats who are not sufficiently to the left. The same story could be told the other way around. Michele Bachmann was, for a time, as beloved on the right as AOC is on the left. She had no patience for "the Democrats." She did not hesitate to ridicule anyone silly enough to be something other than a Republican.

This politics is essential, too. It is the politics that makes government work. As each party rallies its own against the other, it defines a distinctive direction for the nation. And if one party can win a majority, that party should press hard to implement the direction that it had promised. There is no reason to pretend that we all agree in America. There is no reason to be embarrassed about our differences. We each come to these questions along a very different path. The obligation of democracy—for its citizens, not its representatives—is not to tolerate—as in to yield to—views different from our own. The obligation of democracy is to work to convince others that our own views are right.

For almost all of American history, the project of platform, or constitutional, politics was left to the politicians. For almost all of American history, we have relied upon *them* to frame the fundamental changes that we, as a people, needed, and then to bring them into force. Sometimes those changes were inherently partisan—the Twelfth, Thirteenth, Fourteenth, and Fifteenth Amendments were each the product of one-party control in our government. The fundamental (if not constitutionalized) changes ushered in by the New Deal were changes that were made possible only by the utter defeat of the Republican Party by the Democrats in 1936.

But most of the time, constitutional reform has been an inherently cross-partisan effort. Every amendment since the Fifteenth Amendment was endorsed by both major political parties before it was ratified. Some of those amendments were small—who remembers what the Twenty-

Fifth Amendment does? But some are among the most important in the American Constitution—the Sixteenth, permitting an income tax, the Seventeenth, electing senators, the Nineteenth, enfranchising women, the Twenty-Fourth, abolishing the poll tax (in federal elections).

Platform politics is not just about amending the constitution. Platform politics is any politics that aims to reform the system that constitutes America politics. The Voting Rights Act of 1965—again, cross-partisan—is platform politics. It is also the most important example of cross-partisan constitutionalism in the twentieth century.

I fear that ordinary politics has lost the capacity to solve the problems of platform politics. I fear that the partisanship of ordinary politics today—fueled as it is by a media environment that takes no prisoners—has now made the project of platform politics too difficult for the politicians.

Yet the stories that began the Conclusion show that it is not too difficult for us. When we can trigger movements that are understood as beyond politics, when we can motivate ordinary citizens to step up and demand change, and when we can organize the long and difficult campaigns to wrest power back from the insiders, we can do what the ordinary politicians cannot. This is the lesson of Eric Liu's powerful book, *You're More Powerful Than You Think*, applied to the platform of democracy.[11] We can win at constitutional politics when we can convince other citizens that the reforms move us, not left or right, but in the words of the Constitution, toward "a more perfect union."

America desperately needs platform reform. It desperately needs a democracy that all of us can trust. That is the single organizing idea throughout this book. Even without amending our constitution, we need fundamental change within our political system. And if we got that change, we need desperately to complement it with critical changes in our constitution, too.

As difficult as it is to imagine, the reality today is that we are only ever going to get that reform if we can inspire tens of thousands of Americans to, in essence, become Katie or Cara or Helen. We are only ever going to trigger the energy that this kind of change needs if we can nurture the sense in ordinary Americans that this job is their job. Not as politician wannabes. Not on the way to the United States Senate. But as an act of service, like volunteering to go to war to defend the nation, or like agreeing to sit on a jury to judge a fellow citizen.

The only way to change the rules today is to convince everyone that the change is for everyone. The only way to change politics is to convince everyone that the change itself is principle, not politics, that the change is instead simple democracy—expressed in the simple words of ideals that still move practically every single one of us.

THE PROOF IN THAT CLAIM is not just in these successes. It is also in the failures. In one of her first acts as Speaker, at least the second time around, Nancy Pelosi unified the Democratic Party around an extraordinary reform package, referred to as HR 1. HR 1 had practically every statutory reform that I've argued for in this book, from a version of public funding for congressional elections, to the restoration of the Voting Rights Act, to automatic voter registration, to gerrymandering reform. It was the most important civil rights legislation in more than two generations. Pelosi wanted to feature that bill because she wanted America to understand what America would get if America elected Democrats to Congress.

HR1 was the brainchild of one of Congress's greatest leaders, Maryland's John Sarbanes. Sarbanes had been pushing for fundamental reform of campaign finance since 2011. He had crafted a powerful bill to enable congressmen to give up their addiction to big money. And he had worked tirelessly to convince his colleagues to support that reform.

I have known Sarbanes since the beginning of his fight. I have never met a public servant whom I have respected more. He is as committed as anyone and committed for exactly the right reasons. He is a reformer, standing inside the Democratic Party, pushing the party to become the party of reform.

Yet when Sarbanes's work was embraced by the Speaker, and then folded into a package of reform that would certainly make democracy work again, many of us were fearful. For the leaders of the Democratic Party in D.C. to embrace this reform would be for the reform to become essentially partisan. Those fundamental changes—which, as I've argued throughout this book, follow not from the desire to elect Democrats but from the need to make our democracy representative again—would be understood in the public as changes for the Democratic Party. We who were skeptical feared that this success—convincing the most importantly successful Speaker in a generation to take up our cause—would yield an unavoidable defeat—as reform got rendered political. We feared that embrace by the Democrats would be kryptonite.

And of course, it was. After the Democrats introduced the reform, the Republicans identified it as simply partisan. As it was rendered partisan, it moved from platform politics to ordinary politics. And as it moved, its chances at success evaporated. The Republican leader of the Senate, Mitch McConnell, named it a Democratic "power grab."[12] And as absurd as his argument was, no one could miss that he had succeeded completely in melting any idea that this bill was anything more than politics as usual.

On March 8, 2019, the House of Representatives overwhelmingly approved HR 1. Not a single Republican voted for the bill. Immediately after the vote, McConnell repeated his promise never to give the bill even a hearing in the Senate. HR 1 had won, at least in the House. Reform through ordinary politics had lost.

I'm not sure what the movement looks like that could elevate reform above politics. I am just convinced that that is exactly what must happen if reform is ever to have any chance of surviving politics. Yes, the Democrats could hold the House. It is completely possible for the Democrats to take the Senate and the presidency. But if the Democratic Party tries to win platform reform the way they win the battles of ordinary politics—*in the media environment that is today*—then reform will be rendered as Obamacare. It will become the lightning rod of resistance and ultimately fail to bring about the changes that this democracy so desperately needs.

It is possible to imagine something more. I could see a presidential candidate making a pledge equivalent to Nancy Pelosi's—a kind of POTUS 1 to parallel HR 1. If that pledge were central enough to his or her campaign, I could imagine it being accepted that the mandate that president had earned included that POTUS 1 commitment. It is possible, that is, that reform could be made central, and that a winning president would have the political capital to make it something more than the partisan demands of a partisan victory.

This is the essence of what we must fight for. We must find a way to look beyond the forms of ordinary politics. We must find the strategies that the Katie Faheys of America could use. We must build the structures of political change that can rise above the partisan. We need to fight these battles in a manner that strikes both sides as above the interests of either— as battles committed only to the interests of a republic.

A *republic*.

A representative democracy.

A democracy in which we all are represented equally.

That republic we do not have.

That republic we have never had—if you count as citizens the people who obviously are.

That republic, as citizens, we must now fight to achieve. By rallying the best in all of us. As citizens first, to a democracy, that could represent us, all equally.

Acknowledgments

This book is a long time coming. It is the product of a certain fixation that I had with the corrupting influence of money in politics, and a persistent set of questions that others had about how much that single flaw could ever really explain. I had the chance to work through those questions while away from the United States—first in Iceland, during the fall 2016, and then in Rwanda, during the first half of 2017. I am grateful to my puzzled and persistent friends in both places—Katrin Oddsdóttir (Iceland) and Jonathan Stever (Rwanda) especially. I am also grateful to the law school at the University of Reykjavík, and its dean, Ragnhildur Helgadóttir, as well as Aimable Havugiyaremye, director of the Institute of Legal Practice and Development in Kigali, for making it possible for me to stay in those two most extraordinary countries.

I was helped enormously by an army of students who helped me understand the literature and test the theories. Ordinarily, the guidance is the other way around. But in this case, the more they brought me to read, the more my ideas evolved. I am therefore grateful to Sebastian Becker, David Brown, Katie Bruck, Peter Burgess, Suman Dev, Megan Field, Melanie Fontes, Medha Gargeya, Michael Gioia, Emerson Gordon-Marvin, Ross Holley, Steven Jiang, Abraham Moffat, Louis Murray, Catherine Padhi, Steven Palmer, Delany Sisiruca, Kyle Skinner,

Eren Sozuer, Evandro Sussekind, Cassidy Viser, Gege Wang, Steven Wang, Thomas Weber, Jenna Welsh, Daren Zhang, and Adele Zhang. I am especially grateful to Zak Lutz, who inspired the team to do more than I thought was possible. I am grateful as well to my assistant, Valentina de Portu, who kept the sanity. I am thankful as well to David Rose and Sharon Broder for providing the shelter and escape necessary to bringing this work to a close.

Ben Page and Robert Shapiro allowed me to eavesdrop on an extraordinary conversation about how the current media environment might affect their important conclusions in *The Rational Public*. That conversation allowed me to see the difference between a change driven by fragmentation and one driven by polarizing a fragmented public. The Harvard Law School data librarians, especially Jonathan Hack, were enormously helpful when I set out to test some conclusions using data provided by Gallup. Andy Eggers helped guide the reading standing behind what I call "tweedism," and what political science refers to as "candidate selection." I am grateful for his help.

I am especially grateful to my agent, Sarah Chalfant, who had faith in what she saw, and helped me bring these ideas to some closure. Her patient counsel and careful reading helped me enormously, as has the careful hand of my editor, Alessandra Bastagli.

And finally, the one ritual that seems so certainly real: I am grateful to my family, and especially my love, Bettina. All of them accepted the challenge of a year away, with joy and adventure. All of them have accepted the sadness of a Papa too consistently away, struggling to find a way home. Their patience is their love. It is a debt I am eager to repay.

This book is thus a chapter closed. The clean pages of these chapters give me more joy than I can describe.

Appendix: Reformers

Unlike the other books I have written about democracy, this book does not make strategy a core part of its argument. The world has worked hard to convince me I don't understand politics. The world might be right. But in this brief appendix, I point to a range of organizations and movements that I believe could well work. I point not to lead. If the world has learned anything in the last decade, it is that many leaders are needed, not a very few, and certainly not just leaders like me.

FROM THE STATES, UP

There are many great reformers who have left Washington, D.C. Not just, or necessarily, literally, but figuratively. These are leaders who think we're in this for the long haul—that we need to build a movement at the level of the states, first. Once we win there, they believe we can then take on the corruption that is Washington.

I have long admired the work of these reformers. I only fear we don't have the time for that plan to work. But while nothing has been moved effectively at the federal level, reformers at the state level have made enormous progress.

Represent.us is among the most impactful in this space. They've pushed corruption reform across the country, as well as gerrymandering reform and RCV. They live in an insanely beautiful office in an incredibly beautiful town in the middle of Massachusetts. Their leaders have inspired an extraordinary number of talented young people to move to the sticks to help leverage the energy for reform that is everywhere in America.

As well as *Represent.us*, there are others doing the same hard work at the state level. *AmericanPromise.Net* is working state by state to build a movement to support an amendment to the federal constitution that would establish (finally!) political equality. Yet they are building that movement not with top-down diktats, but through an extraordinary process of collaboration to identify what an amendment actually should be. The group has thousands of volunteers across the nation who are building the recognition and support such change will require. They too have adopted the core principle of each of the successes I described in the Conclusion—militantly nonpartisan, grassroots, and engaged.

Finally, there many single-state organizations across the country, working with these national organizations and others (my favorites among the others include the *League of Women Voters* and *Common Cause*). In New Hampshire, for example, *OpenDemocracyNH.org* grew out of the work of Doris Haddock (aka Granny D); it inspired *NH-Rebellion.org,* which rallies attention to reform during the presidential election cycle. All of these organizations (and many more) do the work of platform politics from the state first.

CAPTURING CONGRESS

When I write version 2.0 of this book, the Conclusion will no doubt include a fourth story of success, led by another extraordinary woman, Daniella Ballou-Aares. A Harvard MBA and former staffer in the Clinton State Department, Daniella has launched an inspirational network committed to the fundamental reform of Congress, *Leadership-*

NowProject.org. "Network" here is the key word, because as she and her friends recognized, they could assemble in their friends, and friends of friends, the power it would take to make reform possible. Not from billionaires, but from people with some means and endless motive to save this democracy in time for their kids.

One idea that they are percolating is the election of a "Reform Caucus" in Congress. That caucus—as every story in the Conclusion evinces—must be cross-partisan. It must have leaders who stand above politics, at least for the purpose of reform. But given the close division in Congress, that caucus need not be huge. Thirty members of the House of Representatives would guarantee who could control Congress; those thirty members could then partner with whatever party would agree to their demands: that they would vote for a reform Speaker; that reform Speaker would control the House until Congress passed reform; once the president signs the reform package, the Speaker would resign, and members of the caucus would return to their regular parties.

This idea leverages a quirk in the Constitution. Anyone can be chosen to be Speaker. Literally, anyone. The queen of England. Jennifer Lawrence. Jimmy Carter. Anyone. The requirement to be Speaker is simply that the House votes to select you. There is no requirement for whom the members of the House can vote for.

So imagine a leader—preferably someone above politics, or beyond politics—took up the charge to elect a Reform Caucus in Congress. She would rally the funds to make it a national campaign. Her team would recruit the candidates. Those candidates would run in safe-seat primaries—half Republican and half Democrat, because running in the primary, by the middle of the year of any election cycle, would make it clear whether there will be a Reform Caucus, and if there will be, what kind of changes it would effect.

This is a kind of hack for a political system that does not allow for one-party governance. In Britain, change like this could happen whenever one party gains control of government. But in America, we are too divided for one party to gain the supermajority it would take to withstand the resistance of the other. And with the right leader (think a female Republican with the notoriety and affection of a Tom Hanks), rallying sufficient support (imagine fifty billionaires pledging up to $20 million each to make this happen), it is possible that this hack would work.

"Fifty billionaires?" I am as skeptical as any about the role of billionaires in our democracy. But notice what these fifty would be working for: If the plan wins, then they will have achieved a radical reduction in their own power over our democracy. They would be spending their money to *reduce* their influence. If there's one context in which their money could do good, it is that.

LeadershipNowProject.org is not the only group doing powerful work in Washington. *IssueOne.org* is building a thick collaboration among both Republicans and Democrats, to craft a package of reform that could make Congress work. That work is aided critically by the most important conservative organization fighting for congressional reform, Take Back Our Republic (*TakeBack.org*). It is supported as well by many other critical reform groups, including *Demos.org* and the Brennan Center for Justice. I helped launch one of the most exciting activist organizations pushing for the reform of Congress, *Mayday.US*. Along with *EndCitizensUnited.org,* they are working hard to build recognition for what an uncorrupted democracy could be.

SAVED BY THE THIRTEEN

I believe we need amendments to our Constitution. But more important than the specifics is that we affirm again the idea that we the people—not the judges, and not the politicians—ultimately rule.

As I described in chapter 4, there is an Article V movement to convene a convention to propose amendments to the Constitution. It's never happened before. That fact terrifies people today. As I described then, I don't think those fears are justified. I support that movement.

I've recorded a whole season of a podcast, *Another Way*, season 2, hosted by *Wolf-PAC.com*, to explain why.

But what's obvious about a convention is that if it were partisan, it would fail. Either side would use the threat of a convention by the other side to whip up its base and raise money against fear. That's happening right now within the Democratic Party. It is the right that is close to having enough states to demand a convention. The left is using that fact to terrify its base (and then ask them to donate generously to stop the right).

The issue that is closest to having enough states supporting it is a convention to address a "Balanced Budget Amendment." This idea is supported by many on the right, but not exclusively. Yet regardless of the precise mix, the movement is viewed as *from* the right. If it succeeded in getting thirty-four states behind it, it would be perceived as a right-wing convention. That perception would guarantee that any proposal the convention adopts would be quickly rejected by at least thirteen non-right states.

Put most charitably, the Balanced Budget Amendment seeks to add *fiscal integrity* into our constitutional system. The movement that would grow out of the reforms in this book would add *representational integrity*. These reforms, though supported by people on the right and left, would likely read to the left. If a movement to call a convention to address them were to reach thirty-four states, the right would rally against them, just as we are seeing the left rally against the *fiscal integrity* reforms.

The only convention that could avoid this dynamic—and not certainly, but possibly—would be one that could consider issues from both the right and the left. And given how close the right is, there may be a way to leverage that fact to get a convention that could consider more than just *fiscal integrity*.

To see how, let's first be clear on the numbers. The Constitution says that two-thirds of the states can call a convention. That's thirty-four states. It says that three-fourths of the states must ratify any proposed amendment before it can become part of the Constitution. That's thirty-eight states. That ratification can either be by state legislature or by state convention. Congress gets to choose which. But either way, if thirteen states failed to ratify any proposed amendment, that amendment would be dead.

So imagine leveraging these numbers to a critical end: imagine thirteen states passed the following resolution:

> **We, the Legislature of _____, exercising power granted to us under Article V of the Constitution, do hereby preemptively reject any amendment proposed by a convention that was not free to consider issues of representational integrity.**

The strategy here is clear, if uncertain. By uniting thirteen states against a politically polarized convention, these states could change the calculation of those pushing for such a convention. No one knows whether such a preemptive rejection would work. But it might. And if it did, then the work of the convention would have been for naught. Congress could evade this hack by sending the ratification to state conventions. That has happened once, with the amendment to repeal Prohibition. But that, too, is a risky strategy, especially after the states have passed this resolution.

So rather than risking the outcome, the proponents of a *fiscal integrity* convention might well become open to the idea of a dual convention, or one just after another, that could consider both fiscal and representational integrity issues.

And if it considered both, then each side would have a reason to give the convention a try. At the most, the convention can make just a proposal. That's it. And if the proposal is not supported overwhelmingly (for, again, just thirteen states could stop it), then it won't become part of our Constitution. The worst case then is that nothing happens. The best case is that we get a shot at doing something that will not otherwise happen: proposing amendments to our constitution that will ensure, *finally*, a constitution that protects the political equality of citizens.

EQUAL CITIZENS

None of the organizations I have just described are mine. I've supported all of them, but except for Mayday.US, they were begun and built by others. The last on my list is an organization that I did begin— *EqualCitizens.US*.

Equal Citizens aims to practice the lesson this book wants to teach. By taking on cases and causes that show a commitment to political equality, we want to build a movement of political egalitarians. Our initial strategy was through litigation. Our first cases aimed to reform the Electoral College, by challenging winner-take-all. We have a case pressing the courts to adopt the original meaning of "corruption" so as to allow the regulation of SuperPACs. And we have been pushing the cause of RCV in both presidential primary and general elections.

Equal Citizens should be a model, not just an organization. Ideally there would be a thousand organizations across the country that took its aim and replicated it. In every context in which the insiders have erected walls to block citizen equality, we need people to fight it. I have no desire (or capacity) to build EqualCitizens.US into a huge organization. I want it to remain small and agile. But it will succeed only if there are many others within its network—which there well could be, if you began one where you are. Like, today. Or maybe tomorrow.

Notes

The Internet references linked in this book have been permanently archived using the *perma.cc* system. All the links referenced in these notes can be found at http://represent.lessig.org. If the originally referenced source is no longer available at the original link, *perma.cc* will provide an archived copy, unless the content is behind a paywall.

PREFACE

1. See *Environment*, Gallup, available at link #1; Austin Frakt, "The Astonishingly High Administrative Costs of U.S. Health Care," *New York Times*, July 16, 2018, available at link #2; Tami Luhby, "Millions More American Were Uninsured in 2017," *CNN Business*, January 16, 2018, available at link #3; James McBride, "The State of U.S. Infrastructure," Council on Foreign Relations, January 12, 2018, available at link #4.

INTRODUCTION

1. Timur Kuran, *Private Truths, Public Lies: The Social Consequences of Preference Falsification* (Cambridge, MA: Harvard University Press, 1995), 118–27.
2. Cited in Christopher Achen and Larry Bartels, *Democracy for Realists: Why Elections Do Not Produce Responsive Government* (Princeton, NJ: Princeton University Press 2016), 18.

3.　See, e.g., David Van Reybrouck, *Against Elections* (New York, NY: Vintage, 2018), x ("We have to admit that democracy is experiencing a crisis of confidence."); "Declining Trust in Government Is Denting Democracy," *The Economist*, January 25, 2017, available at link #5. Pew reports high support for "representative democracy," (78%), but find almost half support "rule by experts" (49%); 29% support "rule by a strong leader," and 24% support "rule by the military." Richard Wike et al., "Globally, Broad Support for Representative and Direct Democracy," Pew Research Center's Global Attitudes Project, October 16, 2017, available at link #6.

　　The literature on democracy's collapse is endless. For a brilliant analysis, see Tom Ginsburg and Aziz Z. Huq, *How to Save a Constitutional Democracy* (Chicago, IL: The University of Chicago Press, 2018). Other favorites include Benjamin I. Page and Martin Gilens, *Democracy in America?: What Has Gone Wrong and What We Can Do about It* (Chicago: University of Chicago Press, 2017); Richard L. Hasen, *Plutocrats United: Campaign Money, the Supreme Court, and the Distortion of American Elections* (New Haven, CT: Yale University Press, 2016); Brink Lindsey and Steven Teles, *The Captured Economy: How the Powerful Enrich Themselves, Slow Down Growth, and Increase Inequality* (New York: Oxford University Press, 2017); Steven Levitsky and Daniel Ziblatt, *How Democracies Die* (New York: Crown, 2018); Jacob S. Hacker and Paul Pierson, *Winner-Take-All Politics: How Washington Made the Rich Richer—and Turned Its Back on the Middle Class* (New York: Simon & Schuster, 2010). On remedies, see Frances Moore Lappé and Adam Eichen, *Daring Democracy: Igniting Power, Meaning, and Connection for the America We Want* (Boston: Beacon, 2017).

4.　See, e.g., Achen and Bartels, *Democracy for Realists*.

5.　Numbers drawn from Max Roser, "Democracy," in *Our World in Data* (2016), available at link #7. For a slightly different reckoning, see Robert A. Dahl, *On Democracy* (New Haven, CT: Yale University Press, 1998), 8.

6.　Francis Fukuyama, "The End of History?," *The National Interest* 16 (Summer 1989): 6.

7.　Steven Kull, "Voter Anger with Government and the 2016 Election: A Survey of American Voters," *Voice of the People,* conducted by the Program for Public Consultation, School of Public Policy, University of Maryland (November 2016), available at link #8. The differences between Republicans and Democrats with each of these questions was slight: "big interests" 95%R/89%D; "does not serve the common good"—87%R; 84%D; "corporations and their lobbyists have too much influence"—89%R/90%D; "elected officials think more about the interests of their campaign donors than the common good of the people"—92%R/88%D. In 2018, Pew continued to find high levels of dissatisfaction, though a lower percentage (76%) who say the government is "run by a few big interests." Pew Research Center, *The Public, the Political System and American Democracy* (April 2018), 72, available at link #9.

8.   Pew, *Public, Political System and American Democracy*, 1.

CHAPTER 1: THE UNREPRESENTATIVE "THEM"

1.   The idea of "representative" is of course not self-defining, and there have been many different conceptions across the history of democratic theory. The modern foundational text for mapping that conceptual range is Hanna F. Pitkin, *The Concept of Representation* (Berkeley:, University of California Press, 1967). In the present book, I move between two specific conceptions. The one is roughly consistent with Nicholas Stephanopoulos's view of representative implicit in "alignment." See Nicholas Stephanopoulos, "Aligning Campaign Finance Law," *Virginia Law Review* 101 (2015): 1425. Its focus is on whether representatives are aligned with the interests of citizens (ideally) or voters (in practice). The other is the conception of representative as selected, and then vested with the power to make judgments. This related to the trustee conception described by Pitkin, ch. 7, and advanced as the "selection" model more recently by Jenny Mansbridge. We will return to that conception later. In the main, the analysis I am offering here remains agnostic about these conceptions of representation, until chapter 5. In this way, chapters 1 and 3 are evaluating the mechanisms of democracy and the skew they produce relative to a conception of citizens possessing equal political power. For a powerful account of the other side of representation, namely "virtual representation," see Joseph Fishkin, "Taking Virtual Representation Seriously," *William & Mary Law Review* 59, no. 5 (2018): 1681.

2.   James Madison, "Thursday, July 5, 1787," The Avalon Project: Madison Debates, available at link #10; James Madison, "Tuesday, July 14, 1787," The Avalon Project: Madison Debates, available at link #11.

No doubt, Madison would have turned in his grave if he had read the Supreme Court's elevation of this anti-egalitarian exception into a constitutional rule. In *Whitcomb v. Chavis*, 403 U.S. 124, 167 (1971), the Court criticized "majoritarianism" as "a philosophy which ignores or overcomes the fact that the scheme of the Constitution is one not of majoritarian democracy, but of federal republics, with equality of representation a value subordinate to many others." Without doubt, the American republic is federal. And without doubt, it does not uniformly apply a majoritarian principle, at least with the Senate. But to render inequality as the rule is to invert the basic plan of Madison's republic.

3.   James Madison, "The Federalist Papers, No. 52.," The Avalon Project: The Federalist Papers, available at link #12.

4.   James Madison, "June 30," in *The Records of The Federal Convention of 1787*, ed. Max Farrand 1 (New Haven, CT: Yale University Press, 1966), 490.

5.   Danielle Allen maps the origin and vitality of the ideal of equality within our ur–founding text, the Declaration of Independence, in *Our Declaration: A Reading of the Declaration of Independence in Defense of Equality* (New York: W. W. Norton, 2014).

6.   This project is related to—and as Lawrence Lessig, *Republic, Lost: Version 2.0* (New York: Hachette, 2015), 39 makes clear, builds upon—the systemic account offered by Michael Golden in *Unlock Congress: Reform the Rules, Restore the System* (Pacific Grove, CA: Why Not Books, 2015). Three of his "four defects"—"the money flood," "rigged congressional races," and "the Senate filibuster"—are explicitly grounded upon representational equality. By drawing the frame more narrowly and precisely, I hope to complement his institutional analysis.

7.   Charles Riley, "Tom Perkins' Big Idea: The Rich Should Get More Votes," CNN Business, February 14, 2014, available at link #13.

8.   "Plural voting," in Wikipedia, available at link #14. Don't tell sixty-six-year-old Republican Lincoln Wilson about this: Wilson was prosecuted for registering to vote both in Kansas and Colorado, because he owned property in both places. Wilson would vote for "president in one state, and local issues in both places." After eighteen months and $50,000

in legal fees, he pled guilty to three misdemeanors, and paid a $6,000 fine. See Carol Anderson, *One Person, No Vote: How Voter Suppression Is Destroying Our Democracy* (New York: Bloomsbury, 2018), 86.

9.   Scott Lucas, "The Top Twenty Most Out-There Things Tom Perkins Said Last Night," *San Francisco Magazine*, February 14, 2014, available at link #15; Sam Gustin, "Tom Perkins Says the Rich Should Get More Votes in Elections," *Time*, February 14, 2014, available at link #16; Sarah McBride, "UPDATE 1-Investor Tom Perkins Says Progressive Taxation 'Persecutes' the Rich," Reuters, February 14, 2014, available at link #17; David A. Graham, "Tom Perkins Has a Fascinating, Radical, Un-American Voting Plan," *The Atlantic*, February 14, 2014, available at link #18.

10.   This framing between internal and external is offered by Jacob Katz Cogan in "The Look Within: Property, Capacity, and Suffrage in Nineteenth-Century America," *Yale Law Journal* 107 (1997): 473.

11.   Cogan, "The Look Within," 476–82.

12.   For perhaps the only comprehensive account of state rules regulating the right to vote, see the appendix to Alexander Keyssar's *The Right to Vote: The Contested History of Democracy in America* (New York: Basic Books, 2000).

13.   See Hanes Walton, Jr., Sherman C. Puckett, and Donald R. Deskins, Jr., *The African American Electorate: A Statistical History* (Los Angeles: CQ Press, 2012); Keyssar, *The Right to Vote*, ch. 4.

14.   *Harper v. Virginia Bd. of Elections*, 383 U.S. 663 (1966).

15.   The foundational work describing both the legal background and political science is Stephen Ansolabehere and James M. Snyder, Jr., *The End of Inequality: One Person, One Vote and the Transformation of American Politics* (New York: W.W. Norton, 2008).

16.   *Avery v. Midland County*, 390 U.S. 474, 476 (1968) (applying "one person, one vote" to a Texas county election system); *Lucas v. Forty-Fourth Gen. Assembly of Colo.*, 377 U.S. 713, 734–35 (1964) (applying "one person, one vote" to Colorado General Assembly apportionment); *Davis v. Mann*, 377 U.S. 678, 690 (1964) (applying "one person, one vote" to Virginia General Assembly); *Md. Comm. for Fair Representation v. Tawes*, 377 U.S. 656, 674 (1964) (applying "one person, one vote" to Maryland legislature apportionment); *WMCA, Inc. v. Lomenzo*, 377 U.S. 633, 653 (1964) (applying "one person, one vote" to New York

assembly apportionment); *Reynolds v. Sims*, 377 U.S. 533, 558 (1964) (applying "one person, one vote" to Alabama legislature apportionment); *Wesberry v. Sanders*, 376 U.S. 1, 18 (1964) (applying "one person, one vote" to U.S. congressional districts); *Gray v. Sanders*, 372 U.S. 368, 381 (1963) (formulating the "one person, one vote" principle for legislative districting and applying to the Georgia County Unit System); *Baker v. Carr*, 369 U.S. 186, 237 (1962) (holding that malapportionment claims are justiciable).

17. Anthony Lewis, "Districts Ruling Shocks Capital; Many Surprised by Court's Decision on Legislatures," *New York Times*, June 17, 1964, available at link #19. See also Andrew Hacker, "One Man, One Vote— Yes or No?," *New York Times*, August 16, 1964, available at link #20; "Decision on Reapportionment," *Los Angeles Times*, June 25, 1964 ("sweeping" and "controversial"); David Lawrence, "Supreme Court Oversteps Bounds," *Nashua Telegraph*, June 18, 1964), ("No such usurpation of power by the judicial branch of the government has been recorded before in the whole history of the republic").

18. Republican minority leader Everett Dirksen proposed an amendment in January 1965 to allow states to apportion a unicameral legislature or one house of a bicameral legislature on a basis other than population, based on a popular vote. The proposal had 37 cosponsors. See David Kyvig, *Explicit and Authentic Acts: Amending the U.S. Constitution, 1776–1995* (Lawrence, KS: University Press of Kansas, 1996), 375. The vote on August 4, 1965 was 57 to 39—seven votes short of the two-thirds needed for passage of the amendment. Id. at 376. The second vote on April 20, 1966 was 55 to 38. Dirksen began to call for state legislatures to call for a convention pursuant to Article V. By March 1967, 32 states had called for a convention, but 5 states called for a different amendment and 2 states never submitted their resolutions to Congress. The effort at a convention "collapsed entirely after Dirksen's death in September 1969." Id. at 378.

19. Anderson, *One Person, No Vote*; Carol Anderson, *White Rage: The Unspoken Truth of Our Racial Divide* (New York: Bloomsbury, 2016).

20. Katherine J. Cramer, *The Politics of Resentment: Rural Consciousness in Wisconsin and the Rise of Scott Walker* (Chicago: University of Chicago Press 2016), 164–66.

21. *Shelby County v. Holder*, 570 U.S. 529 (2013).

22.   *United States v. Classic*, 313 U.S. 299, 315 (1941).

23.   U.S. Const., Art. I, § 4.

24.   The effort to measure the health of our democracy is not anything new. Heather Gerken has been arguing for a "Democracy Index" for more than a decade. And the idea of modeling voter participation as a function of cost has been commonplace since Anthony Downs formalized the idea in the late 1950s. See Heather K. Gerken, *The Democracy Index: Why Our Election System Is Failing and How to Fix It* (Princeton, NJ: Princeton University Press, 2009) and Anthony Downs, *An Economic Theory of Democracy* (New York: Harper & Row, 1957).

25.   *Shelby County v. Holder*, 570 U.S. 529, 535 (2013).

26.   *Shelby County v. Holder*, 570 U.S. 529, 547, 558 (Thomas, J., concurring).

27.   Ari Berman, *Give Us the Ballot: The Modern Struggle for Voting Rights in America* (New York: Farrar, Straus and Giroux, 2015), Kindle edition, loc. 5459.

28.   Zoltan Hajnal, Nazita Lajevardi, and Lindsay Nelson, "Voter Identification Laws and the Suppression of Minority Votes," *The Journal of Politics* 79, no. 2 (April 2017): 376–77, available at link #21.

29.   On the partisan effect generally, see Jonathan Brater, Kevin Morris, Myrna Pérez, and Christopher Deluzio, *Purges: A Growing Threat to the Right to Vote*, Brennan Center for Justice July 20, 2018, available at link #22. For the background of Crosscheck, see "Interstate Voter Registration Crosscheck Program," in Wikipedia, available at link #23. For the statistics about racial difference and the quote from *The Root*, see Anderson, *One Person, No Vote*, 88.

30.   Anderson, *One Person, No Vote*, x ("Professor Justin Levitt of Loyola Law School, Los Angeles, found only thirty-one incidents of voter fraud out of hundreds of millions of votes cast since 2000"); Berman, Give Us the Ballot Kindle loc. 4414–73. See also Greg Price, "Donald Trump Makes Absurd Claim That Illegal Voters Change Into Disguise in Their Car and That's Why Republicans Lose," *Newsweek*, November 14, 2018, available at link #24.

31.   See Charles Stewart III, Stephen Ansolabehere, and Nathaniel Persily, "Revisiting Public Opinion on Voter Identification and Voter Fraud in an Era of Increasing Partisan Polarization," *Stanford Law Review* 68 (2016): 1455.

32. Wendy Weiser and Max Feldman, *The State of Voting 2018*, Brennan Center for Justice, June 5, 2018, available at link #25.

33. Berman, *Give Us the Ballot*, loc. 4083.

34. Berman, *Give Us the Ballot*, loc. 4025.

35. Berman, *Give Us the Ballot*, loc. 4230.

36. Berman, *Give Us the Ballot*, loc. 4245.

37. Berman, *Give Us the Ballot*, loc. 4245.

38. Anderson, *One Person, No Vote*, 117. For analysis by the Brennan Center, see Christopher Famighetti, "Long Voting Lines: Explained," Brennan Center for Justice, November 4, 2016, available at link #26.

39. Ari Berman, "There Are 868 Fewer Places to Vote in 2016 Because the Supreme Court Gutted the Voting Rights Act," *The Nation* November 4, 2016, available at link #27.

40. Berman, *Give Us the Ballot*, loc. 5001-04.

41. Jamil Smith, "Mitch McConnell, Enemy of the State," *Rolling Stone*, January 31, 2019, available at link #28.

42. John LaLoggia, "Conservative Republicans Are Least Supportive of Making It Easy for Everyone to Vote," Pew Research Center, October 31, 2018, available at link #29.

43. The graphic is drawn from Steven Nass, available at link #30. It was used by Christopher Ingraham in "This Is the Best Explanation of Gerrymandering You Will Ever See," *Washington Post*, March 1, 2015, available at link #31.

44. David Daley, *Ratf**ked: The True Story Behind the Secret Plan to Steal America's Democracy* (New York: Liveright, 2016), Kindle edition, loc. 644–46. A similar story could be told in North Carolina. Thomas Wolf and Peter Miller, "How Gerrymandering Kept Democrats from Winning Even More Seats Tuesday," *Washington Post,* November 8, 2018, available at link #32.

45. Neal Simon, "To Fix Our Democracy, First End Gerrymandering," *RealClearPolitics*, January 23, 2019, available at link #33.

46. *Bethune-Hill v. Va. State Bd. of Elections*, 137 S. Ct. 788 (2017), SCOTUSblog, available at link #34.

47. David Wasserman and Ally Flinn, "Introducing the 2017 Cook Political Report Partisan Voter Index," *Cook Political Report*, April 7, 2017, available at link #35.

48. Michael J. Barber and Nolan McCarty, "Causes and Consequences of Polarization," in *Political Negotiation*, ed. Jane Mansbridge and Cathie Jo Martin (Washington, DC: Brookings Institution, 2015), 52–53.

49. Jay O'Callaghan, "Republican 2014 Primary Turnout Tops Democrats for the Second Time since 1930," *Human Events*, October 8, 2014, available at link #36.

50. John C. Fortier, Matthew Weil, Michael Thorning, and Joshua Ferrer, "2018 Primary Election Turnout and Reforms," Bipartisan Policy Center, November 2018, 5, available at link #37.

51. Barber and McCarty, "Causes and Consequences of Polarization," 48–49.

52. Elaine Kamarck, Alexander R. Podkul, and Nick Zeppos, "Political Polarization and Voters in the 2016 Congressional Primaries," Center for Effective Public Management at Brookings, January 2017, 3, available at link #38.

53. Robert G. Boatright, *Getting Primaried: The Changing Politics of Congressional Primary Challenges* (Ann Arbor: University of Michigan Press, 2013), 86.

54. Boatright, *Getting Primaried*, 215.

55. Boatright, *Getting Primaried*.

56. See Jamie L. Carson, Michael H. Crespin, Charles J. Finocchiaro, and David W. Rohde, "Redistricting and Party Polarization in the U.S. House of Representatives," *American Politics Research* 35, no. 6 (2007): 878–904; Sean M. Theriault, *Party Polarization in Congress* (Cambridge: Cambridge University Press, 2008); Edward R. Tufte, "The Relationship between Seats and Votes in Two-Party Systems," *American Political Science Review* 67, no. 2 (1973): 540–54.

57. Barber and McCarty, "Causes and Consequences of Polarization," 52.

58. Barber and McCarty, "Causes and Consequences of Polarization," 52.

59. There is a longstanding debate among political scientists about whether America has become more "polarized." Some insist it has. See, e.g., Alan I. Abramowitz and Kyle L. Saunders, "Is Polarization a Myth?," *The Journal of Politics* 70, no. 2 (2008): 542. Some insist it has become instead "sorted." See, e.g., Morris P. Fiorina, Samuel A. Abrams and Jeremy C. Pope, "Polarization in the American Public: Misconceptions and Misreadings," *The Journal of Politics* 70, no. 2 (2008): 556.

Following Sam Rosenfeld, I use the term interchangeably. See Sam Rosenfeld, *The Polarizers: Postwar Architects of Our Partisan Era* (Chicago: University of Chicago Press, 2018), Kindle edition, loc. 5128 n.9.

60. George Reedy, quoted in Sam Rosenfeld, *The Polarizers*, Kindle edition, loc. 735.

61. Rosenfeld, *The Polarizers*, loc. 741-47.

62. Lyndon Johnson, quoted in Rosenfeld, *The Polarizers*, loc. 772.

63. Rosenfeld, *The Polarizers*, loc. 773.

64. Tracking roll call votes is the same technique used to analyze the effect of campaign contributions in Stephen Ansolabehere, John M. de Figueiredo, and James M. Snyder, Jr., "Why Is There so Little Money in U.S. Politics?," Working Paper 9409, National Bureau of Economic Research (December 2002), available at link #39.

65. Lawrence Lessig, *Republic, Lost: How Money Corrupts Congress—and a Plan to Stop It* (New York: Hachette Book Group, 2011), 125–71.

66. See Thomas E. Mann and Anthony Corrado, "Party Polarization and Campaign Finance," Center for Effective Public Management at Brookings (July 2014). We don't have a useful measure of small-dollar polarization either with vouchers alone, or when all fundraising is through small-dollar contributions. For a related analysis that draws stronger conclusions, see Thomas Ferguson, "Big Money, Mass Media, and the Polarization of Congress," in *Polarized Politics: The Impact of Divisiveness in the US Political System*, ed. William Crotty (Boulder, CO: Lynne Rienner, 2015), 95–128.

67. Thomas Mann, "Polarizing the House of Representatives: How Much Does Gerrymandering Matter?," in Pietro S. Nivola and David W. Brady, *Red and Blue Nation? Characteristics and Causes of America's Polarized Politics* (Washington, DC: Brookings Institution Press, 2006), 263–83.

68. *Safe-seat calculation,* available at link #40.

69. Elaine Kamarck and Alexander R. Podkul, "The 2018 Primaries Project: The Ideology of Primary Voters," Brookings Institution, October 23, 2018, available at link #41; Elaine Kamarck and Alexander R. Podkul, "Progressives versus the Establishment: An Updated Score," Brookings Institution, August 9, 2018, available at link #42.

70. Lydia Saad, "Conservative Lead in U.S. Ideology Is Down to Single Digits," Gallup, January 11, 2018, available at link #43.

71. "William A. Clark," Wikipedia, available at link #44. See also *Western Tradition Partnership, Inc. v. Attorney General of State*, 363 Mont. 220, 230-33 (2011); K. Ross Toole, *Montana: An Uncommon Land* (Norman: University of Oklahoma Press, 1959), 184–85.

72. David Graham Phillips, "The Treason of the Senate," *Cosmopolitan*, series published monthly from February through July 1906.

73. "The New Millionaire Senator," *New York Times*, January 17, 1890, available at link #45.

74. John F. Kennedy, *Profiles in Courage* (New York: Harper, 1956), 71. On the history of the evolution to an elected Senate, see Wendy J. Schiller & Charles Stewart III, *Electing the Senate: Indirect Democracy before the Seventeenth Amendment* (Princeton, NJ: Princeton University Press 2014).

75. See Max Farrand, "Alexander Hamilton, Federal Convention," *The Founders' Constitution*, June 18, 1787, available at link #46. Hamilton wasn't the only one with this idea. See Douglass Adair, *Fame and the Founding Fathers: Essays by Douglass Adair* (Indianapolis, IN: Liberty Fund, 1998), 94–96, 166–69; Eric Nelson, *The Royalist Revolution: Monarchy and the American Founding* (Cambridge, MA: Belknap Press of Harvard University Press, 2014), 29.

76. George Mason believed "it would be as unnatural to refer the choice of a proper character for chief magistrate to the people, as it would be to refer a trial of colors to a blind man." But the reason was not the incapacity of ordinary citizens. Instead, it was the size of the country that rendered "it impossible that the people can have the requisite capacity to judge of the respective pretensions of the candidates." See Michael J. Klarman, *The Framers' Coup: The Making of the United States Constitution* (New York: Oxford University Press, 2016), 228, quoting *The Records of the Federal Convention of 1787*, ed. Max Farrand (New Haven, CT: Yale University Press, 1911), 31, available at link #47.

77. See William Blackstone, *Commentaries on the Laws of England: A Facsimile of the First Edition of 1765-1769* (Chicago: University of Chicago Press, 1979), 175 (public voting distinct from voting "privately or by ballot").

78. For an account of this history, see Alexander Keyssar, *The Right to Vote: The Contested History of Democracy in the United States* (New York: Basic Books, 2009), 306–14. For a brief historical analysis of the rise

and fall of property requirements in the eighteenth and nineteenth centuries, see Jacob Katz Cogan, "The Look Within: Property, Capacity, and Suffrage in Nineteenth-Century America," *Yale Law Journal* 107, no. 2 (November 1997): 476–82.

79.   Nathan Bailey, *An Universal Etymological English Dictionary* (Edinburgh: Neil, 1783) (unpaginated) ("defining 'elector as "a chuser"); Samuel Johnson, *A Dictionary of the English Language* (London: J. F. and C. Rivington, 1785) (unpaginated) (giving first definition as "He that has a vote in the choice of any officer").

80.   Modern research concludes that the failure was quite intentional. See Thomas N. Baker, "'An Attack Well Directed': Aaron Burr Intrigues for the Presidency," *Journal of the Early Republic* 31, no. 4 (Winter 2011): 553–98; John S. Pancake, "Aaron Burr: Would-Be Usurper," *William and Mary Quarterly* 8, no. 2 (April 1951): 204–13.

81.   Edward B. Foley, "The Electoral College and Majority Rule: Restoring the Jeffersonian Vision for Presidential Elections," Ohio State Public Law, Working Paper No. 429, November 2017, available at link #48.

82.   Samuel Issacharoff, "Law, Rules, and Presidential Selection," *Political Science Quarterly* 120, no. 1 (Spring 2005): 113–29.

83.   *Swing State Demographics*, available at link #49.

84.   Douglas L. Kriner, *The Particularistic President* (Cambridge: Cambridge University Press, 2015), 2.

85.   Kriner, *The Particularistic President*, 11.

86.   Kriner, *The Particularistic President*, 23.

87.   Kriner, *The Particularistic President*, 41.

88.   Megan Geuss, "New Jersey Wants to Know Why Florida Is Exempt from Trump's Offshore Drilling Plans," *Ars Technica*, October 14, 2018, available at link #50.

89.   Pew, *The Public, the Political System and American Democracy*, 56.

90.   By swing states, I am including Arizona, Colorado, Florida, Georgia, Iowa, Maine, Michigan, Nevada, New Hampshire, North Carolina, Ohio, Pennsylvania, Virginia, and Wisconsin. The demographics of those states are represented here: *Swing State Demographics*, available at link #51.

91.   Kriner, *The Particularistic President*, 177.

92.   James M. Snyder Jr., "Monte Carlo Estimates of the Probability of an Electoral-College/Popular-Vote Split," Department of Government, Harvard University and NBER, July 18, 2018.

93. Ian Stewart, "Report: Americans Are Now More Likely to Die of an Opioid Overdose than on the Road," NPR, January 14, 2019, available at link #52. On the general problem of influence with pharmaceuticals, see Lawrence Lessig, *America, Compromised* (Chicago: University of Chicago Press, 2018), ch. 4; Beth Mole, "Big Pharma Shells Out $20B Each Year to Schmooze Docs, $6B on Drug Ads," *Ars Technica*, January 11, 2019, available at link #53.

94. See Chris McGreal, "FDA's Opioids Adviser Accuses Agency of Having 'Direct' Link to Crisis," *Guardian*, January 24, 2019, available at link #54.

95. Or at least the part of the Sackler family associated with two of the three original Sackler brothers; Arthur Sackler was not involved in the company when it developed and pushed its opioid, OxyContin.

96. At least in the sense of institutional corruption that I describe in *America, Compromised*.

97. Except as indicated, the facts in this section are drawn from the extraordinary article by Patrick Radden Keefe, "The Family That Built an Empire of Pain," *New Yorker*, October 30, 2017, available at link #55.

98. Ethan Barton, "American Cartel: Here Are the Politicians That Took Opioid Tycoons' 'Dirty, Bloody Money,'" *Daily Caller*, March 14, 2018, available at link #56.

99. Chris McGreal, "How Big Pharma's Money—and Its Politicians—Feed the US Opioid Crisis," *Guardian,* October 19, 2017, available at link #57.

100. For the founding rule on recusal statutes, see *Nevada Commission on Ethics v. Carrigan* 564 U.S. 117, 122-25 (2011).

101. Nara Pavão, "Corruption as the Only Option: The Limits to Electoral Accountability," *Journal of Politics* 80 (July 2018): 996–1010, available at link #58.

102. Dennis F. Thompson, *Ethics in Congress: From Individual to Institutional Corruption* (Washington, DC: Brookings Institution, 1995), 2.

103. Here is how James Bryce described him in 1888: "William Marcy Tweed was born in New York in 1823, of a Scotch father and an American mother. His earliest occupation was that of a chairmaker—his father's trade; but he failed in business, and first became conspicuous by his energy in one of the volunteer fire companies of the city, whereof he was presently chosen foreman. These companies had a good deal of

the club element in them and gave their members many opportunities for making friends and becoming known in the district they served. Tweed had an abounding vitality, free and easy manners, plenty of humor, though of a coarse kind, and a jovial, swaggering way which won popularity for him among the lower and rougher sort of people. His size and corpulence made it all the easier for him to support the part of the genial good fellow; and it must be said to his credit, that though he made friends lightly, he was always loyal to his friends. Neither shame nor scruples restrained his audacity. Forty years earlier these qualities would no more have fitted him to be a popular leader than Falstaff's qualities would have fitted him to be the chancellor of King Henry V; and had anyone predicted to the upper classes of New York that the boisterous fireman of 1845, without industry, eloquence, or education, would in 1870 be ruler of the greatest city in the western world, they would have laughed him to scorn. In 1850, however, Tweed was elected alderman, and soon became noted in the Common Council, a body already so corrupt (though the tide of immigration had only just begun to swell) that they were commonly described as the forty thieves. He came out of it a rich man and was presently sent to Washington as member for a district of the city. In the wider arena of Congress, however, he cut but a poor figure. He seems to have spoken only once, and then without success. In 1857 he began to repair his fortunes, shattered at the national capital, by obtaining the post of public school commissioner in New York, and soon afterwards he was elected to the Board of Supervisors, of which he was four times chosen president. There his opportunities for jobbery and for acquiring influence were much enlarged. 'Heretofore his influence and reputation had both been local, and outside of his district he had hardly been known at all. Now his sphere of action embraced the whole city, and his large figure began to loom up in portentous magnitude through the foul miasma of municipal politics.' Tweed was by this time a member of Tammany Hall, and in 1863 he was elected permanent chairman of the general committee. Not long after he and his friends captured the inner stronghold of the Tammany Society, a more exclusive and hitherto socially higher body; and he became grand sachem, with full command both of the Society, with its property and traditional influence, and of the political organization." James Bryce, *The American Commonwealth*, vol. 2, (Indianapolis: Liberty Fund, 1888), 262.

104. Though this is how Tweed is reported to have spoken, there is a good chance the quote is apocryphal. Several variations on the quotation have been attributed to him. The three earliest uses discovered by research assistants are: "Great Welcome Is Given Heney," *Los Angeles Herald*, May 3, 1908, at 3, available at link #59 ("The people can vote for whom they please if they let me do the nominating.") (quotation appears as part of a transcript of a speech by San Francisco assistant prosecuting attorney Francis J. Heney); "Direct Nominations," *Outlook* 95 (July 2, 1910): 468, available at link #60 ("'Let me do the nominating, and I care not who do the electing.' That might well serve a the motto of the commercialized political boss.") (not attributing it to Tweed, specifically); R. H. Blakesley, "Second Negative," *The Speaker* 6 (1911): 91, available at link #61 ("Let me put up the candidates, and I don't care who is elected.").

Political science has made some progress understanding the effects of a nomination filter on a final election. See, e.g., Richard S. Katz, "The Problem of Candidate Selection and Models of Party Democracy," *Party Politics* 7, no. 3 (May 2001): 277–96; Gideon Rahat and Reuven Y. Hazan, "Candidate Selection Methods: An Analytical Framework," *Party Politics* 7, no. 3 (May 2001): 297–322.

105. Primaries were initially very competitive; after their first thirty to forty years, their competitiveness dropped off. See John H. Aldrich, *Why Parties? The Origin and Transformation of Political Parties in America* (Chicago: University of Chicago Press, 1995). See also Stephen Ansolabehere, John Mark Hansen, Shigeo Hirano, and James M. Snyder Jr., "The Decline of Competition in U.S. Primary Elections, 1908–2004," paper presented at the annual meeting of the American Political Science Association, Marriott Wardman Park, Omni Shoreham, Washington Hilton, Washington, DC (September 1, 2005), available at link #62.

106. Our Campaigns, "TX Governor," available at link #63; United States House of Representatives History, Art & Archives, "Election Statistics, 1920 to Present," available at link #64.

107. Tania Branigan, "Hong Kong Activists Vow to Take Over Financial Centre in Election Protest," *Guardian*, August 31, 2014, available at link #65.

108. Jonathan Van Fleet, "Lawrence Lessig Compares the Number of Fundraisers between Presidents Reagan and Obama," *PolitiFact*, January 20, 2015, available at link #66.

109. Lessig, *Republic, Lost*, 13–14.

110. Stephanopoulos, *Aligning Campaign Finance Law*, 1474. While I am confident that the pattern and persistence of fundraising in Congress has changed dramatically since the middle 1990s, see especially Robert Kaiser, *So Damn Much Money* (New York: Knopf Books, 2009), I don't mean to suggest that money has not played a central role in American politics since the founding. See especially Thomas Furgeson, "Beyond Their Means? The Costs of Democracy From Jefferson to Lincoln," *The Journal of the Historical Society* 6, no. 4 (December 2006): 501–12; Thomas Ferguson and Jie Chen, "Investor Blocs and Party Realignments in American History," *The Journal of the Historical Society* 5, no. 4 (December 2005): 503–46.

111. "Speech: Donald Trump in Waterloo, IA—October 7, 2015," *Factbase*, October 7, 2015, transcript and video available at link #67.

112. "Speech: Donald Trump in Green Bay, WI—August 5, 2016," *Factbase*, August 5, 2016, transcript and video available at link #68.

113. Donald Trump, "Third Republican Presidential Candidate Debate, October 28, 2015," *Factbase*, October 28, 2015, transcript and video available at link #69.

114. "Speech: Donald Trump in Beaumont, TX—November 14, 2015," *Factbase*, November 14, 2015, transcript and video available at link #70.

115. *Austin v. Michigan Chamber of Commerce*, 494 U.S. 652, 660 (1990).

116. Stephanopoulos, *Aligning Campaign Finance Law*, 1430.

117. Christopher Ingraham, "Congress Thinks the Public Is Way More Conservative than It Actually Is. Deep-Pocketed Lobbyists Are to Blame, According to New Research," *Washington Post*, November 1, 2018, available at link #71.

118. Stephanopoulos, *Aligning Campaign Finance Law*, 1427. The consequences of this dependency are many, including, prominently, the increased access that the donors get to representatives. See, e.g., Amy Melissa McKay, "Fundraising for Favors? Linking Lobbyist-Hosted Fundraisers to Legislative Benefits," *Political Research Quarterly* 71, no. 4 (December 2018): 869–80. See generally Lessig, *Republic, Lost: Version 2.0*, 102–8.

Jennifer Heerwig has done some of the most comprehensive work to trace this dependence effect. See her masterful "Donations and Dependence: Individual Contributor Strategies in House Elections," *So-*

cial Science Research 60 (November 2016): 181–98, which uses a database that she developed to trace the effects of repeat donors across candidates.

119. Stephanopoulos, *Aligning Campaign Finance Law*, 1476. This relationship is causal, not correlational. Ibid., at 1478.

120. For a brilliant and subtle account, see Lee Drutman, *The Business of America Is Lobbying* (New York: Oxford University Press, 2015). See also Maggie McKinley and Thomas Groll, "The Relationship Market: How Modern Lobbying Gets Done," Harvard Edmond J. Safra Center for Ethics Lab Blog, February 13, 2015, available at link #72; Thomas Groll, and Christopher Ellis, "A Simple Model of the Commercial Lobbying Industry," *European Economic Review* 70 (2014): 299–316. Even worse in this story, but untouched in my analysis, is the growth in "dark money"—contributions that are not transparent to their (human) source. The best account of that dynamic is Jane Mayer, *Dark Money: The Hidden History of the Billionaires Behind the Rise of the Radical Right* (New York: Doubleday, 2016).

121. Lewis Hyde, *The Gift: Imagination and the Erotic Life of Property* (New York: Vintage Books, 1983), 56.

122. There is familiar skepticism among political scientists about whether campaign contributions are affecting policy results. The foundational work substantiating the skepticism is Stephen Ansolabehere, John M. de Figueiredo, and James M. Snyder, Jr., "Why Is There so Little Money in U.S. Politics?," Working Paper 9409, National Bureau of Economic Research (December 2002), available at link #39. That claim has inspired an industry of rebuttal. See Clayton D. Peoples, *The Undermining of American Democracy: How Campaign Contributions Corrupt our System and Harm Us All* (New York, NY: Routledge, 2020). See also Lessig, *Republic, Lost: Version 2.0*, 118–21. Thomas Furgeson, Paul Jorgensen, and Jie Chen have done the most extensive work tracking the relationship between campaign spending and political results. See Thomas Ferguson, Paul Jorgensen, and Jie Chen, "Big Money—Not Political Tribalism—Drives US Elections," Institute for New Economic Thinking, October 31, 2018, available at link #73; Thomas Ferguson, Paul Jorgensen, and Jie Chen, "Fifty Shades of Green: High Finance, Political Money, and the U.S. Congress," Report for the Roosevelt Institute, May 2017, available at link #74; Thomas Ferguson, Paul Jorgensen, and Jie Chen, "How Money Drives US Congressional Elections," Institute for New

Economic Thinking, Working Paper No. 48, August 1, 2016, available at link #75.

123. A similar point was drawn much earlier by Jamin B. Raskin and John Bonifaz in "Equal Protection and the Wealth Primary," *Yale Law & Policy Review* 11, no. 2 (1993): 273, available at link #76. Raskin and Bonifaz go further than I do, concluding the Equal Protection Clause requires reform of the campaign funding system. They develop that argument more fully in Jamin B. Raskin and John Bonifaz, *The Wealth Primary* (Washington, DC: Center for Responsive Politics, 1994).

124. Bernie Sanders, "A World for All of Us, Not Just the Billionaires," *Nation*, June 21, 2018, available at link #77.

125. Tad Dehaven, "Corporate Welfare and the Global Economic Crisis," *Policy Analysis* no. 703 (July 25, 2012), available at link #78; Jason Brennan, "The Right to Good Faith: How Crony Capitalism Delegitimizes the Administrative State," *Georgetown Journal of Law & Public Policy* 317, 334 (2013); Malcolm S. Salter, "Crony Capitalism, American Style: What Are We Talking About Here?," Harvard Edmond J. Safra Center for Ethics, Working Papers No. 50 (October 22, 2014).

126. Benjamin I. Page, Jason Seawright, and Matthew J. Lacombe, *Billionaires and Stealth Politics* (Chicago: University of Chicago Press, 2018).

127. See Theda Skocpol and Vanessa Williamson, *The Tea Party and the Remaking of Republican Conservatism* (Oxford: Oxford University Press, 2016).

128. Indeed, the median household income of the twenty smallest states is below the median household income of the top twenty. See *Per Capita Wealth*, available at link #79.

129. Francis Fukuyama, *Political Order and Political Decay: From the Industrial Revolution to the Globalization of Democracy* (New York: Farrar, Straus & Giroux, 2014), chap. 34.

130. Van Reybrouck, *Against Elections*, xiii.

131. See the analysis by Ciara Torres-Spelliscy in "What Drives Climate Change Denial? Campaign Donations and Lobbying," Brennan Center for Justice, September 19, 2017, available at link #80.

132. See Office of the Director of National Intelligence, "U.S. Intelligence Community Budget," November 2, 2018, available at link #81; Amanda Macias, "Trump Gives $717 Billion Defense Bill a Green Light. Here's What the Pentagon Is Poised to Get," CNBC, August 13, 2018, available at link #82.

133. See "Defense: Top Contributors to Federal Candidates, 2018," Open-Secrets.org, available at link #83.

134. Tim Wu, *The Curse of Bigness* (New York: Columbia Global Reports, 2018), 127–40.

135. Katherine M. Gehl and Michael E. Porter, "Why Competition in the Politics Industry Is Failing America: A Strategy for Reinvigorating Our Democracy," *Harvard Business Review* (2017). Gehl and Porter propose a series of significant reforms to address this single most important problem. Those reforms parallel the recommendations I make in this book.

CHAPTER 2: THE UNREPRESENTATIVE US

1. See "Topics of the Times: Italy Hails Our Dictator," *New York Times*, March 7, 1933; "Italian Fascists Call Roosevelt Rome's Disciple," *New York Herald Tribune*, May 7, 1933; "When Thieves Fall Out," *Daily Worker*, March 9, 1935; Harvey Klehr, "American Reds, Soviet Stooges," *New York Times*, July 3, 2017, available at link #84; Roger Shaw, "Fascism and the New Deal," *North American Review* 238 (1934): 559–64, available at link #85. Roosevelt himself acknowledged the criticism. Franklin Roosevelt, "Fireside Chat 5: On Addressing the Critics," June 28, 1934, available at link #86.

2. Jill Lepore, "Politics and the New Machine: What the Turn from Polls to Data Science Means for Democracy," *New Yorker*, November 16, 2015, available at link #87. Skepticism about polls and the idea of a public will is long-standing. For some representative sources, see Jean M. Converse, *Survey Research in the United States: Roots and Emergence, 1890–1960* (Berkeley: University of California Press, 1987).

3. Peverill Squire, "Why the 1936 Literary Digest Poll Failed," *Public Opinion Quarterly* 52, 1 (1988): 125–33

4. Daniel Robinson, *The Measure of Democracy: Polling, Market Research, and Public Life, 1930–1945* (Toronto: University of Toronto Press, 2019), Kindle edition, loc. 869, n.4. Gallup wasn't the only pollster to predict FDR's reelection: Elmo Roper and Archibald Crossly did as well. See Jean Converse, "The Most Direct Line, Business: Market Research and Opinion Polling," in *Survey Research in the US: Roots and Emergence 1890–1960* (Berkeley: University of California Press 1987), 87.

5. The idea of using a small sample was not original to Gallup. Jill Lepore, "Politics and the New Machine," available at link #87. His method—followed by Roper and Crossley—was the "quota sampling" method: identifying the relevant groups, and interviewing till the right quota from each was found. That method is not the modern randomized technique. The failure of 1948—predicting Truman would lose to Dewey—pushed the industry to adopt the random sampling method.

6. James Bryce, *The American Commonwealth* (London: Macmillan, 1888), 2: 920.

7. George Gallup and Saul Rae, *The Pulse of Democracy* (New York: Simon & Schuster, 1940). For examples of his extensive writing in the popular press, see, e.g., George Gallup, "Public Opinion in Our Cities," *National Municipal Review* 27, no. 2 (February 1938): 69–71, 103; George Gallup, "We, The People, Are Like This—A Report on How and What We Think," *New York Times*, June 8, 1941.

8. David W. Moore, *The Opinion Makers: An Insider Exposes the Truth Behind the Polls* (Boston: Beacon Press, 2008), Kindle edition, 16–18.

9. George Gallup, "Measuring Public Opinion," *Boston Globe*, July 7, 1936, 14.

10. Robinson, *The Measure of Democracy*, loc. 156.

11. Robert S. Erikson and Kent L. Tedin, *American Public Opinion,* 8th ed. (New York: Pearson Education, 2011).

12. James Bryce, *The American Commonwealth* (London: Macmillan, 1888), 2, ch. 78. Bryce acknowledged the difficulty: "How does this vague, fluctuating, complex thing we call public opinion—omnipotent yet indeterminate—a sovereign to whose voice everyone listens, yet whose words, because he speaks with as many tongues as the waves of a boisterous sea, it is so hard to catch—how does public opinion express itself. . . ? By what organs is it declared and how, since these organs often contradict one another, can it be discovered which of them speak most truly for the mass?" Ibid., chapter 79.

13. Susan Herbst, *Numbered Voices: How Opinion Polling Has Shaped American Politics* (Chicago: University of Chicago Press, 1993), 11; Tom W. Smith, "The First Straw? A Study of the Origins of Election Polls," *Public Opinion Quarterly* 54 (1990): 21–36.

14. V. O. Key, *Public Opinion and American Democracy* (New York: Knopf, 1961), 536.

15.   Alexis De Tocqueville, in Herbst, *Numbered Voices*, 73.

16.   Philip E. Converse, "Changing Conceptions of Public Opinion in the Political Process," *Public Opinion Quarterly* 51 (1987): S12–13.

17.   Converse, *Changing Conceptions*, S17. The effect was not limited to the political domains. Or Bassok has demonstrated how the rise of an independent source for determining public opinion profoundly changed the Supreme Court's own conception of its relationship to "the People." See Or Bassok, "The Supreme Court's New Source of Legitimacy," *University of Pennsylvania Journal of Constitutional Law* 16, no. 1 (October 2013): 153–98.

18.   See Figure 9.1 in Tom Rosenstiel and Andrew Kohut, "But What Do the Polls Show? How Public Opinion Surveys Came to Play a Major Role in Policymaking and Politics," Pew Research Center, October 14, 2009, available at link #88.

19.   See Felix Spangenberg, *The Freedom to Publish Opinion Poll Results: Report on a Worldwide Update*, World Association for Public Opinion Research (Amsterdam: Foundation for Information, 2003).

20.   George Gallup defended the role of polls in democracy. See George Horace Gallup and Saul Forbes Rae, *The Pulse of Democracy: The Public-Opinion Poll and How It Works* (New York: Simon & Schuster, 1940). But as Lepore reports, there was deep skepticism about whether polls should exist. Lepore, "Are Polls Ruining Democracy?" See also Lindsay Rogers, *The Pollsters: Public Opinion, Politics, and Democratic Leadership* (New York: Knopf, 1949) (an early work critical of Gallup's optimism). The most compelling account of the sociology of polls in American life—and indeed, how polls helped define America—is Sarah E. Igo, *The Averaged American: Surveys, Citizens, and the Making of a Mass Public* (Cambridge, MA: Harvard University Press, 2007); see also Robert S. Erikson and Kent L. Tedin, *American Public Opinion*, 8th ed. (New York: Pearson Education, 2011).

21.   Markus Prior, *Post-Broadcast Democracy* (New York: Cambridge University Press, 2007), 75.

22.   Prior, *Post-Broadcast Democracy*, 56.

23.   Tim Wu, *The Attention Merchants: The Epic Scramble to Get Inside Our Heads* (New York: Knopf, 2016), Kindle edition, loc. 928.

24.   *TV Penetration 1947–2008* (February 10, 2019, 3:26 P.M.), available at link #89.

25. Prior, *Post-Broadcast Democracy*, 3.

26. Prior, *Post-Broadcast Democracy*, 51–52.

27. Wu, *The Attention Merchants*, loc. 1705.

28. Wu, *The Attention Merchants*, loc. 2497.

29. See *Judgment at Nuremberg*, IMDB, available at link #90.

30. See "#Selma50: What the Media and Hollywood Got Wrong About 'Bloody Sunday,'" NBC News, March 8, 2015, available at link #91.

31. Bernard Grofman, Lisa Handley, and Richard Niemi, *Minority Representation and the Quest for Voting Equality* (New York: Cambridge University Press, 1992), 23.

32. Converse, *Changing Conceptions*, S21.

33. Robinson, *The Measure of Democracy*, loc. 1371.

34. Benjamin I. Page and Robert Y. Shapiro, *The Rational Public: Fifty Years of Trends in Americans' Policy Preferences* (Chicago: University of Chicago Press, 1992), xi.

35. Page and Shapiro, *The Rational Public*, 2–3.

36. Prior, *Post-Broadcast Democracy*, 3.

37. Converse, *Changing Conceptions*, S22.

38. Richard McKinney, "An Overview of the Congressional Record and Its Predecessor Publications: A Research Guide," Law Librarians' Society of Washington, D.C. (last revised January 2019), available at link #92.

39. Frank Noyes, "The Associated Press," *North American Review* 197 (1913): 701–10.

40. Herbst, *Numbered Voices*, 73. For a brilliant history of the emergence of a free press, see Michael Schudson, *Discovering the News: A Social History of American Newspapers* (New York: Basic Books, 1981). See also Alexander Field, "Newspapers and Periodicals: Number and Circulation By Type, 1850–1967," in *Historical Statistics of the United States: Earliest Times to the Present*, Millennial ed. (New York: Cambridge University Press, 2006); Frank Luther Mott, *A History of American Magazines: 1905–1930* (Cambridge, MA: Harvard University Press, 1968); Alfred McClung Lee, *The Daily Newspaper in America: The Evolution of a Social Instrument* (New York: Macmillan, 1937); David Shedden, "Early TV Anchors," *Poynter*, April 4, 2006, available at link #93.

41. Douglas Blanks Hindman and Kenneth Wiegand, "The Big Three's Prime-Time Decline: A Technological and Social Context," *Journal of Broadcasting & Electronic Media* 52 (2008): 119–35, available at link #94.

42. See Paul Starr, *The Creation of the Media: Political Origins of Modern Communications* (New York: Basic Books, 2005); Robert W. McChesney and John Nichols, *The Death and Life of American Journalism: The Media Revolution That Will Begin the World Again* (Philadelphia: Nation Books, 2010); Lessig, *America, Compromised*, 72–74; Herbst, *Numbered Voices*, 73–74 ("It is clear that most newspapers had distinct ideological perspectives in the mid-nineteenth century").

43. In a later paper, Robert Shapiro tracks how political polarization can affect how the public learns. See Robert Shapiro and Yaeli Bloch-Elkon, "Political Polarization and the Rational Public," paper prepared for presentation at the Annual Conference of the American Association for Public Opinion Research, Montreal, Quebec, Canada, May 18–21, 2006, available at link #95.

44. The optimistic: Mike Godwin, *Cyber Rights: Defending Free Speech in the Digital Age* (Cambridge, MA: MIT Press, 1998); Yochai Benkler, *The Wealth of Networks: How Social Production Transforms Markets and Freedom* (New Haven, CT: Yale University Press, 2006); Clay Shirky, *Here Comes Everybody: The Power of Organizing Without Organizations* (New York: Penguin Press, 2008). The dark: Jonathan Zittrain, *The Future of the Internet and How to Stop It* (New Haven, CT: Yale University Press, 2008); Jaron Lanier, *You Are Not a Gadget: A Manifesto* (New York: Knopf, 2010).

45. The quote is from John Gilmore, one of the founders of EFF. See "John Gilmore," *Wikipedia*, available at link #96.

46. Eli Pariser, *The Filter Bubble: How the New Personalized Web Is Changing What We Read and How We Think* (New York: Penguin Press, 2011).

47. Zeynep Tufekci, *Twitter and Tear Gas: The Power and Fragility of Networked Protest* (New Haven, CT: Yale University Press, 2017), 31, 270.

48. David W. Moore, *The Opinion Makers: An Insider Exposes the Truth Behind the Polls* (Boston: Beacon Press, 2008), Kindle edition, loc. 292–93.

49. Anthony Downs, *An Economic Theory of Democracy* (New York: Harper & Row, 1957).

50. On the limits of even this rationality—and of democracy generally—see Achen and Bartels, *Democracy for Realists*, 30; Kirby Goidel, *America's Failing Experiment: How We the People Have Become the Problem* (Lanham, MD: Rowman & Littlefield, 2014), 57. On the potential

contributions of the media to mitigating the Downs effect, see Alexander Dyck, David Moss, and Luigi Zingales, "Media versus Special Interests," *The Journal of Law & Economics* 56, no. 3 (August 2013): 521–53.

51.   Ewan Palmer, "Barack Obama: 'If You Watch Fox News, You're in One Reality, and If You Read the New York Times, You're in a Different Reality,'" *Newsweek*, March 7, 2019, available at link #97.

52.   Tufekci, *Twitter and Tear Gas*, 270.

53.   Stephan Guyenet, "Fast Food, Weight Gain and Insulin Resistance," *Whole Health Source*, May 22, 2011, available at link #98.

54.   Lessig, *Republic, Lost*, 43–52 (discussing food regulation).

55.   Herbert Hoover, quoted in Wu, *The Attention Merchants,* loc. 1624.

56.   Eric Barnouw, quoted in Wu, *The Attention Merchants,* loc. 2907.

57.   Larry Page and Sergey Brin, quoted in Wu, *The Attention Merchants,* loc. 4920.

58.   John Battelle, quoted in Wu, *The Attention Merchants,* loc. 4933–34.

59.   This road has been cleared by others before. For the most compelling accounts, see Wu, *The Attention Merchants*; McChesney and Nichols, *Death and Life of American Journalism.* For the most comprehensive and theorized recent account, see Shoshana Zuboff, *The Age of Surveillance Capitalism: The Fight for a Human Future at the New Frontier of Power* (New York: PublicAffairs, 2019).

60.   Lawrence Lessig, *The Future of Ideas: The Fate of the Commons in a Connected World* (New York: Random House, 2001), 7.

61.   Compare Cass R. Sunstein, "The First Amendment in Cyberspace," *Yale Law Journal* 104 (1995): 1757–1804, available at link #99, with Eugene Volokh, "Cheap Speech and What It Will Do," *Yale Law Journal* 104 (1995): 1805–50, available at link #100. Rick Hasen gives a contemporary view of Volokh's "remarkably prescient article" in "Cheap Speech and What It Has Done (to American Democracy)," *First Amendment Law Review* 16 (2017–18): 200.

62.   Nick Visser, "CBS Chief Les Moonves Says Trump's 'Damn Good' for Business," *Huffington Post*, March 1, 2016, available at link #101.

63.   Gregory J. Martin and Ali Yurukoglu, "Bias in Cable News: Persuasion and Polarization," *American Economic Review* 107, no. 9: 2565–99, (2017) available at link #102. The trick is to use the channel position for the different networks in different markets. That positioning is not itself biased, but it differs in a sufficiently significant way to distinguish

persuasion from selection. Their work confirms the earlier work by Stefano DellaVigna and Ethan Kaplan, "The Fox News Effect: Media Bias and Voting," *Quarterly Journal of Economics* 122, no. 3 (2007): 1187–1234, available at link #103, which had found a similar effect from the presence of Fox News within a jurisdiction. See also Elizabeth Schroeder and Daniel F. Stone, "Fox News and Political Knowledge," *Journal of Public Economics* 126 (June 2015): 52–63; Daniel J. Hopkins and Jonathan M. Ladd, "The Consequences of Broader Media Choice: Evidence from the Expansion of Fox News," *Quarterly Journal of Political Science* 9, no. 1 (2014): 115–35 (finding loyalties of copartisans increase while independents only possibly persuaded). For an earlier analysis, see James G. Webster, "Beneath the Veneer of Fragmentation: Television Audience Polarization in a Multichannel World," *Journal of Communication* 55, no. 2 (June 2005): 366–82.

64. Analysis drawn from Gallup Poll Social Series, on file with author. Trump comparison drawn from Wave 27, May 1–15, 2017; Obama comparison drawn from Wave 7, September 9–October 3, 2014. My thanks to Jonathan Hack, data librarian at Harvard Law School, for help tabulating the differences.

65. This is the important qualification to the debate about polarization offered by Morris Fiorina. Fiorina insists that the nation has not moved "away from the center toward both extremes." Instead, the "ideological consistency in the American electorate . . . has increased." That's a significantly harmful dynamic, too, as Fiorina argues—it is "a fundamental cause of the gridlock and incivility that characterize contemporary politics." But it is different from the idea that Americans are becoming more extreme. See Morris Fiorina, "Americans Have Not Become More Politically Polarized," *Washington Post*, June 23, 2014, available at link #104; Morris P. Fiorina, "The Political Parties Have Sorted," a Hoover institution essay on contemporary American politics, series no. 3, 2016.

66. Yochai Benkler, Robert Faris, and Hal Roberts, *Network Propaganda: Manipulation, Disinformation, and Radicalization in American Politics* (New York: Oxford University Press, 2018), 73–74.

67. Benkler, Faris, and Roberts, *Network Propaganda*, 75-6.

68. Thomas E. Mann and Norman J. Ornstein, *It's Even Worse Than It Looks: How the American Constitutional System Collided with the New Politics of Extremism* (New York: Basic Books, 2012).

69. Hillary Clinton, *What Happened* (New York: Simon & Schuster, 2017), Kindle edition, loc. 4048.

70. Benkler, Faris, and Roberts, *Network Propaganda*, 17.

71. For a related view—that the media "must embrace their solemn duty and educate the population about our great challenges—ratings be damned"—see Rob Cohen, "TV News Is As Much to Blame for Democracy's Decline as Trump Is," *Chicago Tribune*, November 16, 2018, available at link #105.

72. Among the most comprehensive analysis of the news coverage during the 2016 campaign is that conducted by the Harvard Kennedy School's Shorenstein Center. The center published four studies after the election. Part 1: Thomas E. Patterson, "Pre-Primary News Coverage of the 2016 Presidential Race: Trump's Rise, Sanders' Emergence, Clinton's Struggle," Harvard Kennedy School Shorenstein Center on Media, Politics & Public Policy and *Media Tenor* (June 2016), available at link #106; Part 2: Thomas E. Patterson, "News Coverage of the 2016 Presidential Primaries: Horse Race Reporting Has Consequences," Harvard Kennedy School Shorenstein Center on Media, Politics & Public Policy and *Media Tenor* (July 2016), available at link #107; Part 3: Thomas E. Patterson, "News Coverage of the 2016 National Conventions: Negative News, Lacking Context," Harvard Kennedy School Shorenstein Center on Media, Politics & Public Policy and *Media Tenor* (September 2016), available at link #108; Part 4: Thomas E. Patterson, "News Coverage of the 2016 General Election: How the Press Failed the Voters," Harvard Kennedy School Shorenstein Center on Media, Politics & Public Policy and *Media Tenor* (December 2016), available at link #109.

73. Patterson, "News Coverage of the 2016 General Election," 3.

74. Patterson, "News Coverage of the 2016 General Election," 4.

75. Patterson, "News Coverage of the 2016 General Election," 15.

76. Patterson, "News Coverage of the 2016 General Election," 18.

77. Benkler, Faris, and Roberts, *Network Propaganda*, 3.

78. Patterson, "News Coverage of the 2016 General Election," 7.

79. Bernie Sanders: The Democracy Now! Interview, *Democracy Now!*, December 26, 2016, available at link #110.

80. Nara Pavão, "Corruption as the Only Option: The Limits to Electoral Accountability," *Journal of Politics* 80, no. 3 (2018): 996–1010, available at link #111.

81. See Michael Barber and Jeremy C. Pope, "Does Party Trump Ideology? Disentangling Party and Ideology in America," *American Political Science Review* 113 (2019): 38, available at link #112; Elizabeth Kolbert, "Why Facts Don't Change Our Minds," *New Yorker*, February 27, 2017, available at link #113; Hugo Mercier and Dan Sperber, *The Enigma of Reason* (Cambridge, MA: Harvard University Press, 2017).

82. Dan M. Kahan, "The Politically Motivated Reasoning Paradigm, Emerging Trends in Social & Behavioral Sciences, Part 1: What Politically Motivated Reasoning Is and How to Measure It," *Emerging Trends in the Social & Behavioral Sciences* (2016). This is also the focus of the extremely powerful work by Jonathan Haidt. See especially *The Righteous Mind: Why Good People Are Divided by Politics and Religion* (New York: Random House, 2012). Kahan et al. demonstrate that training can dampen the tendency to adopt cultural values. See Dan M. Kahan, David Hoffman, Danieli Evans, Neal Devans, Eugene Luccim, and Katherine Cheng, "Ideology or Situation Sense: An Experimental Investigation of Motivated Reasoning and Professional Judgment," *University of Pennsylvania Law Review* 164 (2016): 349.

83. Graham Vyse, "The Decline of the Fox News Liberal Pundit," *New Republic*, May 24, 2017, available at link #114.

84. Martin and Yurukoglu, *Bias in Cable News*, 2596.

85. Ian Schwartz, "Tucker Carlson: We Are Ruled by Mercenaries Who Feel No Long-Term Obligation to the People They Rule," *Real Clear News*, January 3, 2019, available at link #115.

86. Free Press News, "Tucker Carlson—Time to Ban The Electoral College Because It's Racist—Of Course!" (October 10, 2018) available at link #116.

87. David Roberts, "The Real Problem with the New York Times Op-Ed Page: It's Not Honest About U.S. Conservatism," *Vox*, March 15, 2018, available at link #117.

88. Jacqueline Thomsen, "Cavuto Reads Hate Mail He Got for Criticizing Trump-Putin Summit," *Hill*, July 20, 2018, available at link #118.

89. See Dan M. Kahan, "What Is the 'Science of Science Communication'?" *Journal of Science Communication* 14 (2015), available at link #119. A similar conclusion is drawn by Jonathan Haidt. See *The Righteous Mind*. See also *Why Do They Vote That Way* (New York: Vintage Books 2018) (drawn in part from *The Righteous Mind*). This dynamic

at the macro level is reinforced at the micro level as well. Cass R. Sunstein, "The Law of Group Polarization," *Journal of Political Philosophy* 10, no. 2 (2002): 175–95. For a detailed review of evidence, see Cass R. Sunstein, *Going to Extremes: How Like Minds Unite and Divide* (Oxford: Oxford University Press, 2009), 161–68.

90. Ben Gilbert, "There's a Simple Reason Your New Smart TV Was So Affordable: It's Collecting and Selling Your Data," *Business Insider*, January 12, 2019, available at link #120.

91. Sean Burch, "'Senator, We Run Ads': Hatch Mocked for Basic Facebook Question to Zuckerberg," *SFGate*, April 10, 2018, available at link #121; "Facebook CEO Mark Zuckerberg Hearing on Data Privacy and Protection," C-SPAN, April 10, 2018, available at link #122.

92. My thinking in this respect was inspired by a brilliant article by Jonathan Zittrain, published just at the height of the copyright wars. In "What the Publisher Can Teach the Patient: Intellectual Property and Privacy in an Era of Trusted Privication," *Stanford Law Review* 52 (2000): 1201, available at link #123, Zittrain argued that the problem of the copyright owner in the digital age was the same as the problem of the patient (or person) trying to protect her privacy. In both cases, the architecture of digital technology has made it difficult to control the spread of those data, whether copies of copyrighted material or private data. And at its core, the idea of copy-protection technologies was the same as the idea of privacy-protection technologies: both are about controlling copies in a digital era. That recognition, however, leads to a second: that maybe the law should care less about controlling copies, and more about controlling uses. With copyright, that would entail a freedom to distribute widely, but with certain uses regulated. See, for example, William W. Fisher III, *Promises to Keep* (Stanford, CA: Stanford University Press, 2004). With privacy, it would mean worrying less about the promiscuous sharing of data, and more about how that data could be used. That remains my intuition, as I suggest in this book, but this book is not the context within which to work out all that approach would entail. Suffice to say that it must reject as talismanic the "consent" of individuals. In my view, some uses should be forbidden, and some uses should be permitted, and only very few uses should require specific consent by the person whose data is at issue.

I have also benefitted enormously here (and elsewhere) from the work of Julie Cohen. See, especially, Julie E. Cohen, "The Surveillance-Innovation Complex: The Irony of the Participatory Turn," in *The Participatory Condition in the Digital Age*, ed. *Darin Barney, Gabriella Coleman, Christine Ross, Jonathan Sterne, and Tamar Tembeck (Minneapolis: University of Minnesota Press, 2016), 207–26.*

93. Tim Wu believes there is a wrong here with a remedy, *The Curse of Bigness* (New York: Columbia Global Reports, 2018). Others are clear there's a competitive harm, but unsure about the remedy. For a fantastic analysis of the antitrust problem raised by "free" data, see Dirk Bergemann and Alessandro Bonatti, "The Economics of Social Data" (working paper, January 15, 2019) (while identifying a competitive problem, the authors have no clear remedy beyond data portability).

94. Steven Levy, *In the Plex: How Google Thinks, Works, and Shapes Our Lives* (New York: Simon & Schuster, 2011), 172–73.

95. Microsoft acquired Skype for $8.5 billion on May 10, 2011. "Microsoft Officially Welcomes Skype," *Microsoft*, October 13, 2011, available at link #124. Microsoft revealed its speech recognition capabilities through an announcement that demonstrated Star Trek–like technology (the "universal translator"). "Skype Translator Preview—An Exciting Journey to a New Chapter in Communication," Skype, December 15, 2014, available at link #125. Microsoft assures users that no personally identifiable data is gathered from Skype and that the data is not used for advertising. "Skype Translator Privacy FAQ," Skype, available at link #126.

96. Andrew C. Oliver, "In Memory of Aaron Swartz: Stealing Is Not Stealing," *InfoWorld*, January 17, 2013, available at link #127.

97. Zuboff, *Surveillance Capitalism*, 521.

98. Zuboff, *Surveillance Capitalism*, 92.

99. Zuboff, *Surveillance Capitalism*, 339–40.

100. Zuboff, *Surveillance Capitalism*, 451.

101. Chris Nodder, *Evil by Design: Interaction Design to Lead Us into Temptation* (Indianapolis, IN: John Wiley, 2013).

102. Steve Henn, "Online Marketers Take Note of Brains Wired for Rewards," NPR, July 24, 2013, available at link #128.

103. Hayley Tsukayama, "Video Game Addiction Is a Real Condition, WHO Says. Here's What That Means," *Washington Post*, June 18, 2018, available at link #129. On the neural effects of gaming, see S. Kühn

et al., "The Neural Basis of Video Gaming," *Translational Psychiatry* (2011): 1, e53, available at link #130. All of these gaming techniques build upon the long-practiced technique in casinos of designing the environment and technology of gambling environments to induce addiction. See Natasha Dow Schüll, *Addiction by Design: Machine Gambling in Las Vegas* (Princeton, NJ: Princeton University Press, 2014).

104. See Roger McNamee, *Zucked* (New York: Penguin Random House, 2019), 86. The classic textbook by Fogg is *Persuasive Technology: Using Computers to Change What We Think and Do* (San Francisco: Morgan Kaufmann, 2002). Its insights have been popularized by Nir Eyal in *Hooked: How to Build Habit-Forming Products* (New York: Portfolio, 2016).

105. McNamee, *Zucked*, 86.

106. McNamee, *Zucked*, 88.

107. Harris describes ten hijacking techniques: (1) control the menu, (2) turn the experience into a slot machine, (3) generate a fear of missing something important, (4) create conditions for social approval, (5) create dynamics of social reciprocity, (6) create bottomless bowls, (7) architect instant interruption, (8) bundle your reasons with their reasons, (9) create inconvenient alternatives, (10) create "foot in the door" forecasting errors. See Tristan Harris, "How Technology Hijacks People's Minds—from a Magician and Google's Design Ethicist," TristanHarris.com, available at link #131.

108. Many have tried to measure the net psychological effects of Facebook upon its users. Among the most comprehensive is Hunt Allcott, Luca Braghieri, Sarah Eichmeyer, Matthew Gentzkow, "The Welfare Effects of Social Media," NBER Working Paper No. 25514, available at link #132. Allcott, et al., conducted a randomized evaluation of the welfare effects of Facebook during the lead-up to the 2018 election. Following more than 2,500 users willing to deactivate their account, they measured the effect on a randomized subset that actually did. While they conclude that consumer surplus from the platform is, on balance, positive, they found that deactivating users reduced online activity generally, were less informed and less polarized about news, were happier, and demonstrated a large persistent reduction in Facebook use after the experiment.

109. See Richard Thaler and Cass Sunstein, *Nudge: Improving Decisions about Health, Welfare, and Happiness* (New York: Penguin, 2009).

110. Mark Zuckerberg, "The Facts About Facebook," *Wall Street Journal*, January 24, 2019, available at link #133.

111. Zuboff, *Surveillance Capitalism*, 310.

112. Dirk Bergemann and Alessandro Bonatti, "The Economics of Social Data" (working paper, January 15, 2019).

113. This example is purely hypothetical, although in 2016, Microsoft received a patent for "User Behavior Monitoring on a Computerized Device." The patent envisions a device monitoring behavior, and then alerting different groups, including, Zuboff reports, "insurance companies." See Zuboff, *Surveillance Capitalism*, 411–12.

114. McNamee, *Zucked*, 101.

115. Zeynep Tufekci, "How Social Media Took Us from Tahrir Square to Donald Trump," *MIT Technology Review* (August 14, 2018), available at link #134. See also Laura Hazard Owen, "Facebook Groups Are 'the Greatest Short-Term Threat to Election News and Information Integrity,'" *NiemanLab*, November 9, 2018, available at link #135; Jonathan Albright, "The Shadow Organizing of Facebook Groups," *Medium*, November 4, 2018, available at link #136.

116. Yochai Benkler and his colleagues are not convinced the Russians affected the 2016 election results. Benkler, Faris, and Roberts, *Network Propaganda*, chap. 8. Kathleen Hall Jamieson believes the opposite. Kathleen Hall Jamieson, *Cyberwar: How Russian Hackers and Trolls Helped Elect a President* (New York: Oxford University Press, 2018). It is clear that we are learning more that leads more directly to Jamieson's conclusion. See, for example, Adam Peck, "The Russian Effort to Divert Votes to Jill Stein Was More Extensive than Previously Thought," *ThinkProgress*, December 22, 2018, available at link #137; Peter Weber, "Ex-intelligence Chief James Clapper Says Russia Won the Election for Trump. This Study Backs Him Up," *Week*, May 24, 2018, available at link #138. On the continued interventions in 2018, see Jonathan Albright, "Facebook and the 2018 Midterms: A Look at the Data," *Medium*, November 4, 2018, available at link #139. In March 2019, Mark Zuckerberg announced Facebook would shift its focus to emphasize user privacy more. What was not clear from the announcement was how the shift would affect the business model of advertising— or whether it would at all. See Mark Zuckerberg, "A Privacy-Focused Vision for Social Networking," Facebook, March 6, 2019, available

at link #140. See also Mike Issac, "Facebook's Mark Zuckerberg Says He'll Shift Focus to Users' Privacy," *New York Times*, March 6, 2019, available at link #141.

117. Zuboff, *Surveillance Capitalism*, 509. ("The larger point of the exercise is to find the point of equilibrium between the ability to pull users and their surplus into the site and the risk of repelling them. This is a calculation of radical indifference that has nothing to do with assessing the truthfulness of content or respecting reciprocities with users.")

118. Julia Angwin, Madeline Varner, and Ariana Tobin, "Facebook Enabled Advertisers to Reach 'Jew Haters,'" ProPublica, September 14, 2017, available at link #142.

119. Tim Wu tells this story powerfully in *The Attention Merchants*.

120. Based on Nielsen Media Research, NBC is number one in total viewership with an average of 7.8 million total viewers. See Wayne Friedman, "NBC Wins Season TV Ratings, But Broadcast Nets Lose Ground Overall," *Media Post*, May 21, 2019, available at link #143.

121. The conservatives are wrong, if convinced by a small minority. See Damon Centola, Joshua Becker, Devon Brackbill, and Andrea Baronchelli, "Experimental Evidence for Tipping Points in Social Convention," *Science* 360 (2018): 1116–19, available at link #144. But so too are the liberals. Philip M. Fernbach, Nicholas Light, Sydney E. Scott, Yoel Inbar, and Paul Rozin, "Extreme Opponents of Genetically Modified Foods Know the Least but Think They Know the Most," *Nature Human Behavior*, January 14, 2019, available at link #145.

122. Zuboff, *Surveillance Capitalism*, 469.

123. See Al Gore, *The Assault on Reason* (New York: Penguin Press, 2007). While Gore's view of the past is too optimistic, his view of the present is quite prescient.

124. Zephyr Teachout, "The Anti-Corruption Principle," *Cornell Law Review* 94 (2008): 377, available at link #146.

125. And it turns the question back on the democratic "realists": is the "folk theory" of democracy—which "celebrates the wisdom of popular judgments by informed and engaged citizens"—wrong or just misplaced? Achen and Bartels, *Democracy for Realists*, 9. Achen and Bartels are skeptical about what I'll offer as the ultimate partial solution—deliberative polling—but it is striking that their empirical attack on the folk theory presumes this epistemic weakness regardless.

126. Kirby Goidel, *America's Failing Experiment* (Lanham, MD: Rowman & Littlefield, 2013), 3.

127. Goidel, *America's Failing Experiment*. I don't mean to belittle Goidel's important work. He does capture brilliantly the challenge of engaging a democratic public sensibly—and the opportunistic use that campaigns make of this ignorance. See especially 91–97. His and Achen and Bartels are among the best briefs against the idea of democratic self-governance. But as I've suggested, both embed a presumption about how we speak. That is the assumption this chapter is meant to challenge.

128. "The Public, the Political System, and American Democracy," Pew Research Center, April 26, 2018.

129. Stephen Hawkins, Daniel Yudkin, Míriam Juan-Torres, and Tim Dixon, "Hidden Tribes: A Study of America's Polarized Landscape," *More in Common*, October 2018.

130. Prior, *Post-Broadcast Democracy*, 155–56.

131. See, for example, Herbst, *Numbered Voices*; Justin Lewis, *Constructing Public Opinion* (New York: Columbia University Press, 2001); Diane J. Heith, *Polling to Govern: Public Opinion and Presidential Leadership* (Stanford, CA: Stanford University Press, 2004); George F. Bishop, *The Illusion of Public Opinion: Fact and Artifact in American Public Opinion Polls* (Oxford: Rowman & Littlefield, 2005); Sarah E. Igo, *The Averaged American: Surveys, Citizens, and the Making of a Mass Public* (Cambridge, MA and London: Harvard University Press, 2007); Robert S. Erikson and Kent L. Tedin, *American Public Opinion*, 8th ed. (New York: Pearson Education, 2011).

132. Jill Lepore, "Politics and the New Machine," *New Yorker*, November 16, 2015, available at link #147.

CHAPTER 3: FIXING THEM

1. "Statistical Summary of 24-Month Campaign Activity of the 2017–2018 Cycle," Federal Election Commission, March 15, 2019, available at link #148.

2. Michael Beckel, "Dark Money Illuminated," *Issue One*, 2018; Nicholas Confessore, "The Families Funding the 2016 Presidential Election," *New York Times*, October 10, 2015, available at link #149.

3.   *Buckley v. Valeo*, 424 U.S. 1, 45 (1976) (per curiam).

4.   *Buckley v. Valeo*, 424 U.S. 1, 48–49 (1976) (per curiam).

5.   Richard L. Hasen, "Clipping Coupons for Democracy: An Egalitarian/Public Choice Defense of Campaign Finance Vouchers," *California Law Review* 84 (1996), available at link #150.

6.   The idea of using vouchers to fund campaigns is not new. Senators Russell Long (D-LA; 1948–87) and Lee Metcalf (D-MT; 1961–78) proposed an early and modest version in 1967. See Thomas Cmar, "Toward a Small Donor Democracy: The Past and Future of Incentives for Small Political Contributions," *Fordham Urban Law Journal* 32 (2005): 475. David Adamany and George Agree built on the Metcalf plan to propose their own voucher program in *Political Money: A Strategy for Campaign Financing in America* (Baltimore: Johns Hopkins University Press, 1975), 189–99. The more recent debate pushing vouchers as a small-dollar public funding system begins with Ed Foley's work, "Equal-Dollars-Per-Voter: A Constitutional Principle of Campaign Finance," *Columbia Law Review* 94 (1994) (arguing for public funding proposals such as vouchers as a matter of constitutional obligation). Rick Hasen followed up shortly thereafter in Richard L. Hasen, *Clipping Coupons for Democracy: An Egalitarian/Public Choice Defense of Campaign Finance Vouchers*, California La Review 84 (1996): 1. Bruce Ackerman and Ian Ayres build on that work in *Voting with Dollars: A New Paradigm for Campaign Finance* (New Haven, CT: Yale University Press, 2002), Kindle edition, which proposes a voucher system tied to an "anonymous donation booth"—a device that permits anonymous contributions beyond the contributions funded by vouchers. Pam Karlan separates out again the voucher proposal and adds important support in "Elections and Change Under Voting with Dollars," *California Law Review* 91 (2003), available at link #151. I advanced a voucher proposal in the first edition of this book, *Republic, Lost: How Money Corrupts Congress: And a Plan to Stop It* (New York: Hachette Book Group, 2011), which conditioned receipt of vouchers on a candidate's giving up contributions beyond $100. For an informed and experienced view of that proposal, see Michael J. Malbin, "Small Donors: Incentives, Economy of Scale, and Effects," *Forum* 11, no. 3 (2011): 385, 400–06, available at link #152. Richard Painter has a version in his masterful (and politically conservative) work, *Taxation Only with Representation:*

The Conservative Conscience and Campaign Finance Reform (Auburn, AL: Take Back Our Republic, 2016).

7. Kelsey Hamlin, "Seattle's Democracy Vouchers: They Worked," Capitol Hill Seattle Blog, December 1, 2017, available at link #153. See also Jennifer Heerwig and Brian J. McCabe, "Expanding Participation in Municipal Elections: Assessing the Impact of Seattle's Democracy Voucher Program," University of Washington Center for Studies in Demography & Ecology, available at link #154.

8. Note, to avoid a substantial budget effect, the number of candidates you could give your credits to would have to be limited, as any splitting would increase the total cost per contributor above $100. So, for example, if you split your 10,000 SCs evenly between two candidates, that would cost the treasury $141.42 (square root of 5,000, times 2); among 3 candidates, $173.21. The system would also have to restrict the ability of candidates to transfer the value of SCs to another campaign to avoid coordinating committees inducing donors to split contributions which would then be reallocated by the committees.

9. Michael Walzer, *Spheres of Justice: A Defense of Pluralism and Equality* (New York: Basic Books, 1983).

10. See Michael J. Malbin, "Small Donors: Incentives, Economy of Scale, and Effects," *Forum* 11 (2011): 385, 395–97. See also Michael J. Malbin, Peter W. Brusoe, and Brendan Glavin, "Small Donors, Big Democracy: New York City's Matching Funds as a Model for the Nation and States," *Election Law Journal* 11 (2012): 3–20, available at link #155; Neil Malhotra, "The Impact of Public Financing on Electoral Competition: Evidence from Arizona and Maine," *State Politics and Policy Quarterly* 8 (2008): 263 (systems had helped competitors); "A Look at H.R. 1826, and the Public Financing of Congressional Campaigns: Hearing on H.R. 1826 Before the H. Comm. on House Admin., 111th Cong. 206 (2009), statement of Jeffrey Garfield, Exec. Dir., Conn. State Elections Enforcement Comm'n," (stating that in the 2008 Connecticut state elections more women had run for office than ever had previously) available at link #156; Steven M. Levin, "Keeping It Clean: Public Financing and American Elections," Center for Governmental Studies (2006): 12 (increased women's participation in Maine), available at link #157; Mimi Murray, Digby Marziani, and Adam Skaggs, "More Than Combating Corruption: The Other Benefits

of Public Financing," Brennan Center for Justice, October 7, 2011, available at link #158. Keith M. Phaneuf, "The Clean-Election State," *American Prospect*, January 5, 2012, available at link #159 (found grassroots influence increased in Connecticut after public funding was adopted, while lobbying influence waned); Wesley Joe, Michael J. Malbin, Clyde Wilcox, Peter W. Brusoe, and Henrik M. Schatzinger, "Individual Donors in Connecticut's Public Financing Program: A Look at the First Election Under the New System," paper presented at the Annual Meeting of the American Political Science Association, Toronto, Ontario, Sept. 3–6, 2009, available at link #160 (found that in the first election, donors to incumbents were essentially the same as before , but donors to nonincumbents were more representative); Seth E. Masket and Michael G. Miller, "Does Public Election Funding Create More Extreme Legislators? Evidence from Arizona and Maine," *State Politics and Policy Quarterly* 15 (2015): 24–40, available at link #161 (could find no measurable difference in ideological extremity between publicly funded and non–publicly funded candidates for nonincumbents). See also Raymond J. La Raja, "Campaign Finance and Partisan Polarization in the United States Congress," *Duke Journal of Constitutional Law and Public Policy* 9 (2014): 223–58 (party participation reduces polarization), available at link #162.

11. *Austin v. Michigan Chamber of Commerce*, 494 U.S. 652, 657 (1990).

12. Stephanopoulos, *Aligning Campaign Finance Law*, 1481–82. Some of this moderation is a function of PACs giving to both sides to ensure access (and preserve threat value). Lessig, *Republic, Lost*, 258. But as Stephanopoulos reports, scholars find moderation beyond just that. Stephanopoulos, *Aligning Campaign Finance Law*, 1482. For this reason, Stephanopoulos argues that limits on PAC contributions might be unnecessary (1483). This argument brings out the important difference in our perspectives. If limits on contributions were removed, more fundraising would come from business interests. That increased dependence would conflict with the equal dependence that representativeness requires.

13. See Lessig, *Republic, Lost*; Lessig, *Republic, Lost: Version 2.0*; Lessig, *America, Compromised*. This argument distinguishes fundamentally between *Citizens United* speech (expenditures made by corporations or unions independently of a campaign) and SuperPACs (contributions

made to an organization that would spend independently). I make the argument for the regulability of the latter type in "On the Legitimate Aim of Congressional Regulation of Political Speech: An Originalist View," in *The Free Speech Century* (New York: Oxford University Press, 2019), 95–105. See also Robert Post, *Citizens Divided: Campaign Finance Reform and the Constitution* (Cambridge, MA: Harvard University Press, 2016).

14. Adam Bonica, "Expert Report of Adam Bonica, Ph. D," *Equal Citizens*, available at link #163.

15. Stephanopoulos, *Aligning Campaign Finance Law*, 1495.

16. James Madison, "The Federalist Papers, No. 52," Avalon Project, available at link #164; "The Federalist Papers, No. 57," Avalon Project, available at link #165.

17. Lessig, *Republic, Lost: Version 2.0*, ch. 12. Compare Richard L. Hasen, "Is 'Dependence Corruption' Distinct from a Political Equality Argument for Campaign Finance Laws? A Reply to Professor Lessig," *Election Law Journal* 12 (2013). In this way, I agree with Burke that a theory of corruption depends on a theory of representation. See Thomas F. Burke, "The Concept of Corruption in Campaign Finance Law," *Constitutional Commentary* 14 (1997): 127, 128 ("Any adequate standard of corruption . . . must be grounded in a convincing theory of representation"). "Dependence corruption" is related to the notion of "soft corruption," explicated in "Unstacking the Deck: A New Agenda to Tame Corruption in Washington," The Roosevelt Institute, May 2018, available at link #166 (expanding the dimensions along which the dynamic of soft corruption flows).

18. These reforms together would create representative institutions that were properly dependent. That dependence would produce an influence that was likewise representative. Nicholas Stephanopoulos has argued that we should instead press for representative democracies that produce representatives who are "aligned"—both within a district and across districts. Stephanopoulos, *Aligning Campaign Finance Law*. While the reforms I have described here would not produce the same kind of alignment, the standards are complementary. If a properly dependent legislature were representative, that would tend to alignment.

19. H.R. 3057, The Fair Representation Act, 115th Congress (2017–18), available at link #167. The *New York Times* has endorsed this plan. See

Editorial Board, "A Congress for Every American," *New York Times*, November 10, 2018, available at link #168. For a contrary view, see Thomas F. Schaller, "Multi-Member Districts: Just a Thing of the Past?," *Sabato's Crystal Ball*, March 21, 2013, available at link #169. Of course, the United States Supreme Court has repeatedly considered the question of partisan gerrymandering, and there is some chance it might render this debate moot by declaring the practice unconstitutional. I am skeptical that any such judicial remedy would be sufficient. If the Court does enter this field, it will be under the guidance of research such as this: Nicholas O. Stephanopoulos and Eric M. McGhee, "Partisan Gerrymandering and the Efficiency Gap," *University of Chicago Law Review* 82, no. 2 (Spring 2015): 831–900.

20.   For a description of the idea, see Fair Vote, The Fair Representation Act, available at link #170.

21.   For a similar conclusion for distinct reasons, see Shigeo Hirano and James Snyder, *Primary Elections in the United States* (forthcoming).

22.   Hirano and Snyder, *Primary Elections in the United States,* 4. ("Imperfect as they are, primaries on balance enhance the U.S. electoral system. They bring an essential element of democracy—competitive elections from time to time that offer the voters of at least one party a real choice—to the vast areas of the U.S. where the general elections do not. Thus far, our limited imaginations have not come up with anything obviously better.")

23.   I agree with Baker and Dinkin that the real barrier here is political. Lynn A. Baker and Samuel H. Dinkin, "The Senate: An Institution Whose Time Has Gone," *Journal of Law and Politics* 13 (1997): 68–70, available at link #171 (explaining possible ways to avoid the Equal Suffrage Clause and concluding each is highly unlikely). Others have been encouraged to think around the "Equal Suffrage Clause." That thinking is interesting (if wild): see Arthur Machen Jr., "Is the Fifteenth Amendment Void?," *Harvard Law Review* 23, no. 3 (1910): 169 (arguing the Equal Suffrage Clause precluded passing the Fifteenth Amendment); Eric Posner and Adrian Vermeule, "Legislative Retrenchment: A Reappraisal," *Yale Law Journal* 111 (2002): 1681–82, available at link #172 (arguing the Equal Suffrage Clause means legislative retrenchment is constitutional); Benjamin Lieber and Patrick Brown, "On Supermajorities and the Constitution," *Georgetown Law Journal* 83 (1995):

2367–70 (arguing the Equal Suffrage Clause would preclude constitutional amendments imposing a supermajority requirement on any Senate legislation, such as tax increases); Burt Neuborne, "One-State/ Two-Votes: Do Supermajority Senate Voting Rules Violate the Article V Guaranty of Equal State Suffrage," *Stanford Journal of Civil Rights and Civil Liberties* 10 (2014), available at link #173 (arguing the Equal Suffrage Clause may make the filibuster unconstitutional). By contrast, the Supreme Court has been quite relaxed in its reading of the constraints of the clause. See *National Prohibition Cases*, 253 U.S. 350, 388 (1920) (White, J., concurring) (lamenting that the Court did not explain more thoroughly why the Equal Suffrage Clause does not prohibit the Eighteenth Amendment). See also Elai Katz, "On Amending Constitutions: The Legality and Legitimacy of Constitutional Entrenchment," *Columbia Journal of Law and Social Problems* 29 (1995): 278–79 (explaining the limited consideration of the Equal Suffrage Clause). At most, the Court has simply insisted that the clause is permanent. *Dodge v. Woolsey*, 59 U.S. 331, 348 (1855) (explaining the sovereign states agreed to forgo some sovereignty through a national amendment process but required some limits on that national amendment procedure, including the two "permanent and unalterable exceptions to the power of amendment" in Article V: the clause preventing any amendment regarding slavery until 1808 and the Equal Suffrage Clause). It seems plain that unanimous consent would work. See Michael B. Rappaport and John McGinnis, "Symmetric Entrenchment: A Constitutional and Normative Theory," *Virginia Law Review* 23 (2003): 412 (arguing that because every state agreed to the terms to which it entered the union as an equal Senate sovereign, every state must agree to change the norm of equal suffrage in the Senate).

Many believe you could amend Article V and then amend the "Equal Suffrage Clause." See George Mader, "Binding Authority: Unamendability in the United States Constitution: A Textual and Historical Analysis," *Marquette Law Review* 99 (2016): 864–70, available at link #174 (arguing Article V expressly does not require unanimous consent to amend Equal Suffrage Clause); Peter Suber, *The Paradox of Self-Amendment: A Study of Law, Logic, Omnipotence, and Change* (Peter Lang International Academic Publishers, 1990), 64, available at link #175 (claiming the Equal Suffrage Clause is amendable by normal amendment procedures); Lynn A. Baker and Samuel H. Dinkin, "The Senate: An Institution Whose Time Has Gone," *Journal of Law and Policy* 13 (1997): 69 (claiming the Equal Suffrage Clause is "arguably" amendable by normal amendment procedures); Lynn A. Baker, "Federalism: The Argument from Article V," *Georgia State University Law Review* 13 (1997): 947 (same); Jeffrey K. Tulis, "The Demon at the Center," *University of Chicago Law Review* 55 (1988), available at link #176 (framing the question as a debate over whether the Constitution's core commitment is procedural process or substantive). One opponent of amending the Equal Suffrage Clause has described the clause as "constructively unamendable"—that is, a political promise, albeit one deeply embedded in our political culture, not to alter the Senate's equal suffrage. Richard Albert, "Constructive Unamendability in Canada and the United States," *Supreme Court Law Review* 67 (2014): 196, available at link #177. No doubt, some would insist that the clause can't be amended directly or indirectly. But the theory of popular sovereignty that justified our abandoning the Articles of Confederation would certainly justify our amending Article V. Akhil Reed Amar, "Philadelphia Revisited: Amending the Constitution Outside Article V," *University of Chicago Law Review* 55 (1988), available at link #178. On the idea of abolishing the Senate, see Douglas Linder, "What in the Constitution Cannot Be Amended?," *Arizona Law Review* 23 (1981): 726. But see Baker and Dinkin, "The Senate": 70 (arguing that Article 1, Section 1 requires only the House).

And on the idea of limiting the Senate's powers, see Linder, "What in the Constitution": 727; see also *National Prohibition Cases*, 253 U.S. 350, 389-90 (1920) (White, J., concurring) (explaining the Equal Suffrage Clause was assumed not to prevent the Eighteenth Amendment); Elai Katz, "On Amending Constitutions: The Legality and Legitimacy of Constitutional Entrenchment," *Columbia Journal of Law and Social Problems* 29 (1995): 278–79. I am especially grateful to Zak Lutz for the extraordinary research that supported this note.

24.   For the interpreted source, see "Rules and Procedure," United States Senate, available at link #179.

25.   Bruce Ackerman, *We the People,* vol. 3, *The Civil Rights Revolution* (Cambridge, MA: Harvard University Press, 2014), Kindle edition, loc. 1002–32.

26. See Richard S. Beth, "Procedures for Considering Change in Senate Rules," *Congressional Research Service*, January 22, 2013 (explaining in some detail the procedures for changing Senate rules and the variants of the "nuclear option"), available at link #180; see also Walter J. Oleszek, "Changing the Senate Cloture Rule at the Start of a New Congress," *Congressional Research Service*, December 12, 2016, available at link #181 (discussing many efforts to reform the filibuster).

27. A Resolution to Establish as a Standing Order of the Senate that a Senator Publicly Disclose a Notice of Intent Objecting to Any Measure or Matter, S. Res. 28, 112th Cong. (2011), available at link #182.

28. Nolan D. McCaskill, "McConnell to Trump: The Filibuster Is Here to Stay," *Politico*, June 27, 2018, available at link #183.

29. See Elizabeth Rybicki, "Filling the Amendment Tree in the Senate," *Congressional Research Service*, August 14, 2015, available at link #184.

30. Thomas H. Neale and Andrew Nolan, "The National Popular Vote (NPV) Initiative: Direct Election of the President by Interstate Compact," *Congressional Research Service*, 7 (October 25, 2018), available at link #185.

31. The National Popular Vote project has a FAQ that offers evidence to answer this and other concerns. See *Answering Myths*, available at link #186.

32. This point is described by Jon Fasman in "Why American Elections Cost So Much," *Economist*, February 9, 2014, available at link #187.

33. This is the point made powerfully in John R. Koza, Barry F. Fadem, Mark Grueskin, Michael S. Mandell, Robert Richie, and Joseph F. Zimmerman, *Every Vote Equal: A State-Based Plan for Electing the President by National Popular Vote* (Los Altos, CA: National Popular Vote Press, 4th. ed. 2013).

34. Scandalously, the Supreme Court has read Congress's Section 5 power narrowly. That's scandalous because it's clear the framers intended Congress to have broad power under that clause. See James W. Fox Jr., "Re-Readings and Misreadings: Slaughter-House, Privileges or Immunities, and Section Five Enforcement Powers," *Kentucky Law Journal* 91 (2002): 67.

35. The Twelfth Amendment requires electors to name "the person voted for as president." A strict reason would read that as limiting the vote to just one person ("the" person). But as the purpose of the Twelfth

Amendment could be advanced through fractional voting as much as through whole voting, there would be no need to restrict the voting to a single person—especially if fractionated voting would serve another important constitutional purpose.

36.   The Constitution requires that if no candidate for president receives a majority of the Electoral College votes, then the election is decided in the House. But the House must vote state by state, with each state casting one vote. That creates a huge gap between the popular vote of the nation and the vote if cast state by state—assuming, at least, that members voted for the candidate of their own party. If the 2016 election had gone to the House, and members had voted according to their party, Trump would have received 70 percent of the vote in the House (35 states out of 50), even though he received just 46 percent of the popular vote, and the Republicans held only 55 percent of seats in the House. A state could well justify avoiding a system that produced that gap based on the principle of "one person, one vote" as applied to presidential elections. The Supreme Court affirmed that application in *Bush v. Gore*, 531 U.S. 98 (2000). So under this proposed system, a state would first calculate the RCV winner of the state, by dropping candidates and reallocating the vote to those candidates until there are just two. The electoral votes would then be allocated to those two proportionally.

37.   Automatic voter registration has had an enormous effect on increasing participation. See, for example, Caitlin Oprysko, "Oregon Governor Calls Automatic Voter Registration a 'Phenomenal Success,'" *Politico*, February 22, 2019, available at link #188. For a comprehensive account of state changes to improve voting rights, see Daniel Nichanian, "The Voting Rights Manifesto: A State-by-State Plan to Defend Democracy," *Vox*, December 15, 2016, available at link #189.

38.   The complexity here is caused by the Eleventh Amendment, which has been read to grant the states substantial immunity from monetary liability imposed by the federal government. The exception to this ban is grounded in amendments that come after the Eleventh, like the Fourteenth. That suggests that if we relied upon Article I to ground the right to vote equally, the Eleventh Amendment would bar monetary damages for violating that rule. This weakness strengthens the argument in favor of a federal right to vote secured through a constitutional

amendment. On the Eleventh Amendment, see Lawrence Lessig, *Fidelity and Constraint* (New York: Oxford University Press, 2019), ch. 10.

39.   Ben Nadler, "Voting Rights Become a Flashpoint in Georgia Governor's Race," AP News, October 9, 2018, available at link #190.

40.   Mark Niesse and Tyler Estep, "High Rate of Absentee Ballots Thrown Out in Gwinnet," *Atlanta Journal-Constitution*, October 15, 2018, available at link #191; Jonathan Brater, Kevin Morris, Myrna Pérez, and Christopher Deluzio, "Purges: A Growing Threat to the Right to Vote," Brennan Center for Justice, June 2018, available at link #192.

CHAPTER 4: FIXING US

1.   Jürgen Habermas, "Discourse Ethics: Notes on a Program of Philosophical Justification," in *Moral Consciousness and Communicative Action*, trans. Christian Lenhardt and Shierry Weber Nicholsen (Cambridge, MA: MIT Press, 1990), 43–115. The reference to an "ideal speech situation" comes from page 88. For a useful reply, see Michael Schudson, "Was There Ever a Public Sphere? If So, When? Reflections on the American Case," in *Habermas and the Public Sphere,* ed. Craig Calhoun (Cambridge, MA: MIT Press, 1992), 143–63.

2.   The process is described in James S. Fishkin's *Democracy When the People Are Thinking: Revitalizing Our Politics Through Public Deliberation* (Oxford: Oxford University Press, 2018), 189–95. An earlier deliberative poll conducted on participatory budgeting for the city of Ulaanbaatar is described at 91–100. See also "Mongolia Celebrates 27th Anniversary of Modern Constitution," *Xinhua News,* January 31, 2019, available at link #193.

3.   General statistics drawn from "Mongolia," Central Intelligence Agency, July 2016, available at link #194.

4.   "Distribution of Family Income: GINI Index," Central Intelligence Agency, July 2016, available at link #195.

5.   "The World Factbook: Internet Users," Central Intelligence Agency, July 2016, available at link #196.

6.   His latest book is Fishkin, *Democracy When the People Are Thinking.* Fishkin of course did not create the idea of deliberative democracy. For the best introduction and analysis, see Amy Gutmann and Dennis Thompson, *Why Deliberative Democracy?* (Princeton, NJ: Princeton

University Press, 2004); André Bächtiger, et al., *The Oxford Handbook of Deliberative Democracy* (Oxford: Oxford University Press, 2018); and Zsuzsanna Chappell, *Deliberative Democracy: A Critical Introduction* (Basingstoke, UK: Palgrave Macmillan, 2012); "The Prospects & Limits of Deliberative Democracy," ed. James S. Fishkin & Jane Mansbridge, special issue of *Daedalus: Journal of the American Academy of Arts & Sciences*, 146, no. 3 (Summer 2017).

7.   The story is a bit more complex. The election of the drafting committee was thrown out by the Icelandic Supreme Court, in one of the most extraordinary election law opinions in the history of the free world. The outrage was so great that the government simply appointed the people who had been previously elected. For a full account of the Iceland experience, see Hélène Landemore, "Inclusive Constitution Making: The Iceland Experiment," *Journal of Political Philosophy* 23 (2015): 166, available at link #197; Katrin Oddsdóttir, "Iceland: The Birth of the World's First Crowd-Sourced Constitution?," *Cambridge Journal of International & Comparative Law* 3 (2014): 1207; Jon Elster, "Icelandic Constitution-Making in Comparative Perspective," in *Iceland's Financial Crisis: The Politics of Blame, Protest, and Reconstruction,* Valur Ingimundarson, Philippe Urfalino, Irma Erlingsdóttir, eds. (New York: Routledge, 2016); Thorvaldur Gylfason, "From Collapse to Constitution: The Case of Iceland," in *Public Debt, Global Governance and Economic Dynamism,* ed. Liugi Paganetto, (Milano: Springer, 2013). As of this writing, Iceland has not ratified a constitution based on that draft.

8.   For an excellent review of Ireland, see Jane Suiter, David M. Farrell, and Clodagh Harris, "The Irish Constitutional Convention: A Case of 'High Legitimacy'?," in *Constitutional Deliberative Democracy in Europe,* ed. Min Reuchamps and Jane Suiter (Colchester, UK: ECPR Press, 2016), 33–51, and see the book generally for a review of other similar examples in Europe. For an account of Canada, see Genevieve Fuji Johnson, "Deliberative Democratic Practices in Canada: An Analysis of Institutional Empowerment in Three Cases," *Canadian Journal of Political Science* 42 (2009): 679, available at link #198. See also Genevieve Fuji Johnson, *Democratic Illusion: Deliberative Democracy in Canadian Public Policy* (Toronto: University of Toronto Press, 2015); Claudia Chwalisz, *The People's Verdict: Adding Informed Citizen Voices to Public Decision-Making* (London: Rowman & Littlefield, 2017).

9. See Laura Cahillane, "Delaying Tactics or Useful Deliberative Exercises? The Irish Citizens' Assembly and the Convention on the Constitution," IACL-AIDC blog, December 3, 2018, available at link #199.

10. See Fishkin, *Democracy When the People Are Thinking*. Fishkin's book is an excellent introduction to a wide range of examples of deliberative democracy.

11. There is a growing political movement of scholars and activists pressing for practices related to deliberative polling. The most hopeful are collected by Democracy R&D on its website, available at link #200. Democracy R&D describes itself as an "international network of organizations and associations helping decision makers take hard decisions and build public trust." It organizes those projects according to three principles—representative, deliberative, and impartial. As of this writing, the site collects more than twenty-five separate projects experimenting with techniques like Fishkin's. More about the evolution of this movement in democracy reform can be found on an essay by Adam Cronkright, "Sharing Sortition with Some Soul," available on the sortition blog Equality by Lot, available at link #201. For an exploration of something close to sortition applied to budgeting, see Josh Lerner, *Everyone Counts: Could "Participatory Budgeting" Change Democracy?* (Ithaca, NY: Cornell Press 2014).

12. Larry M. Bartels, "Is 'Popular Rule' Possible? Polls, Political Psychology, and Democracy," *Brookings Review* 21 (2003): 12; see also Achen and Bartels, *Democracy for Realists*. Bartels is skeptical about deliberation.

13. "5 of the Largest Personal Injury Verdicts Ever," McCune Wright Arevalo LLP, March 28, 2017, available at link #202.

14. Lessig, *America Compromised*, 105–7.

15. Lessig, *America Compromised*, 139–52. See also Ezra Klein, "How Politics Makes Us Stupid," *Vox*, April 6, 2014, available at link #203.

16. For a full account of this institutional brilliance, see Lessig, *Fidelity & Constraint*, ch. 2.

17. Lessig, *Republic Lost*; Lessig, *Republic, Lost: Version 2.0*. The fear of convention opponents is that an Article V convention is a "constitutional convention," and thus would possess the constituent power of the people. With that power, it could amend the existing constitution—even without complying with the rules of the existing constitution. All that is just so much bunk. My view is the same as expressed by Lord James

Bryce in his *American Commonwealth* in 1888: "Originally a convention was conceived of as a sovereign body, wherein the full powers of the people were vested by popular election. It is now, however, merely an advisory body, which prepares a draft of a new constitution and submits it to the people for their acceptance or rejection. And it is not deemed to be sovereign in the sense of possessing the plenary authority of the people, for its powers may be, indeed now invariably are, limited by the statute under which the people elect it." James Bryce, *The American Commonwealth*, vol. 1 (1888; reprint, Indianapolis, IN: Liberty Fund, 1995), 606.

18.   Van Reybrouck, *Against Elections,* 66.

19.   Van Reybrouck, *Against Elections,* 75.

20.   Van Reybrouck, *Against Elections,* 83, 88.

21.   Oliver Dowlen, *Sorted: Civil Lotteries and the Future of Public Participation* (Toronto: MASS LBP, 2008), available at link #204.

22.   David Bellhouse, "Decoding Cardano's *Liber de Ludo Aleae,*" *Historia Mathematica* 32 (2005): 180–202; Alan Hájek, "Interpretations of Probability," in *Stanford Encyclopedia of Philosophy*, December 19, 2011, available at link #205.

23.   Terrill Bouricius recommends a similar idea in "Democracy Through Multi-Body Sortition: Athenian Lessons for the Modern Day," *Journal of Public Deliberation* 9, no. 1 (2013): article 11, available at link #206.

24.   The movement is described by Slow Food USA, available at link #207, and by one of its leaders, Carlo Petrini, *Slow Food Nation: Why Our Food Should Be Good, Clean, and Fair,* trans. Clara Furlan and Jonathan Hunt (New York: Rizzoli Ex Libris, 2007).

25.   This movement is described by *Slow Democracy*, available at link #208, and by the wonderful book by Susan Clark and Woden Teachout, *Slow Democracy: Rediscovering Community, Bringing Decision Making Back Home* (White River Junction, VT: Chelsea Green, 2012). I have been inspired in this more structural way to think about reforming a political culture by the work of Ethan Zuckerman, most clearly in *Digital Cosmopolitans: Why We Think the Internet Connects Us, Why It Doesn't, and How to Rewire It* (New York: Norton, 2014). Though Zuckerman is not directly considering the mechanisms of democracy, the interventions to produce a culture better able to function with, among other things, a democracy is at the core of his project, too.

26. Christopher Ingraham, "Too Much Democracy: Do We Really Need to Put Obscure Local Offices to the Popular Vote?," *Washington Post*, November 4, 2014, available at link #209; Evan Horwitz, "We Have Too Many Elections," *Boston Globe*, September 8, 2016, available at link #210.

27. Pew Research Center, *The Public, the Political System and American Democracy*, 4.

28. Claire S. H. Lim and James M. Snyder Jr., "Is More Information Always Better? Party Cues and Candidate Quality in U.S. Judicial Elections," *Journal of Public Economics* 128 (August 2015): 107–23.

29. James Bryce, *The American Commonwealth*, vol. 2 (1888; reprint Indianapolis, IN: Liberty Fund, 1995), 765–68.

30. Charles A. Beard, "The Ballot's Burden," *Political Science Quarterly* 24, no. 4 (December 1909): 589, 598–99, available at link #211.

31. On the psychology of negative advertising, see Erik J. Bolinder, "The Dynamics of Negative Political Advertising: History, Thematic Designs, and Effectiveness," *Sigma: Journal of Political and International Studies* 10 (1992): 42–57. On the political incentives and effects, see Conor M. Dowling and Yanna Krupnikov, "The Effects of Negative Advertising," *Oxford Research Encyclopedia of Politics*, November 2016, available at link #212. On the effect of ads generally, see Michael M. Franz and Travis N. Ridout, "Political Advertising and Persuasion in the 2004 and 2008 Presidential Elections," *American Political Research* 38, no. 2 (March 2010): 303-329 (finding an effect); Alan S. Gerber, "Does Campaign Spending Work?: Field Experiments Provide Evidence and Suggest New Theory," *American Behavioral Scientist* 47, no. 5 (January 2004): 541–74 (finding effect among challengers especially); Alan S. Gerber, James G. Gimpel, Donald P. Green, and Daron R. Shaw, "How Large and Long-Lasting Are the Persuasive Effects of Televised Campaign Ads? Results from a Randomized Field Experiment," *American Political Science Review* 105, no. 1 (February 2011): 135–50 (finding ephemeral effects from television advertising); Mark Gius, "The Effects of Campaign Expenditures on Congressional Elections," *American Review of Political Economy* 7, nos. 1 & 2 (June/December 2009): 51–66 (finding differential effects between winners/losers); Mark Paul Gius, "An Analysis of the 2006 Congressional Elections: Does Campaign Spending Matter?," *Applied Economics Letters* 17, no. 7 (May 2010):

703–6 (finding clear effect, and clear incumbent advantage); Brett R. Gordon and Wesley R. Hartmann, "Advertising Effects in Presidential Elections," *Marketing Science* 32, no. 1 (January–February 2013): 19–35 (finding clear effects from television ads but less than with branded goods); Gary C. Jacobson, "Campaign Spending Effects in U.S. Senate Elections: Evidence from the National Annenberg Election Survey," *Electoral Studies* 25, no. 2 (June 2006): 195-226; Gary C. Jacobson, "Measuring Campaign Spending Effects in U.S. House Elections," in *Capturing Campaign Effects*, ed. Henry E. Brady and Richard Johnston (Ann Arbor: University of Michigan Press, 2006): 199–220; Mitchell J. Lovett and Ron Shachar, "The Seeds of Negativity: Knowledge and Money," *Marketing Science* 30, no. 3 (May–June 2011): 430–46 (modeling the incentives to go negative).

32.   See Lisa Hill, "Voting Turnout, Equality, Liberty, and Representation: Epistemic Versus Procedural Democracy," *Critical Review of International Social and Political Philosophy* 19 (2016): 283, 286–87; David Darmofal, "The Political Geography of Macro-Level Turnout in American Political Development," *Political Geography* 25 (2006): 123, 127–28.

33.   Erika Franklin Fowler, Travis N. Ridout, and Michael M. Franz, "Political Advertising in 2016: The Presidential Election as Outlier?," *Forum* 14, no. 4 (2016): 445, 464–66, available at link #213.

34.   Morris P. Fiorina and Samuel J. Abrams, *Disconnect: The Breakdown of Representation in American Politics* (Norman: University of Oklahoma Press, 2009), 47.

35.   Though this is not likely. See *Ancheta v. Watada*, 135 F. Supp. 2d 1114 (D. Haw. 2001); *Arizona Right to Life Political Action Committee v. Bayless*, 320 F.3d 1002 (9th Cir. 2003). Because the temptation to regulate is so great, the literature about regulation is massive as well. See Erika Franklin Fowler, Michael M. Franz, and Travis N. Ridout, *Political Advertising in the United States* (Boulder, CO: Westview, 2016), 13–40; Randolph Kluver et al., *The Internet and National Elections: A Comparative Study of Web Campaigning* (New York: Routledge, 2007); Yochai Benkler, Robert Faris, and Hal Roberts, *Network Propaganda: Manipulation, Disinformation, and Radicalization in American Politics* (New York: Oxford University Press, 2018), 367–68; Clifford A. Jones, "Campaign Finance Reform and the Internet: Regulating Web Messages in the 2004 Election and Beyond," in *The Internet Election:*

Perspectives on the Web in Campaign 2004, ed. Andrew Paul Williams and John C. Tedesco (Lanham, MD: Rowman & Littlefield, 2006), 5-20; Abby K. Wood, and Ann M. Ravel, "Fool Me Once: Regulating Fake News and Other Online Advertising," *Southern California Law Review* 91 (September 2018): 1223–78; Becky Kruse, "The Truth in Masquerade: Regulating False Ballot Proposition Ads Through State Anti-False Speech Statutes," *California Law Review* 89, no. 1 (January 2001): 129–81; Clifford A. Jones, "Regulating Political Advertising in the EU and USA: A Human Rights Perspective," *Journal of Public Affairs* 4, no. 3 (2004): 244–55; Craig Holman, "The Bipartisan Campaign Reform Act: Limits and Opportunities for Non-Profit Groups in Federal Elections," *Northern Kentucky Law Review* 31, no. 243 (2004): 243–87; Cynthia L. Bauerly, "The Revolution Will Be Tweeted and Tbml'd and Txtd: New Technology and the Challenge for Campaign-Finance Regulation," *University of Toledo Law Review* 44, no. 3 (Spring 2013): 525–40; Irina Dykhne, "Persuasive or Deceptive? Native Advertising in Political Campaigns," *Southern California Law Review* 91, no. 2 (January 2018): 339–73; Jeffrey P. Hinkeldey, "The 140-Character Campaign: Regulating Social Media Usage in Campaign Advertising," *Rutgers Computer & Technology Law Journal* 40, no. 1 (2014): 78–105; Kenneth Goldstein, David A. Schweidel, and Mike Wittenwyler, "Lessons Learned: Political Advertising and Political Law," *Minnesota Law Review* 96, no. 5 (May 2012): 1732–54; Lee Goldman, "False Campaign Advertising and the 'Actual Malice' Standard," *Tulane Law Review* 82, no. 3 (February 2008): 889; Lili Levi, "Plan B for Campaign-Finance Reform: Can the FCC Help Save American Politics after *Citizens United*?," *Catholic University Law Review* 61, no 1 (Winter 2011): 97–174; Peter F. May, "State Regulation of Political Broadcast Advertising: Stemming the Tide of Deceptive Negative Attacks," *Boston University Law Review* 72, no. 1 (January 1992): 179–216; Scott Holleman, "Regulating the Mother's Milk of Politics: Why Washington's Campaign Finance Law Constitutionally Prohibits State Parties from Spending Soft Money on Issue Ads," *Washington Law Review* 80, no. 1 (February 2005): 191–218; Seth Grossman, "Keeping Unwanted Donkeys and Elephants out of Your Inbox: The Case for Regulating Political Spam," *Berkeley Technology Law Journal* 19, no. 4 (Fall 2004): 1533–76.

36. Joe Flint, "Cable TV Shows Are Sped Up to Squeeze in More Ads," *Wall Street Journal*, February 18, 2015, available at link #214.

37. Michelle Greenwald, "What's Really Driving the Limitless Growth of Podcasts," *Forbes*, October 4, 2018, available at link #215. See also George P. Slefo, "Women Are Driving Podcast Growth, A New Study Says," *AdAge*, September 5, 2018, available at link #216; Rose Leadem, "The Growth of Podcasts and Why It Matters," *Entrepreneur*, December 23, 2017, available at link #217.

38. For commentary about the series, see Diane Negra and Jorie Lagerwey, eds., "In Focus: *Homeland*," *Cinema Journal* 54, no. 4 (Summer 2015): 126–60, available at link #218; James Donaghy, "Why Homeland Deserves to Go Out on Top," *Guardian*, April 19, 2018, available at link #219; Robert Arp, ed., *Homeland and Philosophy: For Your Minds Only* (Chicago: Open Court, 2014). For a less affirmative view of the series, see Sophie Gilbert, "The Trouble With *Homeland's* Political Realism," *Atlantic*, April 10, 2017, available at link #220.

39. The criticism is endless. See, for example, Laura Durkay, "'Homeland' Is the Most Bigoted Show on Television," *Washington Post*, October 2, 2014, available at link #221.

40. See Andrew Bacevich, *America's War for the Greater Middle East: A Military History* (New York: Random House, 2016); Andrew Bacevich, *Breach of Trust: How Americans Failed Their Soldiers and Their Country* (New York: Metropolitan Books, 2013); Andrew Bacevich, *Washington Rules: America's Path to Permanent War* (New York: Metropolitan Books, 2010).

41. Emily Nussbaum, "'Homeland': The Antidote for '24,'" *New Yorker*, November 29, 2011, available at link #222.

42. Goidel, *America's Failing Experiment*, 161.

43. See, for example, Morten M. Warmedal, "The Future of High Quality Documentaries Reaching a World Audience," *Medium,* December 10, 2017, available at link #223.

44. "Romer v. Evans," *Wikipedia*, available at link #224.

45. "2008 California Proposition 8," *Wikipedia*, available at link #225.

46. "*Philadelphia (film)*," *Wikipedia*, available at link #226.

47. *Lawrence v. Texas*, 539 U.S. 558 (2003).

48. *Obergefell v. Hodges,* 135 S. Ct. 2584 (2015).

49. Damon Centola, Joshua Becker, Devon Brackhill, and Andrea Baron-shelli, "Experimental Evidence for Tipping Points in Social Convention," *Science* 360 (June 2018): 1116–19; the editor's summary of this work is available at link #227.

50. Jack M. Balkin and Jonathan Zittrain, "A Grand Bargain to Make Tech Companies Trustworthy," *Atlantic*, October 3, 2016, available at link #228.

51. Aleecia M. McDonald and Lorrie Faith Cranor, "The Cost of Reading Privacy Policies," *Journal of Policy for the Information Society*, 4, no. 3 (2008), available at link #229.

52. There are many roads that lead to the conclusion of a significant effect. Adding the effect of Cambridge Analytica, see Mark Scott, "Cambridge Analytica Helped 'Cheat' Brexit Vote and US Election, Claims Whistleblower," *Politico*, March 27, 2018, available at link #230. On the relationship between the groups Facebook enabled and the contours of polarized opinion, see Michela Del Vicario, "Mapping Social Dynamics on Facebook: The Brexit Debate," *Social Networks* 50 (2017): 6, 6–16. On the relative effect of the Leave versus Remain campaign, see Vyacheslav Polonski, "Impact of Social Media on the Outcome of the EU Referendum," *EU Referendum Analysis 2016*, available at link #231. For the claim that fake news was spread and Russia almost certainly had some illicit hand, see "Disinformation and 'Fake News,'" *House of Commons: Digital, Culture, Media, and Sport Committee*, February 14, 2019, 72–77, available at link #232; Dan Sabbagh, "Facebook to Expand Inquiry into Russian Influence of Brexit," *Guardian*, January 27, 2018, available at link #233.

53. *Burson v. Freeman,* 504 U.S. 191 (1991), upheld a ban on politicking within one hundred feet of a polling place. In *Minnesota v. Mansky*, 138 S.Ct. 1876 (2018), the Court struck down a law banning the wearing of political clothing in a polling place as too broad.

CHAPTER 5: WHAT "FIXED" WOULD GET US

1. Jane Mansbridge, "A 'Selection Model' of Political Representation," Harvard University John F. Kennedy School of Government, Working Paper No. RWP08-010, issued March 18, 2008, available at link #234.

Compare Donald J. McCrone and James H. Kuklinski, "The Delegate Theory of Representation," *American Journal of Political Science* 23 (1979): 278; Pitkin, *Representation*, 127.

2.   Mansbridge, *A Selection Model*, 21–23.

3.   The Congressional Research Institute has done extensive work to demonstrate how the Legislative Reorganization Act of 1970 enabled, rather than disabled, rent-seeking in Congress. See the research collected on its site, available at link #235.

4.   Mansbridge, *A Selection Model*, 42.

5.   Nancy Rosenblum, *On the Side of the Angels: An Appreciation of Parties and Partisanship* (Princeton: Princeton University Press, 2008).

6.   Khorri Atkinson, "Democrats Won the House with the Largest Midterms Margin of All Time," *Axios*, November 26, 2018, available at link #236.

7.   Lessig, *Republic, Lost: Version 2.0*, 224–29.

CONCLUSION

1.   Interview with Katie Fahey, executive director, Voters Not Politicians, February 23, 2018.

2.   Not all states give citizens as much power as Michigan. See "States with Initiative or Referendum," *Ballotpedia*, available at link #237.

3.   "Michigan Proposal 2, Independent Redistricting Commission Initiative (2018)," *Ballotpedia*, available at link #238.

4.   Their ads included the following posted on YouTube. See *Vote Yes on Proposition 2*, available at link #239; *The System Is Rigged*, available at link #240; *Michigan Is Gerrymandered*, available at link #241; *Gerrymandering*, available at link #242; *It's Time, Michigan*, available at link #243.

5.   Joel Kurth, "Emails: Michigan Republicans Brag that Redistricting 'Protects Incumbents,'" *Bridge*, October 13, 2018, available at link #244.

6.   John R. Hibbing and Elizabeth Theiss-Morse, *Stealth Democracy: Americans' Belief About How Government Should Work* (New York: Cambridge University Press, 2002).

7.   Or at least most of the system: In addition to the rejection by the legislature, as in Michigan, the courts were asked to step in. For reasons I'll leave to these notes, the Maine Supreme Court concluded that because of the Constitution, some offices had to be decided by plurality (as op-

posed to RCV). So without amending the Constitution, the People's Veto would restore the vote for federal offices and just some of the state offices as well. See *Opinion of the Justices of the Supreme Judicial Court*, 2017 ME 100 (May 23, 2017), available at link #245.

8. Because it could not be used on statewide officers referred to in the Constitution as requiring "plurality" voting, it did not apply to all state offices. See id.

9. Ranked-choice voting does not always eliminate the "spoiler effect," at least where the additional candidate is not a weak candidate. See "The Spoiler Effect," Center for Election Science, available at link #246. This leads some—the Center for Election Science in particular—to advocate "approval voting" over RCV. Under approval voting, voters indicate support for every candidate they would like. As Common Cause characterizes this concern, "proponents of either system over the other can give fairly complicated mathematical scenarios where each system fails to prevent the spoiler effect." Andrea Bloom, "Instant Runoff Voting (IRV) vs. Approval Voting (AV)," Common Cause, December 5, 2013, available at link #247. I would very much like to see more experiments with approval voting, as well as "star voting," where candidates are rated with a score similar to an Amazon book review, and then there is an instant run-off among the top candidates. But "approval voting" has been tried in just one jurisdiction so far—Fargo, North Dakota. Star voting has yet to be adopted in any jurisdiction.

10. Princeton Gerrymandering Project, available at link #248.

11. Eric Liu, *You're More Powerful Than You Think: A Citizen's Guide to Making Change Happen* (New York: PublicAffairs, 2017).

12. Felicia Sonmez, "McConnell Says Bill That Would Make Election Day a Federal Holiday Is a 'Power Grab' by Democrats," *Washington Post*, January 30, 2019, available at link #249; Ari Berman, "Mitch McConnell Admits That Republicans Lose When More People Vote," *Mother Jones,* January 30, 2019, available at link #250.

Index

Page numbers enclosed in square brackets indicate main text references to notes.